The
RAILWAY
DILEMMA

The RAILWAY DILEMMA

The Perpetual Problems of Ownership,
Costs & Control

Sim Harris

Ian Allan

First published 2016

ISBN 978 0 7110 3835 6

Published by Ian Allan Publishing

an imprint of Ian Allan Publishing Ltd, Addlestone, Surrey KT15 2SF.
Printed in Bulgaria.

Visit the Ian Allan Publishing website at www.ianallanpublishing.com

Contents

List of Tables in Text

Part of the country's collective psyche, the railway is important for economic and social development, requires substantial public investment, carries us around – daily for some, on occasion for others – has significant impacts on our built environment and landscape, and is, mostly, photogenic. These things, together with the colourful characters who have worked on, designed, managed and regulated the system, mean that rail is regularly featured in the British media and discussed around kitchen tables, on social media, and in Parliament.
— Nicola Shaw, The Shaw Report (November 2015)

Preface

I am very grateful to a number of people who have helped me to research the *Railway Dilemma*. They include Dr John Gough, who patiently worked his way through several drafts and made some invaluable suggestions. Chris Green read the first part while on a train journey to Bristol and generously encouraged me to continue. Sir William McAlpine provided essential and much-appreciated access to a number of previously unpublished documents, while my *Railnews* colleague Alan Marshall shed some very useful light on various events in the 1980s and by doing so improved that part of the narrative considerably.

I have resisted the temptation to convert old currency into modern units (until 1971, 12 pence equalled a shilling and 20 shillings made a pound), because the tremendous changes down the years in the real value of money make such comparisons not just meaningless but quite misleading. As an example, the 3d (three old pence) by which the Liverpool & Manchester Railway increased its fares in the 1830s (see Chapter 30) would be at least the equivalent of £1 today – but most people earned a lot less in real terms, and so in some ways 3d then was worth much more than £1 is now. I have used metric measurements and 24-hour clock throughout, for the sake of consistency.

Finally, although I have received a great deal of help, the responsibility for any errors which remain is entirely mine.

Sim Harris
Dunstable
November, 2015

www.railwaydilemma.com

Introduction

Railways in Britain are booming. Passenger and freight traffic totals are rising every year, and major investment between now and 2019 has been approved by the Government, including several important extensions of electrification.

More schemes lie further ahead, including the highly controversial but also exciting project to build the nation's first domestic high-speed line.

On the other hand, the industry appears to be in yet another crisis.

In a country where many people have got into trouble in recent years by 'maxing out' their credit cards, it seems curiously appropriate that the nation's track authority is currently heading in the same direction, while also losing control of its project timetables and costs.

Network Rail borrows to invest in its infrastructure. It is no different in this from many previous railway administrations.

The original companies raised capital by selling shares or issuing debentures. The ill-fated British Transport Commission was allowed to obtain funds by issuing government-guaranteed stock and also benefited from state support for its modernisation plan. Its successor, the British Railways Board, was less able to deploy capital but still managed to do so from time to time by persuading the Treasury that this project or that was vital to the economy.

In the modern railway, which is sometimes described (inaccurately) as 'privatised', there are several sources of capital. One, at least, is truly provided by the private sector, in the form of funds used by the leasing companies to buy new rolling stock.

The private sector passenger operators also need capital to reassure the Department for Transport.

Apart from the actual cost of bidding, which must be regarded as an investment to procure an intangible asset, namely a Government contract to run trains, an operator must also provide a financial safety net in the form of a bond to protect season ticket holders, who pay for their travel up to a year in advance.

The Department for Transport – the DfT – also now requires a further buffer in the form of a 'subordinated loan', which may be partly or wholly forfeited in the event of franchisee failure. This is intended, among other things, to reimburse the DfT's costs if it has to run an unscheduled replacement franchise competition.

The funds to satisfy these requirements are usually loans from the parent company of the bidder that will be repaid during the duration of the franchise, then followed, in theory, by profits. If the bid fails, then the costs of the bid itself – £10m is often quoted as typical – must be written off, while the other items do not arise.

In other words, franchises are not long-term capital investments comparable with buying rolling stock and still less with building a new railway, which is expected to last for more than a century.

A typical franchised passenger operator has almost no assets. The trains are usually leased, the stations are rented (from Network Rail), and access to the network is only possible if the relevant charges are paid, also to Network Rail.

Indeed, a franchised operator may own very little apart from such incidentals as staff uniforms, the crockery in First Class and intellectual property rights in its design and branding.

So, if we are looking for railway capital we can step over the franchised operators. In this context, they are insignificant.

Other operators, known as open access, may own a little more, because they are discrete passenger or freight businesses. But even they are likely to lease their rolling stock and must also pay access charges, although as with franchise-holders there is nothing to prevent them from owning property (or indeed trains) outright.

As in previous times, the major asset base is the railway and its trains. Now that rolling stock is mainly owned by large financial houses, the infrastructure is all that is left. This is in the charge of Network Rail, but although it is a registered company it has been a 'not-for-dividend' enterprise limited by guarantee, without shareholders.

In one sense Network Rail was a fiction – a shell company created by the state so that railway assets had an owner-manager, but a change of obscure European statistical rules placed it wholly in the public sector as a government body on 1 September 2014. Until then the nation – and especially the Government – had been able to keep the railway industry at arm's length.

This position was not only convenient during Parliamentary questions ('The information sought by the Honourable Lady is not kept at the Department for Transport but by Network Rail, who may be contacted at King's Place, 90 York Way, London N1 9AG...'), but also gave the industry a mask of independence, notwithstanding the supervision of the Office of Rail and Road (ORR – formerly the Office of Rail Regulation), which may be a creature of Government but is not a Department of State.

Network Rail was the successor of Railtrack, which had shareholders and was a genuine member of the private sector. It was also a genuine failure, suggesting that it is no longer possible to recreate a commercial railway in the sense of an industry that makes a real cash profit when the books have been balanced.

The country's need for an efficient, comprehensive railway is quite a separate matter, and the cost of supporting it must in fairness be set against the possible effects on the economy if the railway was not there, in the same way that the country would suffer grievously if it was deprived of the (unprofitable) health service.

So a new crisis is looming, and that is one reason why this book was written, although it is not intended to be a plea for any particular structure. In other words, it is not a tract urging either renationalisation or greater free market deregulation.

But there are real problems once again. What is clear, as the storm clouds gather, is that we have been here before, and in arguably less favourable circumstances too.

This commentary does not reach the present post-1993 Railways Act era until Part 3, but the purpose of the earlier chapters is to set the situation in some kind of context, however feeble the reader may judge the result to be.

In other words, if the author does have one strong belief (apart from a conviction that railways will be essential for the foreseeable future) it is that we cannot usefully discuss what might happen next until we have considered how we got here.

An examination of historical records (some of which are discussed in this book for the first time) suggests that there has rarely been a period during the last hundred years when the industry sailed in placid waters.

The occasional conflicts between operators and their colleagues (or Network Rail) over such matters as paths and routeings occasionally make a headline or two in the trade press at least, but they are as water unto wine compared to some of the turbulent events of the past.

This is not a reference to those well-documented serio-comic dramas of the mid-19th century in which one company locked a competitor's locomotive in a shed, or navvies braced themselves for a pitched battle, but rather the vigorous exchanges in Parliament and elsewhere over the rights and wrongs of such issues as Government payments to railway shareholders in wartime, or how many companies should exist, and, of course, the fundamental question of who should actually own the railways.

Privatisation triggered fresh conflicts after 1994, particularly in the first decade, when the Rail Regulator focused on Railtrack with such determination that at times the relationship seemed to resemble a minor war rather than a regulatory regime. There was bitterness on both sides, which came to a head when the Government decided that Railtrack had to go, while the heat of the battle for control rose still further when the short-lived and often pilloried Strategic Rail Authority was added to the matrix. The result was confusion, so much so that in 2004 a critical Committee of MPs would report that there was 'astonishing and fundamental disagreement'.

The amount of public money that should be provided for the industry often makes headlines now (and not just in the trade press), but MPs were already debating this issue in the 1930s, when the railways were theoretically private sector enterprises through and through. The resulting debts were later just one more straw on the back of the camel that was the unhappy British Transport Commission. It thought it had won the war for capital when the Government agreed to fund its modernisation plan, only to discover to its discomfort that it was being held to its promises of restored profitability.

However, the Commission surely did have cause for complaint when Governments from both sides of the House tampered brazenly with its affairs in the name of political expediency.

Winston Churchill discovered that fare rises might affect election results, so he took on the Commission in much the same spirit with which he had confronted Hitler ten years earlier.

In short, the railways have been a political football for a long time, and the often ill-informed decisions of briefly appointed Ministers will probably continue to be one of the hazards of the game.

The industry has a long, complex history, much of which it may be proud, but we are only in the middle of yet another chapter.

Envisage, if you will, a broad and fertile valley. This green landscape can stand as a metaphor for the later 19th century, when the industry was approaching its most prosperous period.

Well-established giants like the London & North Western and the irritatingly innovative Midland have traced their metal tentacles across the face of the nation, transforming it for ever. One or two hillocks in our otherwise smooth valley represent the less fortunate members of the family – such as the locally promoted enterprises that had gone all out to connect their town with the nearest main line, only to find that they could not stay in business.

But generally all is calm as Victoria gives way to Edward, and the railways revel in a near golden age, which is tarnished only by the restrictions on their rates imposed by the Railway & Canal Traffic Acts and the insistence of the Board of Trade that they pay for expensive luxuries like block working and continuous brakes.

It is true that the embryo unions are muttering about nationalisation and occasionally staging strikes, but the effects are small.

Edward is replaced by George, and now there are foothills ahead. The ground rises more steeply as the international situation worsens, and suddenly the skies are red over Europe. War changes the world for ever, and when peace returns the railways must reassess their position if they wish to survive.

To pursue this metaphor further, the industry seems to have been roaming through mountainous regions ever since. Many books have been written over the years with such titles as *How to make the British railways pay*, *The rail problem* and *The train that ran away*. Perhaps they were reflecting a more general disquiet.

Governments, too, have repeatedly tried to untangle the rails, and there have been various landmark years when momentous decisions were made – 1921, 1947, 1962, 1968 and 1993 were just some of them.

The nation continued to pursue the ideal of net railway profits for far longer than was sensible in an internal combustion age. Ministers and their officials remained entranced by the possibility of a return to a self-supporting – indeed profitable – industry, and they were not alone.

The 1968 Transport Act opened the door to formal payments from public funds for loss-making but 'socially necessary' passenger services, and reality really began to take over in 1982, when Serpell concluded that the only truly commercial railway would be a very small one at best.

Fortunately, in spite of the hard-nosed Government then in power, the post-

Serpell decision was that railways were still needed.

Within a decade of Serpell an older controversy came alive again: should the railways be the property of the state?

It might have been thought that the nationalisation of 1948 had settled this point for good (and there were sound reasons for believing it to be so, as discussed in Chapter 9).

But an ingenious Treasury and a Government living on borrowed time would not accept this, so a new structure was pushed through in some haste, intended to be complete and irreversible before the General Election of 1997.

The early consequences were mixed. Some of the new franchised operators settled down reasonably well, but others tried to apply the principles of the bus industry to railways or lost their grip on performance. The result was burnt fingers and in some cases early terminations.

The private sector infrastructure owner made poor decisions and duly came to grief, having promoted an unachievable modernisation project while being (it has been said) almost unhealthily obsessed with its share price.

Even the last decade has not been entirely smooth. Some over-optimistic operators have been forced to fall on their swords, while the debate about renationalisation is still alive and well.

But against this background of turmoil (which is no more than an echo of every decade since the First World War) something remarkable has happened.

Passenger figures dipped below 1,000m in the early 1960s, but after reaching dismal lows 20 years later they have now recovered spectacularly to the point where comparisons with traffic levels in the 1920s begin to be justified. An industry thought to be in terminal decline has turned round and bitten its accusers – hard.

Success is rarely an unmixed achievement. The new demands have strained the physical assets, particularly after several decades of rationalisation.

Former talk of closures and 'singling' has been replaced by urgent discussions about what lines should be reopened or even built from scratch, or which sections should be redoubled or quadrupled.

Successors of the hands that removed goods loops and demolished stations a few decades ago are now being employed to put them back, while the passenger rolling stock fleet is set to almost double in size by 2040, according to one Network Rail report.

But that fertile valley of net profits is further away than ever, and the reason is not hard to find. When the railways were paying dividends, they could do so because of their revenues from freight.

Passenger railways are rarely profitable on their own account. British Railways Board Chairman Richard Marsh remarked in 1976:

'I doubt whether the railway will ever produce a conventional commercial return on capital invested and, indeed, I know of no passenger railway in the world which does.

If the problem was simply one of "over-manning", "incompetent management" or "awkward unions", someone would have solved it long ago.'

In spite of this, the Board went on to maintain in the later 1980s that its InterCity business had become self-standing, but a semblance of profitability was achieved only by a judicious separation of the various flows and by loading some of the more inconvenient costs on to the other BRB businesses, which included freight as well as Regional Railways and Network SouthEast.

Even if InterCity could cover its direct movement costs it seems unlikely that it could have also supported all the infrastructure and headquarters organisation it was using, as the Board had already suspected in private and Serpell later suggested in public.

What matters now is that privatisation in the 1990s separated the freight and passenger businesses, apparently for good.

Several freight operators have survived without public sponsorship or support (apart from occasional railfreight facilities grants), but their profits no longer cross-subsidise the passenger trains.

One passenger operator more or less inadvertently acquired a railfreight business during a period of wheeling and dealing over franchises, but has since chosen to dispose of it again.

So although the challenges of the next decade may be more about the problems of success than failure, that does not mean we can return to the happy days of net profits.

The upgrading of the railway, which is being fuelled by growing demand, is being paid for to a great extent by borrowing. That cannot go on for ever, as the British Transport Commission proved more than 50 years ago.

It has been said that those who will not heed the mistakes of the past are destined to repeat them. In an attempt to avert that unhappy outcome, it is in the past that this narrative begins.

Part 1:

The luxuries of competition

Chapter 1

'Laborious, dangerous work'

British governments have customarily regarded the country's railways with a certain reserve.

From a standing start in the early 19th century, the industry grew rapidly under the impetus of high-pressure steam.

Within a generation, a short line connecting two obscure north-eastern towns had proved to be the cradle of a mighty enterprise.

This vigorous – sometimes almost frantic – expansion was calculated to cause official frowns in Whitehall, not least because it was unprecedented.

Politicians and civil servants were particularly concerned on the grounds of safety. This was not only because travel by train posed numerous and often novel hazards, but also because the rail was an unpredictable influence on society – and that implied a risk to national security. Governments do not care for new sources of power and influence that may prove hard to control.

The railways had quickly proved themselves as effective mass-movers, and had become sufficiently mature to bring thousands of provincial visitors to London for the Great Exhibition in 1851.

Naturally the Exhibition benefited, but this kind of efficiency was calculated to alarm the ruling classes, who had already feared that revolutionaries could be transported with ease around the country, allowing them to gather in huge multitudes for the purpose of fomenting unrest.

Sometimes the multitudes did indeed gather – such as the Chartists, who held a notable rally at Kennington Common in south London on 10 April 1848.

The *Illustrated London News* reported that:

'The trains which arrived at the London and North-Western Railway [in other words, Euston] brought several persons from Manchester, Birmingham, Rochdale, Liverpool, and other parts of Lancashire, to be present during the proceedings of the day; and there were some from as far even as Edinburgh and Glasgow.'[1]

This was new. It had been possible to travel from Scotland to London by stagecoach before the railways came, but only over many days and at a price that was beyond the means of most people.

The railways were spreading into every corner of national life: they were even a major influence on an easing of company law in the middle of the century, so that limited liability enterprises could now be set up without the cumbersome requirement of a Private Act of Parliament – although new railways normally needed at least one enabling Act for other reasons, such as the gaining of powers to make compulsory purchases of land and build across highways.

In spite of this rapid growth, the Government had not been particularly quick to control the railways in any detail.

The Stockton & Darlington had opened for business in 1825 as the first recognisably modern railway, but the first public Act of Parliament that attempted to regulate railways in general did not appear until 1840, although minor legislation had been passed in 1835, 1838 and 1839, requiring railway companies to operate level crossings safely and to carry mail for the General Post Office. (Section 71 of the 1835 Highways Act provided that 'whenever a Railroad shall cross any Highway for Carts or Carriages, the Proprietors of the said Railroad shall make and maintain good and sufficient Gates at each of the said Crossings, and shall employ good and proper Persons to attend to the opening and shutting of such Gates…')

The various regulatory Acts passed from 1840 did much to control how railways should be run. They created (and then belatedly empowered) government inspectors who investigated accidents and whose approval was needed before a new line could be opened, while also imposing obligations on companies to run 'cheap' trains and make statistical returns, among many other matters.

1844 to 1846 also saw the first 'railway mania', in which hundreds of new railways whose promoters sought Private Acts competed for Parliamentary time as well as investors' funds. At its peak, this flood placed a severe strain on the legislative process.

In Britain, private enterprise had been entirely responsible for developing the system so far, and system was now the right word. By the early 1850s a future network could be seen, although many important links and indeed main lines had yet to be added.

Scotland and England were connected via Carlisle, which was how Chartists from north of the border had been able to reach London in 1848, thanks to the newly opened Caledonian line.

The East Coast route lay in the future (although the embryo Great Northern built a temporary London terminus in 1850, with King's Cross following in 1852), while the Midland Railway only gained its own London station at St Pancras in 1868, but even so many towns were already on the map.

The Great Western extended its influence in a south-westerly direction using the connecting lines that were built through Devon and Cornwall from Bristol, eventually connecting places like Falmouth and Penzance directly with London once the Royal Albert Bridge at Saltash had been opened in 1859. The GWR would later regret its adoption of Brunel's broad gauge, but only completed the conversion of its network to the standard gauge used in the rest of the country in 1892.

The beginnings of a railway clearing service had emerged in 1842, so that the revenue from through transits of both passengers and freight could be apportioned between the companies involved. This machinery gained statutory authority in 1850.

(Due the 21st Decem: 1866)

Bristol & Exeter Railway Company.

DEBENTURE BOND.

No. ~~NBC~~ £1000

One Thousand Pounds

By Virtue of an Act passed in the sixth year of the reign of his late Majesty, King William the Fourth, intituled *"An Act for making a Railway from Bristol to Exeter, with Branches to the Towns of Bridgewater, in the County of Somerset, and Tiverton in the County of Devon,"* and of a certain other Act passed in the first year of the reign of her present Majesty, Queen Victoria, intituled *"An Act for making several Branches in the County of Somerset from the line of the Bristol and Exeter Railway, and for amending the Act relating to such Railway,"* and of another certain Act of Parliament passed in the third year of the reign of her said present Majesty, intituled *"An Act to amend and enlarge the powers and provisions of the Acts relating to the Bristol and Exeter Railway,"* WE, THE BRISTOL AND EXETER RAILWAY COMPANY, incorporated by and under the said first recited Act, in consideration of the Sum of *One Thousand* Pounds to us, in hand paid by *Henry Bennett, of High Street Exeter, Draper*

do assign unto the said *Henry Bennett*

his Executors, Administrators, and Assigns, the said Undertaking, and all and singular the Rents, Rates, Tolls, and Sums of Money arising by virtue of the said several Acts, and each and every and either of them and all the Estate, Right, Title, and Interest of the said Company in and to the same,

To Hold unto the said *Henry Bennett*

his Executors, Administrators, and Assigns, until the said sum of *One Thousand Pounds* together with Interest for the same after the rate of *Four Pounds* for every One Hundred Pounds for a Year, shall be fully paid and satisfied.

And it is hereby stipulated that the said Principal Sum of *One Thousand Pounds* shall be repayable and paid on the *twenty first* day of *December* which will be in the year One Thousand Eight Hundred and *Sixty Six* and that in the mean time, the said Company shall, in respect of Interest as aforesaid, on the said Principal Sum, pay to the bonâ fide Holder hereof, or to the Agents of such Holder, or to Persons duly authorized to receive the same, the several Sums mentioned in the Coupons or Interest Warrants hereto annexed, at the times specified therein. And that after the said *21st* day of *December* all liability of the said Company for the payment of Interest shall cease.

Given under our Common Seal, this *twenty ninth* day of *August* One Thousand Eight Hundred and *fifty nine*

James Buller
Chairman

J. W. Harwood SECRETARY.

Payable on presentation, when due, at the Bank of Messrs GLYN, MILLS & Co., LONDON.

Transport itself would not get its own department of state until after the First World War, and the early railways were included within the responsibility of the Privy Council Committee for Trade and Foreign Plantations (which officially adopted its alternative and simpler title of *Board of Trade* in 1861).

But although the railways were being increasingly regulated, the Government of the day stopped short of a complete takeover. The 1844 Railway Regulation Act took matters to the brink by including powers to compulsorily purchase future railways but not existing ones. This may have been a tactic to discourage high railway rates, but in any event the powers were never exercised.

Notwithstanding the provisions of the 1844 Act, the concept of nationalisation probably did not come easily to Victorians. The structure of government was far smaller than it is today, with primitive welfare arrangements depending on parish vestries, medical care mostly provided by self-employed doctors or local charitably funded hospitals, and many elements of modern administration yet to be added to the Whitehall matrix.

Neither would nationalisation have been popular among those investors who were drawing worthwhile dividends from their railway shareholdings.

There were variations, naturally, but in 1870 the London & North Western's annual dividend was 6⅝% – a fairly typical figure for the period, which was matched precisely by the Great Northern. Other shareholders had less cause to celebrate: the Great Eastern often struggled, but after several years in the 1860s when nothing was paid at all, it managed to find 15 shillings in 1869 (¾%) and 17s 6d at the end of 1870 (⅞%).

At the other extreme double-figure dividends were not unknown, although many more were predicted in overoptimistic prospectuses than actually realised. Even so, the little Maryport & Carlisle paid 11% in 1870 and 12¾% the following year, while the happy shareholders in the Taff Vale received an almost unbroken succession of

LEFT: Railway investor, 1859.

BELOW: Railway expansion (*The Times*, 1854).

GREAT WESTERN RAILWAY.—Extension to Wolverhampton.—Notice is hereby given, that on Tuesday, November 14, the BIRMINGHAM, WOLVERHAMPTON, and DUDLEY LINE, connecting the Great Western Railway at Birmingham with Wolverhampton, Wellington, Shrewsbury, Oswestry, Chester and Birkenhead for Liverpool, will be OPENED for public traffic. On and after that day passengers may proceed by certain trains to and from stations between Paddington and Wolverhampton without change of carriage. Those proceeding to and from stations north of Wolverhampton will have to change carriages in the Birmingham station for the present, every facility and accommodation for which will be provided there. Train bills for the remainder of the month may be procured at all stations after the 11th inst.—Paddington, Nov. 9, 1854.

double-figure dividends between 1870 and 1888, which peaked at a remarkable 17½% in 1882.

The influence of the railway companies also penetrated the chambers of the Houses of Parliament. In 1883 there were 67 railway directors sitting as MPs and 56 in the Lords.

So the companies were permitted to continue, but the details of their business became the subject of particularly detailed official scrutiny in the 1880s, when the Government felt forced to take action in response to traders' complaints.

Select Committees sat in 1881 and 1882 to investigate railway charges, and one eventual result was the passing of the Railway & Canal Traffic Act of 1888. However, a further prolonged period of bargaining followed, so that a uniform General Classification of Goods did not come into force until 1 January 1893.

This was not the end of the matter, because some traders who had enjoyed 'exceptional' status under the former arrangements now found themselves required to pay higher, although legal, rates.

In response to their protests a further Parliamentary investigation was held into the rates charged for goods, and this (to quote a later commentary) decided that the companies had 'unreasonably disturbed the trade of the country, and that it ought to be placed out of their power to act in a similar manner in future'.

This ominous conclusion, which should perhaps have been engraved on the wall of every railway boardroom, triggered the passing of another Railway & Canal Traffic Act in 1894. If a complaint was made about any increase imposed from 1 January 1893, even within legal limits, the railway company now had to satisfy the Railway & Canal Commissioners that it was reasonable.

Firm financial regulation had arrived with a vengeance. It would hamper the industry until nationalisation – and beyond.

Despite such interventions, many people had reason to be more or less satisfied with the status quo, but the fundamental question of who should own the railways was debated with increasing frequency later in the 19th century, particularly by supporters of the emerging political left wing.

One of them, a socialist campaigner called Keddell, had argued in 1887 that money was wasted under private ownership.[2] Among the headings he cited were 'excessive and ridiculous compensation paid for land' (at this time many new railways were still being built, so land purchases were continuing) and 'money wasted on legal expenses'. This latter objection would prove to have a long life and indeed is still heard today.

Another pamphleteer urged nationalisation with an unusual twist in 1890, by urging that Third Class rail travel should be free, with the costs of running the network being met mainly from rates and taxes.[3] He speculated that a superior class might survive on some routes, for which a paid-for ticket would still be required, but did not consider the question of goods traffic.

Unsurprisingly, this particular form of nationalisation did not find favour with either the railway companies or the Government, but state ownership in general would continue to be debated into the following century.

The railway companies were now reaching their peak, but financial and industrial stresses were looming too.

The railway industry had become a significant source of employment in many parts of the country well before the end of the 19th century. The total number of staff ('servants') employed by the companies would have grown rapidly as the network expanded, but statistics are elusive because the companies were not required to provide staff totals in the annual Railway Returns that they prepared for the Board of Trade.

Census returns provide some clues, but general labourers and platelayers were not classified as railway company servants before 1901, and the number of people employed by firms that supplied the railway industry is also very difficult to assess.

However, it has been recorded that 9,130 people were employed by the railways in the London area in 1861, and that the total had more than quadrupled to 39,501 by 1901.[4]

The main 'railway towns' in the provinces, such as Doncaster, Derby and Swindon, also employed large numbers of men in the various companies' works, while there were also significant workforces in the railway hotels and ships.

Although reliable statistics are rare, we do know that when the railways were grouped in 1923, the newly amalgamated companies inherited some 676,000 staff.

The 19th-century companies had probably been no worse than many other Victorian employers, but a peculiarity of railway work was the unusual degree of 'safety critical' responsibilities, as they are now known.

It was true that many industries involved hazards, and people like mill hands working with fast-moving machinery could be hurt or even killed if they failed to take care, but an inattentive signalman or driver could cause a major accident, particularly before the development of the most basic safety devices such as mechanical interlocking of points and signals in the 1870s.

Until then, the safety of railway working depended entirely on the vigilance of the staff, while the long hours that they were routinely expected to work occasionally aroused public disquiet. A particularly tragic example of this was provided by one signalman in November 1892, who was overcome by sleep while on duty at Manor House – a North Eastern Railway box between Northallerton and Thirsk. When he awoke a few minutes later he mistakenly gave a 'line clear' signal, having forgotten that a stationary goods train had come to a stand near his box. An overnight express from Scotland collided with it, and eight people died.

He was charged with the manslaughter of the goods train guard, but there was an outcry when it emerged in evidence that his child had been taken seriously ill and that he had not been able to sleep. Having searched for a doctor, he returned home to find that the child had died and his wife so distraught that he did not like to leave her.

Exhausted, he had then reported himself as unfit for duty that night, but his plea was refused on the grounds that no relief was available. It also seems that the extent of his unfitness was not made clear when the message seeking another signalman was sent.

The jury found him guilty, but the judge took the circumstances before the accident into full account and ruled that he should be discharged – a highly popular decision.

The Board of Trade accident inspector Major Marindin later wrote:

'I think it right to record my opinion that a tour of duty of ten hours is the outside which ought to be allowed in main line signal-cabins, and that the employment of signalmen for a greater number of hours, consecutively, especially at night, upon lines where they have to deal with considerable traffic of all kinds, including fast express traffic, is an element of danger…'

Signalmen's working hours were reduced after this report had been published, and a better system of organising reliefs was introduced.

It was incidents like these that encouraged the formation and growth of the railway unions, but the companies refused to recognise them until the second decade of the 20th century, and even then only did so with great reluctance (see Chapter 2).

The unions also supported public ownership of railways. We get a taste of worker sentiment in this period from a discussion of the issue at the annual conference of the Amalgamated Society of Railway Servants held in Glasgow in October 1908, where a motion urging railway nationalisation received overwhelming support, with just two opposing votes.

It was not really as simple as that, because contemporary records suggest that the various left-wing factions were actually divided over the merits of nationalisation.

Although socialists continued to press for it, an 'anti-Socialist tract'[5] addressed to railway workers, which was published in 1909 by the National Movement Against Socialism, a moderate Labour group, maintained that the staff would be worse off under state control. Its author, T. R. Threlfall, disparaged the Glasgow resolution and assured his readers that 'there was every reason to believe that the delegates who had voted for it have not closely studied the subject from your point of view'.

Mr Threlfall did not reveal how he knew this, but claimed that state control would mean the loss of 120,000 jobs – or 20% of the workforce – as a result of 'unified management', and a reduction in working expenses of some 20-25%.

This was never tested, but it does appear – and the Glasgow vote in 1908 went some way to confirm it – that many railway workers were becoming increasingly dissatisfied.

It is not therefore surprising that they sought an alternative, and the only realistic reform that they could imagine was to allow the state to take over the railways.

Meanwhile, the newly named Labour Party had won 29 seats in the election of 1906, but this modest representation at Westminster could not prevent a worsening of railway industrial tensions until they culminated in the major strike of August 1911, which was essentially about union recognition.

It also divided railwaymen. After the strike had ended, the Guildhall police court was told how a Central London Railway signalman named Hands had assaulted a colleague:

'During the recent strike the complainant remained loyal and kept to his work, but the defendant went on strike, and that was the explanation of the trouble. During a dispute after the men had returned to work at the Post Office station Hands rained blows on Neal's face, knocking him on to the instruments.'[6]

This strike did have some longer-lasting effects: it revived the debate about railway nationalisation and it forced the Government to reconsider the relationship of the railways and the state.

'Even many of those people who are of the opinion that railway workers should be denied the right to strike, as in the Army and Navy, are compelled to admit that if this is done, the railway service, like the Army and Navy, should be operated by the state…,' said the author of an Independent Labour Party pamphlet in 1912.[7]

He went to outline what appeared to be a singular paradox, conceding that many railway shareholders received low dividends, but traders complained 'rightly' that goods rates were 'the highest in the world' while 'the majority' of railway workers 'receive for their laborious and oftentimes dangerous work so low a wage that it is absolutely impossible to lead a decent life'.

'Herein lies the case,' he continued, 'and it is an unanswerable one, for nationalisation of our railways.' He said that there were 217 individual railway companies and that, of their total nominal paid-up capital of some £1.3bn, some £197m was 'fictitious', because it consisted of 'nominal additions' to shareholdings that had not been paid for with cash. Plainly, creative accounting is not a new idea. However relevant this might have been, such arguments would soon become overtaken by events.

Chapter 2

'The luxuries of competition'

There had been a tendency for railway companies to amalgamate or take over rivals since the pioneering days, and this process continued into the early years of the 20th century.

The companies did not always get their way: for example, a Bill seeking a relatively late unification (in 1909) of the Great Central, Great Eastern and Great Northern was withdrawn when the extent of opposition to it became clear, but many others took place, sometimes because minor companies had found that they could not survive alone. Others chose to accept a tempting offer from a larger neighbour.

Over the decades this process had helped to create the giants of the industry, such as the London & North Western and the Great Western, although a number of smaller companies continued to exist as well.

But in spite of the Railway Clearing House, which provided a focus for cooperation at the most essential level – that of day-to-day accountancy – those companies that had survived the amalgamations were still separate enterprises until the First World War. However, some were members of joint working arrangements – the Somerset & Dorset was a classic example – or various kinds of management committees, such as the Cheshire Lines or the London Underground tube railways.

The early years of the 20th century have been called a golden age, but in fact the gold was already tarnishing by the time the new century dawned.

Net receipts in 1901 (including Ireland) had been just over £39m. They then rose fairly consistently until 1913, when they reached £52m. The percentage of gross revenue available as net was also steady at about 36-37% during the period, but if this was a golden age it was one on which the sun was rapidly setting. In any case, by 1910 the sunlight was being increasingly obscured by the storm clouds of industrial unrest and a bitter controversy over railway rates.

Beyond that lay the gloomy uncertainty of a world war and its aftermath.

Although their results were still healthy at first sight in the early 1900s, the companies had found that electric trams and London Underground extensions were starting to erode their passenger receipts, while the firm control of goods rates imposed by a succession of Railway & Canal Traffic Acts was also hurting them. Their determined opposition to union recognition was failing to change the tide of opinion in the workers' favour, even after the strike of 1911.

The conclusions of a Royal Commission later that year, which set out the terms of a compromise settlement involving an amended conciliation scheme, failed to heal the wounds of industrial division. In fact, both sides were disappointed.

One gleam of hope had been ignited by the prospect of an amendment to the

1894 Railway & Canal Traffic Act, which the Government was willing to contemplate so that goods rates could be legally increased to cover higher labour costs.

After the Royal Commission had produced its findings, Asquith's Government contemplated the amendment of the 1894 Act with some repugnance. Increases in railway rates were all too likely to bring traders into conflict with the companies once again, and that conflict could spill over into Parliament.

After some deliberation, a detailed Railways Bill was given its first reading on the unfortunate date of 1 April 1912. It did provide legal justification for increasing railway rates to cover greater costs, but the companies also discovered that there would be a steep price to pay for this concession, because regulation was to be extended to cover passenger fares in general for the first time and also any proposals by the companies to withdraw facilities. Against this, there were to be new powers allowing the companies to draw up working agreements.

Angry protests were heard from all sides. The *Daily Herald* described the proposed measure as a 'betrayal of the workers', because the provisions concerning working agreements did not include any security for staff who might have their jobs placed at risk by amalgamations.

Meanwhile, the traders and their associations remained implacably opposed to any increase in railway rates, as the Government had feared.

Under fire from all sides, the unhappy Government withdrew the unfortunate Bill before its Second Reading, and it was eventually replaced by a further Railway & Canal Traffic Act in 1913, which permitted changes in railway rates.

Armed with their new powers, the companies announced a general increase in goods rates of 4%, to apply from July.

As the traders seethed afresh, the Government contemplated the increasing paradoxes presented by the railways. Were they private entities or public utilities? How much state control was unavoidable? Its response was to appoint yet another Royal Commission, chaired by Lord Loreburn, to consider 'the relations between the railway companies as business concerns on the one hand, and the State as representing the community on the other'.

Meanwhile, the TUC had been maintaining its campaign in favour of railway nationalisation, and at the 1913 Congress a resolution was carried that instructed the TUC Parliamentary Committee to press for legislation.

A further conference was held early in 1914 by the Railway Nationalisation Society, which repeated the call, but the sittings of the Royal Commission had not been completed when war was declared and its proceedings were adjourned indefinitely.

The threat that the country faced in August 1914 changed the situation for ever, because it was realised that the railway companies had to be effectively unified in the interests of Imperial defence. This was achieved by the immediate activation of an executive committee, whose members were senior managers from the ten largest companies and which had existed in shadow form since 1912.

The Railway Executive Committee, as it soon became known, was now the Government's interface with the industry via the Board of Trade, whose President was the ex-officio chairman.

This was not nationalisation, because there was no change of ownership and company-level management continued, but nonetheless the Crown was 'in possession'.

In fact, the Committee was so effective that, although peace returned in 1918, it carried on for the time being while the Government considered how the railways should be managed in the longer term. There were still several interests in conflict, and to add to these problems the industry itself had been left on its knees by the excessive burdens of war.

The Government had agreed to pay the railways annual sums while the war continued, which would maintain their receipts at the 1913 level – a year in which gross revenues reached a record (at that time) of £139.2m.[1] In 1916 the agreement was revised, extending the control period for two years after peace had returned.

Although revenues rose sharply in the war years, so did working expenses, increasing from £87.2m in 1913 to £261.8m in 1920.

Railway profits remained flat, and the amount available to the companies to invest in asset renewal was severely limited. It is possible that only the amounts receivable under the continuance of the Government wartime control agreement staved off disaster.

In short, the worn-out, poverty-stricken railways were ripe for a change, and the voices that had been raised in favour of nationalisation before the war were heard once again.

They were joined by a newcomer to this controversy. This was Winston Churchill, who during a speech in the election of 1918 suggested that railway nationalisation was an idea whose time might have come.

He told his audience in Dundee (where he won the seat):

'So long as the railways are in private hands they may be used for immediate profit. In the hands of the state, however, it might be wise or expedient to run them at a loss if they developed industry, placed the trader in close contact with his market and stimulated development.'

In spite of this mildly phrased proposition, which was reinforced by a resolution in more forthright terms (this called for the railways 'to be worked, unhampered by any private interest ... exclusively for the common good') at the 1918 Labour Party Conference, nationalisation was not an easy option for the Government. This was partly because such a reform could have proved unpopular, and the Cabinet finally ruled it out in mid-1920. Under some pressure from the industry, it instead adopted two separate, less radical measures.

The first of these was a new department, unveiled as a key element of a Ministry of Ways & Communications Bill in February 1919. By the time of Royal Assent, later in the same year, its name had changed to the Ministry of Transport Act.

When Sir Eric Geddes introduced the Bill in the Commons, he told MPs:

'We must forego the luxuries of competition; we must forego private interest and local interest in the interest of the State. In the past private interest made for development, but today I think I may say that it makes for colossal waste.'[2]

These sentiments echoed the arguments made by at least one socialist more than three decades earlier, and the railway companies were challenged even further by one particular clause of the Bill, which appeared to allow the Minister to run his own trains:

'It shall be lawful for the Minister to establish and work transport services by land or water, and to acquire either by agreement or compulsorily such land or easements or rights in or over land, to construct such works, and to do all such other things as may be necessary for the purpose.' (Ministry of Ways & Communications Bill 1919, Clause 8(1))

This was alarming indeed, because the legislation as proposed appeared to authorise the Government to set up transport businesses – including railways – on its own account.

The same clause would have arguably permitted the Minister to attach existing railways to his new 'transport services', as he was also empowered to 'do all such other things as may be necessary'.

After a debate during which the Conservative MP Sir Frederick Banbury, who would prove to be the last Chairman of the Great Northern Railway, had told the Commons that 'it is really by a side wind carrying out nationalisation', the Bill was amended. However, the final Act still included a broadly drafted long stop, which applied to undertakings not already subject to the 1871 Regulation of the Forces Act (this had provided the government with powers to take control of the railways in a national emergency on a renewable weekly basis).

Now the Minister could go beyond the 1871 Act for up to two years, and take control of other undertakings too. This was intended to allow time 'for the consideration and formulation of the policy to be pursued as to the future position of undertakings to which this section applies'. In other words, the new Act was not necessarily the last word as far as the railway industry was concerned.

One safeguard remained: if an undertaking lodged an objection to being acquired by the Minister, his proposal had to be considered first by an advisory committee drawn from a preselected 'panel of experts', who could invite evidence from third parties.

Meanwhile, the railway companies had not been silent during the nationalisation

controversy. They had been bringing pressure to bear via the Railway Companies' Association, latterly supported by the Federation of British Industry, although the presence of many railway directors such as Sir Frederick in the Commons or Lords, which had been a factor for decades, was now mattering less and would soon become even less relevant after the companies had been 'grouped' in 1923.

In practice, the acquisitive provisions of the 1919 Act were never exercised, and the second of the Government's measures proved to be an ambitious programme of railway amalgamation. Private enterprise would be allowed to stay on the rails, at least for the time being.

Although the Ministry of Transport was duly established under its new Act, the Government's proposals for the future shape of the railway industry were set out in a White Paper published in the summer of 1920, which made it plain that nationalisation was no longer being considered. Instead, it was proposed that the railways should be amalgamated into seven groups – six for England and Wales and one for Scotland.

Although the *Railway Gazette* accepted that some form of grouping was necessary, it did not believe at first glance that the proposed structure was necessarily the best:

'It is not clear from the White Paper whether the larger railways forming the component parts of the new "grouped railways" will retain their separate entities as statutory companies and be worked by a managing committee, as in the case of the South Eastern & Chatham system. It is also to be noted that what may be termed extra-territorial lines are left untouched by the system of grouping. We shall still have the North Western lines in South Wales, the Southern group lines in North Cornwall, and Western lines at Chester and Birkenhead and so forth. Presumably these lines are to be left as bartering counters, and it does not require much inside knowledge to justify the belief that there will be considerable trouble in adjusting these and other matters.'[1]

By the time its next issue had appeared, a week later, the *Gazette* had found some further reasons for objecting to the proposals:

'The scheme appeared with provision for keeping a hand deep in the ... companies' pockets by proposing wages boards..., yet there was to be no financial guarantee. Small wonder that the ... five Scottish railway companies unanimously resolved: "That the scheme ... as outlined ... is open to many objections and would afford no protection ... and that any Bill framed on similar lines must be strenuously opposed." Indeed, rumour has it very similar views were expressed at a meeting of the Railway

The RCA (now TSSA) drafted two bills proposing nationalisation. Although these failed, the union claimed to have influenced the 1921 'Grouping' Act.

Companies Association. But second thoughts are notorious in differing from first ideas ... it is clear that the railways have not been consulted ... they are, therefore, in no way committed to the scheme, which represents a basis for negotiation.'[3]

The negotiations had only just started, and before they were completed the number of newly amalgamated groups had been whittled down to four, although two of them would now include part of Scotland in their territories.

Three were new companies, and a correspondent in the *Railway Gazette* suggested in mid-1922, after the Railway Act had been passed the previous year, that the four groups defined by the Act should not be called 'railways' at all: even the Great Western would be renamed the 'South Western Transportation Service'.[4]

This did not find favour with the editor of the *Gazette*, who offered his own titles. These were Great Western, Great Southern, Midland & North Western, and North Eastern – or Great Northern.

Despite this shower of helpful suggestions, the three new companies resolved to be known as the Southern Railway, the London Midland & Scottish Railway and the London & North Eastern Railway.

In all, 123 companies had been amalgamated or absorbed, and the 'Big Four' were able to take over on 1 January 1923 (six months earlier than originally envisaged), although the major joint railways such as the Midland & Great Northern and the Somerset & Dorset continued to be controlled by more than one company.

One important requirement of the new Act was that fares and charges would continue to be regulated. Section 20 created a 'Railway Rates Tribunal', which would be a court of record. It was to have three permanent members. These were to be 'a person of experience in commercial affairs', 'a person of experience in railway business' and the third, to serve as president, would be 'an experienced lawyer'. This trio was able to call on the services of additional members as required, who would be drawn from one of two panels set up for the purpose.

The companies were obliged to submit their proposed standard charges for the Tribunal's approval by the end of 1922. In general terms, their rates were to be based on the 'aggregate net revenues' that had been earned in 1913, plus specified allowances for capital expenditure since then.

Only the Great Western had been able to preserve its pre-Grouping identity, and the legal entity incorporated in 1835 continued to exist. The 'new' GWR was rather larger, however, having been amalgamated with a number of other companies as a result of the Act, particularly in Wales.

This continuity must have caused a good deal of celebration at Paddington, where tradition was always valued, and this was recognised by one Welsh newspaper cartoon in which a Great Western porter was seen to exclaim: 'Hooray: never even blew me cap off'.

Chapter 3

'Undue or unfair disadvantage'

As 1923 dawned, the amalgamated companies were accordingly launched on their new path, with just four managements now responsible for running the main system of British railways.

The companies whose lines made up the London Underground had remained outside the scope of the recent Act, but in 1923 the capital city was experiencing its own transport difficulties, largely because of the exuberant exploits of omnibus 'pirates'. Their excesses would encourage a major change to the organisation of transport in London within a decade.

The 'Big Four' also had numerous challenges to overcome. Industrial relations continued to be a sore point, which would reach a crisis with the calling of the General Strike in 1926, while the spread of the internal combustion engine was also starting to hurt them.

Their predecessors had already been losing short-distance urban traffic to the electric tram for more than 20 years, but now it was country passengers who were increasingly taking to the roads, as bus companies multiplied in rural areas.

The response of the railways was to increase the number of stopping places for local trains, usually by building inexpensive halts that did not need staff.

Unfortunately, although the new halts did attract some traffic, the country lines were not always well placed to compete on even terms with the buses, because they did not serve the centres of many smaller towns and villages so conveniently.

The Great Western, in particular, already operated an extensive Road Motor Department, the origins of which could be traced back almost to the beginning of the century, and there were railway-owned buses in other parts of the country as well.

These buses had originally been provided to extend a company's network beyond the limits of its railways: for example, the GWR took passengers by road onwards from Kingsbridge station to Salcombe, and from Helston to The Lizard. Similar arrangements existed in many other places.

Although railway bus routes normally served at least one station, local passengers were also carried. This brought the railways into direct competition with other operators. They, in turn, were not interested in complementing the train service, preferring to simply abstract its traffic where they could. This was a problem that became more serious for the railway companies as the decade wore on.

The situation was further complicated by the fact that the powers of the Big Four to operate buses were actually far from clear. Certainly the 1921 Railways Act provided no comfort, because its only mention of carriage by road concerned goods traffic.

Placed on the back foot, the companies concluded, not surprisingly, that they needed to fight fire with fire. In 1928 the Big Four and the Metropolitan Railway promoted Private Bills containing powers to run bus, coach and merchandise road services of any kind, not necessarily as railway feeders.

The applicants naturally urged that the powers they sought should be granted, saying:

'If the nation is to obtain the cheapest possible form of transport, and this is one of the first needs of the country, it is essential that the railways should have powers to operate road vehicles as part of their organisation.'[1]

As might have been expected, they did not have the easiest of rides. MPs briefed by existing road interests and their customers claimed during Parliamentary debates on the Bills that granting the railways the powers they sought could have the effect of reducing competition, and thus tend to increase rather than contain freight rates.[2]

Also, to judge by some of the statements made in Parliament, it did seem that the railways had been playing fast and loose with the rules, such as they were:

'In 1924, the Omnibus Owners' Association called the attention of the Great Western Railway to the fact that they were running an omnibus service for which they have had no legal power, in the opinion of the Association. The railway company replied that, notwithstanding that perhaps they had no legal power, they were not prepared to drop the service … but would be prepared to discuss with various omnibus companies the question of co-ordination or working agreements. Some omnibus companies refused; others … agreed to negotiate.'[3]

The same speaker (Sir Joseph Lamb, Conservative MP for Stone) also commented rather wryly that the Canal Commission had remarked that it was 'almost impossible to put in safeguards which you could make a railway company observe'.

Faced with such revelations, it is perhaps surprising that six of the seven Bills (there were two additional measures for the LMS and LNER in Scotland) were in fact passed, although with some amendments. The loser was the Metropolitan Railway, which was forced as a result to place a bus service it operated in Watford in the hands of a contractor until the Metropolitan was absorbed by the new London Passenger Transport Board in 1933.

With their confirmed road powers safely gathered in, it might have been thought that the Big Four would begin a strenuous (and legalised) campaign of road competition.

After some consideration, they evidently decided that discretion might be the better part of valour, perhaps because the Government was poised to licence and regulate bus services, which in fact came about in 1930.

The new Traffic Commissioners were not expected to sanction unbridled competition, which is probably why the railways often chose to invest in existing bus companies, usually taking a maximum share in any concern of no more than 50%, although directly railway-owned feeder road services continued for some time on the LMS and LNER.

In some cases of overlapping territories two railway companies took shares in the same bus operator, but in other parts of the country the share-out was simpler.

In the south-west of England, for example, the Great Western and the Southern each joined forces with an existing operator – the National Omnibus & Transport Company – which had started as an operator of steam buses in London and later expanded into the English provinces.

Almost all of the south-west peninsula was now to be divided up according to the railway company territories, and two new bus companies were created, to be owned equally by National Omnibus and the GWR or SR respectively.

All parties transferred virtually all their bus services to the new firms, which began business in 1929 as the Western National and Southern National Omnibus Companies.

But even while these companies were being formed, it soon emerged that negotiations had been taking place behind the scenes with the powerful bus combine owned by Thomas Tilling, which shortly afterwards bought out National Omnibus.

As a result, Tilling and the two railway companies then jointly owned most of the bus services in the South West until after the Second World War, when the rules would be changed again by an incoming Labour Government intent on nationalisation.

But before this could happen, the 1930s would present the railways with other difficulties. Some of these stemmed from obligations that had their origins in the previous century.

The railways had been 'grouped' – and indeed had come close to nationalisation – partly because they had been financially damaged by a world war. It had been hoped that the larger, amalgamated companies would have been able to prosper, partly as the result of what we would now call the economies of scale. The Grouping had made more than 1,000 railway directors redundant alone.

But although passenger figures reached record levels soon after the First World War, the 1920s became increasingly unkind as the decade advanced. We have already examined the effects of the internal combustion engine on passenger transport in this period, but railway goods traffic was also increasingly under siege, as motor lorries proliferated. All too often the railways found that they were being deprived of lucrative outbound traffic while they were still obliged to return the empty packing cases in the reverse direction.

This obligation stemmed from their status as common carriers, which had been imposed in the early days of the industry by a Government nervous of the effects of what it perceived as a steam-driven monopoly.

In the 19th century heyday of the railways, when nearly all road transport was animal-hauled, there was some justification for this view, but the restrictions from the horse-and-cart era continued when the lorry, car and bus had become commonplace.

In a free market the railways could have changed their rates to compete more effectively with road hauliers, and also increased their charges for carrying 'empties', but railway charges continued to be rigorously regulated by the Railway Rates Tribunal on behalf of the Government, which was apparently reluctant to make significant changes in the companies' favour.

If this was not bad enough, the Wall Street crash of 1929 and the recession that followed reduced the total freight market, while passenger figures were also depressed.

The burden of rates payable to local authorities was eased in 1928, when £4m was allocated to the railways to reduce their liabilities, but they in turn were obliged to pass on this nominal gain by reducing their goods charges for selected trades.

Thus a Government measure to help wider industry was channelled via the railway companies, and it is not clear if they directly benefited.

There was some more tangible relief for the companies shortly afterwards, when the last vestiges of Railway Passenger Duty were abolished in 1929. This was another Victorian relic that, although already partly abandoned, had still been raising some £400,000 a year (mainly from First Class fares) for the Government in the mid-1920s.[4]

The Government completed the abolition (the word used was 'remitted') of the duty on condition that the railway companies invested the money they retained in capital works.

The total amount does not sound very great now but, to place it in perspective, a major scheme providing a flyover at Cogload Junction, quadrupling the track through Taunton and the virtual rebuilding of Taunton station, together with other works that included the reconstruction of 16 bridges, cost the Great Western a grand total of £360,000 in 1930.[5]

Even so, the remission of the passenger duty by itself would not, even then, have allowed significant improvements in more than a few places on the Big Four's network of more than 32,000 route kilometres.

Of greater assistance in 1929 was a series of guaranteed Treasury grants made to the companies for capital works, intended to relieve unemployment, which were worth some £4.5m to the Great Western alone – roughly £300m at 2013 values.

Injections of capital that could be used to pay for infrastructure improvements were naturally welcome but, in spite of the hopes of improvement, the Big Four's revenues continued downwards in the early years of Grouping:

Advertising by a new bus company in 1930. Western National was partly railway-owned, although that fact was not apparent

Table 1: Revenue and journeys, 1923-1933

Year	Total receipts (£m)	Net revenue (£m)	Passenger journeys (m)
1923	195.6	45.6	1,319
1929	182.8	45.0	1,187
1930	172.6	37.7	1,161
1931	158.5	33.4	1,097
1932	145.4	26.4	1,069
1933	145.3	28.8	1,084

Source: Railway Research Service

Most of the other trends were also negative. Passenger receipts fell from £70.3m in 1923 to £51.1m in 1933 (although by now a slight recovery was evident: only £50.9m had been earned in the previous year), while freight receipts fell more sharply still, from £107.4m in 1923 to £78.5m in 1933 – and here no recovery could be seen.

The real danger sign as shown in Table 1 was, of course, the net receipts. As they tumbled, dividends inevitably followed them downwards; the companies paid £46.7m in dividends and interest in 1923, while by 1932 (a trough year in many ways) this total had dropped to only £28.1m – or 60% of the 1923 figure.

Dividends and interest paid were often slightly higher than the net receipts, being supported by raids on the reserves.

Although railway finances were mostly weak between the wars, there was still some significant capital investment in this period.

The Southern, uniquely among the Big Four, electrified substantial parts of its network. The newly grouped company had inherited 105km of electric railways from its constituents, but handed on 1,123km to the British Transport Commission 25 years later.[6]

In the same period the LNER invested in limited electrification (18km in south Tyneside in 1938) together with some highly publicised express locomotives and services, while the GWR built several main-line 'cut-offs', designed new locomotives, began using diesel railcars, modernised some major stations, and replaced semaphore signalling with colour lights at Paddington and Bristol Temple Meads.

The LMS accelerated its services, extended suburban electrification (such as the Manchester and Altrincham line in 1931), introduced diesel shunters, and developed several important new classes of locomotive, particularly in the Stanier era. It also began a major scheme to rebuild Euston, but this was interrupted by the war. A new station was not then achieved until the 1960s when the West Coast Main Line was also electrified, almost two decades after the industry had been nationalised.

The railways had no reason to deliberately drag their feet, but they were constrained by the doleful financial position, the problems of competition from road transport, and the unpromising traffic statistics that resulted, Government assistance notwithstanding.

Electrification of main lines remained on the back burner (the Southern's schemes were considered to be essentially suburban). The Government-sponsored Weir inquiry reported in 1931 that although suburban electrification was likely to spread, 'we have been unable to find any strong spirit of conviction in railway circles to warrant a belief that any schemes … dealing with main lines are likely…'[7]

The GWR did investigate converting its line between Taunton and Penzance, partly because of the rising price of steam coal, but this scheme was finally put to rest when consultants concluded in 1939 that the return on capital was unlikely to be sufficient.

Even so, capital schemes were given a modest boost after more loans became available under the Railways (Agreement) Act of 1935. This measure created a company known as the Railway Finance Corporation Ltd (it was dissolved in 1952), which arranged capital loans for the railway companies, drawing on a fund of £32m.

The companies were to provide security for their borrowing with specially issued 4% debenture stock, returnable on repayment of the loan, although the actual rate of interest would be the lowest the Finance Corporation (owned by the Treasury) could command.

The Second Reading of the Railways (Agreement) Bill on 13 December 1935 gave rise to some lively discussion about the role of the state, and whether it should be providing financial assistance in this way to privately owned companies.

Opening the debate[8], Neville Chamberlain referred to criticisms that had been made by some opposition MPs (one of them was Herbert Morrison). Mr Chamberlain said they had suggested that 'this project was merely the opening phase of a sort of Rake's Progress upon which the Government were about to embark, so that they might bolster up a decaying capitalist system by the indiscriminate use of public credit to finance private enterprise. There is no foundation for a belief of that kind.'

A little further on, Mr Chamberlain explained why his critics were mistaken:

'We make a definite distinction between what I have described as the indiscriminate use of Government credit or Government finance for private enterprise, and a project of this kind, which deals with statutory undertakings … these statutory bodies are also carrying on a great public service, which affects not only those who are employed … but the whole public who are served by the undertakings.'

This did not convince Albert Alexander, who represented Sheffield Hillsborough for Labour. He told the House:

'Even if the Government, against all sound argument, adhere to the doctrine of the maintenance of private control of this great and necessary national service, this scheme … falls short through lack of co-ordination. The scheme is four-sided; four companies are to be allowed to come separately for finance …each one of the four sides in the scheme is incomplete and lacks cohesion.'

These exchanges in the Commons are illuminating because they imply that opinions about the railway industry were evolving. It was now being seen (in some quarters, at least) as an essential service meriting some public support, rather than just a set of private enterprises that should be able to survive by themselves.

However, at this stage the proponents of assistance in some form came from the right, while the left opposed it so long as private ownership continued.

Even so, once the principle of state support is admitted, the next question is inevitably how much there ought to be.

Meanwhile, the problem of freight competition had refused to go away. The licensing of bus services from 1930, and investment by the railways in bus companies, had narrowed if not closed the previous divisions between buses and trains, although express coaches would continue to snap at the heels of the railways' long-distance passenger business.

A Royal Commission on Transport had been appointed in August 1928, and earlier recommendations (in its Second Report)[9] had led to the 1930 Road Traffic Act and the national licensing of bus routes and operators.

More recently it had suggested that something similar should apply to road hauliers.[10] However, this idea had been allowed to lie on the table for a while, not least because the hauliers lobbied hard against it. Before any decision was made, a Ministry of Transport conference (the Salter Conference) had been convened in July 1932, and this also favoured regulation of road freight carriers.

But Salter did not prove to be as helpful as the railways could perhaps have wished, saying:

'We conceive that, in the main, transport will divide itself between road and rail as the demand of those who require it, and the facilities offered by those who provide it, determine … we believe that the best division of function will be obtained mainly through the deliberate effort of those engaged in road and rail transport to coordinate their services and give the public the full advantages of complementary service.'[11]

This argument, or something like it, would be repeated many times over the following decades in connection with debates about how tightly transport should be regulated in the public interest, but Salter went on to observe (somewhat fruitlessly, as later events would demonstrate) that 'there has hitherto been a competition between road and rail of an embittered character which we hope our proposals will help to end'. Salter's main plea, then, was for collaboration rather than competition, aided by a degree of regulation on both sides, even if the details of the regulation were not identical.

The customary private sector plea for freedom to innovate and take its own decisions would be disregarded by Attlee's Government after 1945 as nationalisation approached, but it would be discussed at length when bus deregulation was proposed in the early 1980s, and would surface again in the 1990s during railway privatisation.

However, the immediate consequence of Salter was not necessarily unfavourable to the railways.

The Ministry of Transport now had the conclusions of two bodies of inquiry at the top of its list, and the consensus was that road hauliers should be regulated.

The result was the Road & Rail Traffic Act of 1933, which included a hierarchy of licences – 'A', 'B' and 'C'. The last of these was required by a vehicle conveying goods only for the vehicle owner's purposes, while the first permitted carriage for hire and reward. 'B' licences were a combination of the two.

Debates during the passage of the Bill included some points made by Honourable Members that might kindly be described as obscure, including whether a baker delivering bread to a military camp could claim Crown immunity, and therefore avoid the need to hold any licence at all.[12]

The real difficulty with the 1933 Act, from the railway point of view, was that it did not control road hauliers' charges.

The fact that 'A' and 'B' licence-holders whose permits had expired after the original issue would have to satisfy the Licensing Authority that a renewal was justified by the needs of their area was not enough by itself.

Railway charges would still be decided by the Railway Rates Tribunal in accordance with the 1921 Railways Act, while licensed road hauliers would be free to charge whatever the traffic would bear.

On the other hand, owners of coastal shipping and harbours were to be given special powers to object to railway charges, which provoked Harold Macmillan, who was at that time the Conservative member for Stockton-on-Tees and also a director of the Great Western Railway, to sum up why his industry felt bemused:

'There are today three competing forms of transport for this traffic – rails, merchant shipping and roads. Two of them are absolutely free to quote whatever rates they like on any class of goods. The other is bound, and it is somewhat anomalous that it should not be the transport system which is bound that is protesting against unfair competition.'[13]

After pointing out that shipping operators had been paying dividends varying between 5% and 15% over the previous seven or eight years, Mr Macmillan continued:

'Last night an Hon. Member made an attack on one of the great railways because it charged too much. The whole object of this Clause is to prevent them from charging too little. But we are also frequently attacked, especially by the independent dock and harbour authorities, on the ground that the charges are too low, and are unfairly attracting traffic … so that we find ourselves in the peculiar position of a double attack both on the ground of dearness and of cheapness.'[14]

These apparent contradictions of the Road & Rail Traffic Bill notwithstanding, it received Royal Assent on 17 November 1933, complete with the clauses (at Section 39) that gave protection to coastal carriers. In particular it set out their right of appeal, should they be placed 'at an undue or unfair disadvantage' by a railway company.

Chapter 4

'Commercial and sensible lines'

The Road & Rail Traffic Act received Royal Assent less than five months after another important piece of transport legislation had come into effect, creating the London Passenger Transport Board or LPTB. This new body took over most of the capital's public transport on 1 July 1933, ending the careers of companies like the Metropolitan Railway in the process.

Apart from the Big Four's services, which remained outside its remit, the reach of 'London Transport', as the Board was generally known, was almost all-embracing, taking in the Underground (both subsurface and tube) and street tramways, as well as buses and Green Line coaches. Trolleybus routes recently introduced in south west London by one of the tram operators were also included.

One Underground route stayed outside LT's control: this was the short Waterloo & City line, which had just two stations – the termini at Waterloo and Bank. This had been promoted by the London & South Western Railway in the late 19th century to provide a convenient route to the office for the multitudes of LSWR passengers who worked in the City, and it had been inherited by the Southern Railway in 1923.

The line was undoubtedly an exception to the otherwise neat pattern of the capital's urban transport, but 'the Drain', as it was semi-affectionately known, would continue to be the responsibility of the Southern and its successors until railway privatisation, when it was transferred to the Underground.

The London changeover was unification rather than nationalisation, but it was a major reform.

The new LPTB was a statutory body and public authority, and it had been able to exercise compulsory purchase powers to create its new network. It had the duty to be self-supporting and received no Government subsidies, apart from its inheritance of certain time-limited Treasury grants that had been payable to some of its constituents before the takeover.

Its acquisitions were financed by the issue of interest-bearing stock with a capital value of some £110m. This, plus about £3m in cash, was shared out among 169 undertakings.[1]

The creation of London Transport (or LT) was significant because, unlike the Big Four, it was not a private enterprise: any profits after the payment of working expenses and interest could be used to fund new projects or repay loans of capital.

LT also marked a step forward in the regulation of public transport because it could make its own decisions about bus and tram routes within its substantial Passenger Area, although the problems posed by 'pirate' omnibuses ten years earlier had already been largely dealt with by restricting the streets they could serve under powers contained in the London Traffic Act of 1924.

London Transport's largely unassailable monopoly status made it unique among transport operators, but the ever-vigilant Railway Rates Tribunal still exerted some influence over LT's rates and charges.

This kind of monopoly was only acceptable where there was no private profit motive, although many years later 'not-for-dividend' Network Rail would not be given the same degree of liberty and would indeed be tightly regulated – at least in theory.

London Transport was one example of those public corporations that became popular in Britain between the wars – the BBC, which had been converted from a commercial company about six years before LT was created, was another.

There were some differences: the LPTB had issued non-voting interest-bearing stock, whereas there was no such thing at the BBC, but even so the relative commercial disinterest of corporations like the LPTB or BBC was perceived to be a public good, partly because there were no shareholders to press for high dividends.

Meanwhile, although LT made a vigorous start by investing in new buses, beginning design work on the next generation of tube stock and also announcing, in 1935, that its tram network would be replaced by trolleybuses, the Big Four had less cause to be happy.

It is true that there were some publicity-driven developments in this period associated with streamlined locomotives, faster expresses and (unprofitable) railway air services.

In 1938 the LNER set an enduring steam speed record with *Mallard*, although this was a stunt that slightly damaged the locomotive and did not pave the way for significantly higher speeds on scheduled services, at least while they remained steam-hauled.

But the essential paradox remained, with no relief in sight. This was that although the Government had provided some financial assistance in 1929 and 1935, the companies continued to be treated in the main as powerful monopolies that had to be regulated in the public interest, while other less restricted modes of transport – particularly freight hauliers – were prospering at their expense.

The growing London Underground also posed a threat to suburban revenue. There had been occasional conflicts in the later 19th century, as companies such as the District jostled for position among the main-line companies and sometimes threatened to penetrate their territories, but the electric tubes were barely established – the first, critical phase of their development deep below central London was complete by 1907 – before they too were striding into the suburbs. Here they mostly ran on the surface, because this was cheaper than tunnelling.

Many of the favoured suburbs grew rapidly once the Underground had given them modern stations, often of considerable architectural merit, where clean electric trains called at frequent intervals.

They also provided an attractive alternative to the grimy Victorian establishments, wreathed in steam, which had typically confronted London area commuters until then – apart, perhaps, from those who lived in the growing Southern Electric territory.

Even the Southern's electrification schemes tended to concentrate on tracks and trains, so that some of the stations on electrified lines remained gas-lit, in the name of economy.

The tube companies were naturally restrained by the need to raise capital, but this did not prevent some significant expansion, which was sometimes aided by Government-guaranteed debentures.

This growth reached a peak after the First World War, just as the Big Four were coming under increasing financial pressure.

The first tube to extend beyond the centre was the City & South London, whose tunnels had reached Clapham Common in 1900. Then the Hampstead Tube (officially the Charing Cross, Euston & Hampstead Railway) reinforced this suburban invasion in 1907. It was to have two branches, to Euston and Hampstead, but more powers were gained to extend one branch to Highgate and the other to a country crossroads at undeveloped Golders Green. This terminus was chosen by a newly arrived promoter, the larger-than-life Chicago financier Charles Tyson Yerkes. He played a key part in the development of the tubes until his death in 1905, and predicted in 1900 that within a generation 'people will think nothing of living 20 or more miles from town owing to electrified trains'.

Subsequent developments proved him right. The 1906 Baker Street & Waterloo Railway (the 'Bakerloo') was soon extended westwards, arriving at Edgware Road in 1907. The pace then slackened, but the Bakerloo brought tube trains to Paddington by 1913 and reached the surface at Queen's Park in February 1915. This proved to be the line's suburban springboard, because within another three months its trains were thrusting much further into Middlesex, using a pair of lines that had recently been built by the London & North Western.

For a while the Bakerloo terminated at Willesden Junction, until conductor rails were available through to Watford. This was finally achieved in 1917, the work having been delayed by the war.

Tube trains were now providing direct, frequent services to the West End for the fortunate inhabitants of places such as Kenton and Bushey. This was the result of a joint agreement with the LNWR, which ran its trains on the same line from Watford to Euston or Broad Street, mostly running alternately with Bakerloo services.

Other tubes were also courting suburban traffic, not always with such cooperation from the main line companies. Some schemes were uncontentious, such as the Central London reaching Ealing Broadway in 1920, while the Hampstead Tube, now well established at Golders Green, forged on to Hendon and Edgware in 1924.

Meanwhile the pioneering City & South London Railway, which had opened as the first true tube railway in 1890, was also keen to expand. Its original southerly terminus was Stockwell, but it had already reached Clapham Common, as we have seen. However, when it contemplated a further extension south it collided head-on, figuratively speaking, with the newly unified Southern Railway and its redoubtable General Manager, Sir Herbert Walker.

A glance at the railway map of London soon reveals that the systems on either side of the Thames have different characteristics.

North and, indeed, east and west London are threaded by mainly radial main lines, which are overlaid by a number of Underground routes: most of these, as has already been said, come to the surface once they are outside central London.

The majority of significant suburban centres – from Ealing in the west through Ruislip, Harrow, Edgware, High Barnet and Cockfosters to Hainault and Epping in the east – are served by the Underground. Some boroughs, particularly in the north-west, even possess multiple Underground stations on two or three lines.

South London is different. Underground lines cross the river at 11 points, it is true, but most are confined to the inner suburbs (such as the Bakerloo to Elephant & Castle and the Victoria to Brixton), and only one tube railway gets much further.

To compensate for this, south London possesses a more complex system of what are now known as National Rail lines, and these are not only radial but also provide many other connections.

112

3rd Cl   LT

CHARING CROSS

9d to

Harlesden

(via Queens Park)

Kew Gardens

(via Sloane Sq.)

Osterley
Sudbury Town
Enfield West
Canons Park
Preston Road

p6   or intermediately

Issued subject to the Bye-Laws, Regulations and Conditions of the Board. Available day of issue only

CHARING CROSS

112

This LPTB ticket from the late 1930s includes two stations that had been added to the network earlier in the decade as a result of Underground expansion into the outer suburbs. Canons Park had opened in 1932, originally as part of the Metropolitan Railway, and Enfield West (later renamed Oakwood) followed when the Piccadilly Line was extended in 1933.

Today this network is served by at least four operators, but after the Grouping of 1923 all these lines passed to the Southern Railway, which then seems to have regarded the London suburbs south of the River Thames as its own.

It is possible, then, to imagine the consternation at Waterloo when the City & South London Railway deposited a Parliamentary Bill in late 1922, seeking powers to extend its line from Clapham Common to Morden. Indeed, little imagination is needed, because Sir Herbert Walker, arriving post-haste at Westminster in 1923 to defend the Southern's interests, assured the Bill Committee that although his company had no objection to a tube extension as far as Tooting, anything more would be an invasion of the Southern's territory.

The scheme included a junction at Morden with another proposed line between Wimbledon and Sutton, for which the District had gained powers before the war, after some negotiations behind the scenes. This implied that the Underground might be regarding Morden as a mere staging point on its way into the heartlands of the Southern Electric.

A compromise was eventually hammered out. The Southern would be conceded the powers to build the Wimbledon & Sutton (which it did), while the C&SLR would be extended to Morden, although there would be no connection with the future Sutton line. In addition, no application to build further 'tube' lines in the Southern area would be made without 12 months' notice to the company.

Unlike many tube extensions the Morden line is in tunnel, apart from the terminus, because its route was already built up. The greater need to tunnel (in less favourable geological conditions than north of the river), together with the Southern's restrictive covenant, may help to explain why only one tube penetrates very far into south London.

The Southern had now gained the right to build the Wimbledon & Sutton, blocking further Underground expansion in the area, but the full reasons for its change of heart remain obscure, especially as the company's counsel concluded that the agreement had been made at a 'considerable sacrifice to their own interests'.

This assessment proved to be uncomfortably accurate: the Morden extension opened in 1926 and the Southern later calculated that the new tube had attracted four million of its former passengers in the following year alone.

The ashes of the Morden debate had barely cooled when a similar conflict flared on the other side of London, in reaction to a proposal to extend the Piccadilly Line into parts of outer suburban North London that the LNER regarded as its territory.

The LNER objected to the proposal, which was for an extension from Finsbury Park to Cockfosters, and put forward a plan to electrify its Great Northern suburban lines with 1,500V overhead equipment instead. The argument in favour of extending the Piccadilly rested partly on the confusion and overcrowding at Finsbury Park in the peak, as arriving Underground passengers transferred to buses and trams. It was also suggested that the Piccadilly provided a route to the West End, while the LNER's main traffic was to the City.

The extension received Royal Assent in June 1930, while the LNER gloomily calculated that in the new circumstances GN electrification would be making annual losses of £84,000 within 15 years. Unsurprisingly, the scheme was dropped, and would not be revived until the main East Coast line was electrified in the 1980s.

The LNER also lost nearly all the business at formerly busy Bowes Park to the Underground at nearby Bounds Green, where the electric trains proved irresistible. However, a 'pool' of passenger revenue authorised by the London Passenger Transport Act provided some compensation from July 1933, and the threat of Underground competition was at least modified from then on.

The mid-1930s saw a modest but progressive recovery for the Big Four, until this progress went into sudden reverse in 1938. Most traffic contracted during that year, and net revenue was down by an alarming 23%. Not only did the passenger total fall back, but merchandise also dropped from some 297m tons to little more than 264m. Faced with this new and serious downturn, the industry launched its 'Square Deal' campaign in November 1938.

Table 2: Revenue and journeys, 1933-1938

Year	Passengers (billion)*	Passenger revenue (£m)	**Freight revenue (£m)	net revenue (£m)
1933	1.16	51.13	80.80	26.52
1934	1.20	52.27	85.47	28.80
1935	1.23	53.75	86.24	30.30
1936	1.26	55.77	90.24	33.41
1937	1.30	58.59	94.56	35.26
1938	1.24	58.62	87.82	27.06

* including season ticket holders
** excluding revenue from mail and parcels. This remained at around £16m throughout this period, reaching £16.6m by 1938.
Source: Ministry of Transport Railway Returns

The railway case was set out in a widely distributed booklet called *Clear the lines!*, which pointed out that the number of larger lorries (those over two tons) had virtually doubled since 1930, and reiterated some familiar arguments:

'The railways are not allowed to run their business on commercial and sensible lines. After all, a railway lives by selling transport just as a confectioner lives by selling sweets … but unlike other concerns, the railways are compelled to run in accordance with laws and restrictions which are obsolete and ought to be abolished as quickly as possible.'

Although the railways had stated their case in unequivocal terms, it emerged within a few weeks that there were apparently some matters that the industry would prefer to keep to itself.

Two deputations waited on the Minister of Transport, whose response had been to refer the industry's plea for a relaxation of controls to a body known as the Transport Advisory Council, on which all transport modes had a representative.

The state of play was revealed in the House of Commons on 21 December 1938 during a debate on a motion that road transport was an 'essential feature of modern industrial life', and that called for better roads to be built.

The motion had been proposed by Walter Higgs, Conservative member for Birmingham West, who argued that:

'There are 220 Acts and Orders in existence adversely affecting road transport. The rail came before road transport, and my belief is that if road transport as we know it to-day had come before the railway, probably rail transport would never have been developed [Hon Members: "Oh!"]. That is my opinion, and I think it is justified.'[2]

And so battle was joined. Although the motion was theoretically about roads, it was inevitable that the railways would be called to account as well, especially as the 'Square Deal' campaign had only been launched in the previous month. Mr Higgs continued:

'Last March the road industry started asking for price-fixing and rate-fixing, and the railway companies have now come with their bombshell, asking to be relieved of rate-fixing. A state of chaos now exists. The position is an absurd one. Free competition is the only method of settling rates. Leave them alone. …I believe that if the road transport industry is freed of the restrictions it is labouring under at the present time, it will be to the benefit of the industry and the nation as a whole.'[3]

Later on the Labour member for Bermondsey Rotherhithe, Benjamin Smith, who was a former taxi driver, enlightened the House about what the railway industry had been up to:

'We are told that the claim of the railway companies is for a so-called square deal. After the Minister had received two deputations of the railway representatives he referred this matter, I understand, to the Transport Advisory Council. But what happened? I am credibly informed that the railway companies pressed that their case should not be publicly heard. I want to protest against that.'[4]

MPs proceeded to vote in favour of the motion, but the railway industry's plea to the Transport Advisory Council, whether *in camera* or otherwise, would not, rather like the motion itself, have any lasting effects, although the TAC duly published its report in the spring of 1939.

It recommended the scrapping of many legal restrictions on the railways, including the complex General Classification of Goods and regulated railway rates.[5]

The Government accepted the TAC's conclusions, but its subsequent report came too late to gain legislative attention, because of the increasingly serious international situation.

The country had already tested its plans for transition to war during the Munich crisis in the autumn of 1938 and, although that had proved to be a false alarm, next time it would be the real thing.

Chapter 5

'A very meagre return'

It has been recorded that there was a sense of relief when the Prime Minister, Neville Chamberlain, decided that the German advance into Poland on 1 September 1939 – the latest in a series of provocative moves by Adolf Hitler – could not be tolerated. The formal declaration of hostilities was announced by Chamberlain on the morning of Sunday 3 September but, together with the rest of the country, the railways had already been placed on a war footing.

The key development had taken place just two days earlier, when the Minister of Transport signed an order under the authority of the comprehensive Emergency Powers (Defence) Act, which had only received Royal Assent on 24 August.

A small part of this Act – Regulation 69 – allowed the Government to take control of 'such railway undertakings as may be specified', recalling the unused provisions of the 1919 Ministry of Transport Act.

However, the powers provided by that Act, even if they had not expired, would have been insufficient for a wartime emergency, particularly because Hitler could not be expected to wait while any proposed railway takeover was subjected to the deliberations of an advisory group, however expert.

The immediate result of the Ministerial order was the revival of the Railway Executive Committee – sometimes abbreviated to the REC. As in 1914, railway ownership did not change, but control of the industry was again the joint responsibility of a group of selected senior managers from the main-line companies, reporting to the Ministry of Transport.

The industry had been preparing for war since 1937 at least, when the LMS designed a medium tank for the War Office.[1]

The following year saw the start of training of railway staff for Air Raid Precautions, while the special timetables for evacuation trains had been precisely calculated before the official decision was made on 31 August 1939 to take children and expectant mothers out of the big cities to safety.

The trains began running early the following day, and one official history reported that 4,349 trains carried 1,428,425 passengers away from London alone during these first evacuations.[2]

Evacuation specials marked the real beginning of the railway war. Between 1939 and 1945 the industry kept the country moving, carrying millions of troops, refugees, war workers and – from the back of a very long queue – as many ordinary passengers who could be squeezed on board.

The requirements of wartime posed a tremendous strain on the railway industry, and it could only cope with the deluge of new traffic by cutting back sharply on regular services. These had already been trimmed considerably to provide space and resources for evacuation trains when hostilities seemed imminent, but it became clear very quickly that the railway and its users – together with the rest of the country – could be in for a long haul.

The initial evacuation specials had hardly returned to their sidings when the Railway Executive Committee announced the shape of wartime railway services with effect from 11 September 1939.

Although the nightly blackout had started, it would be a few months before many wartime measures really began to make themselves felt – food rationing did not begin until January 1940, for example – but railway travel was affected almost at once.

Train services were 'considerably curtailed and decelerated', and all restaurant cars were withdrawn (although this particular restriction proved to be short-lived, at least for a time). Only a 'very limited number' of sleeping cars continued to run, but most passengers were probably more concerned about the peremptory withdrawal of most 'cheap' fares. Only weekend and monthly returns were spared, together with early morning workmen's tickets.

A further sign of the new austerity was the withdrawal of seat and compartment reservations, while it was also no longer possible to book 'saloons for private parties', a phrase that irresistibly recalled the more spacious days of the Victorian and Edwardian eras.

The next few weeks saw a series of relaxations in the light of experience, but these were combined with further restrictions.

Cash on delivery arrangements for traders were withdrawn on 14 September, and the opening hours of goods depots were shortened on 2 October so that as far as possible they functioned only during daylight.

On the other hand, passenger timetables were strengthened on 18 September, cheap day returns came back on 9 October, and restaurant cars were restored on principal trains a week after that (the relatively few still running in 1944 disappeared again as D-Day approached – this time, as it turned out, for the duration).

Changes continued through the winter. On the London Underground, First Class on all District and most Metropolitan trains was withdrawn from 1 February 1940 (the two Pullman cars on the Metropolitan had already been sacrificed to increase capacity on 7 October 1939), and although Metropolitan trains to Watford and Aylesbury kept their First Class compartments until the following year they became Third Class only on 6 October 1941, together with all other trains running wholly within the London Passenger Transport Area (the LPTA was bounded approximately by Luton and Crawley).

Most trains operated by the Big Four ran beyond the boundaries of the LPTA, and

Evacuation, 1939.

RAILWAY PASSENGER
SERVICES
DURING EVACUATION

The Main Line Railways announce that during Evacuation, alterations in the existing Passenger Services will be necessary, and the public are requested to limit their train travel to essential journeys.

The following information will be of guidance :—

LONDON SUBURBAN SERVICES.

Before 8.0 a.m. and after 5.30 p.m. services will be as near as possible normal.

Between 8.0 a.m. and 5.30 p.m. skeleton services only will operate.

PROVINCIAL SUBURBAN SERVICES.

During the hours of evacuation, skeleton services only will operate.

MAIN LINE SERVICES.

The Railways expect to maintain Main Line services, but no guarantee can be given as extensive alterations to existing time tables may have to be made without notice.

The Railways will make every endeavour to provide the best possible services, and are confident that they may rely upon the co-operation of the public in their efforts.

on these First Class bookings continued, but as it was not apparently possible to find enough solely Third Class coaches for trains in the London area, some existing stock was 'declassified' for the purpose. The official historian of the LMS disapproved of the results, describing the reform as 'of doubtful use'.

He recorded that the situation was 'often farcical', because 'it was a regular occurrence for passengers to seek out the former first class compartments and fill them to overflowing, with the result that they were frequently standing in them, while other parts of the train were sparsely occupied'.

Most wartime travellers would have been thankful to find any part of a train that was sparsely occupied. Timetables were slashed repeatedly to provide more capacity for Government traffic (the most extreme year was 1944). This traffic included almost countless tons of munitions, building materials and food which had to 'go through', even though 113,000 railway staff had joined the forces by 1945.[3]

Although travel was discouraged, passenger totals increased and the length of an average journey went up even more sharply. This may have been partly because many military travellers had far-flung destinations, but also because civilians who needed to make longer journeys had few alternatives after the basic petrol ration had been withdrawn in 1942, together with the remaining express coaches.

The result was that space on board trains became just one more of the many commodities that were in critically short supply.

Table 3: Passenger totals and distances travelled, 1938-1948

Year	Passengers (million)	Passenger kms*	Year	Passengers (million)	Passenger kms*
1938	1,235.9	30,566**	1944	1,345.3	51,393
1939	1,225.5	***	1945	1,371.8	56,726
1940			1946	1,266.0	47,043
1941	1,023.3	***	1947	1,076.7	***
1942	1,218.3	***	1948	996.1	34,213
1943	1,334.6	51,938			

* Estimated
** Sept 1938 to Aug 1939
*** Not available

Sources: Ministry of Transport. Railway Returns (1938-46); British Transport Commission, Annual report and accounts (1947-48)

Restrictions of war, 1940.

ON AND AFTER FEBRUARY 1, 1940

FIRST CLASS
WITHDRAWN

ON LONDON TRANSPORT TRAINS
EXCEPT ON THROUGH TRAINS
RUNNING BETWEEN THE METROPOLITAN LINE
AND MET. AND GREAT CENTRAL JOINT LINES
AYLESBURY AND WATFORD

For journeys where first class accommodation will be wholly withdrawn, first class quarterly (and broken period) season tickets will not be issued after November 1, 1939, or first class monthly season tickets after January 1, 1940

The whole operation was controlled throughout by the REC as the agent of the Government, but the companies remained privately owned and their shareholders expected dividends to continue.

Therefore, although the REC periods have been described as 'nationalisation', this is, strictly speaking, an exaggeration.

There was undoubtedly state control, demonstrated by the numerous changes imposed – such as the withdrawal of cheap fares and the drastic rewriting of timetables to cater for special traffic.

But state ownership, the foundation of nationalisation, was still absent – although the Government's treatment of railway profits perhaps did take the industry some way down that road. Even if the railways had not been nationalised they had certainly been conscripted. Like all conscripts, they had to do what they were told.

Although the outbreak of war had been met by a prompt response from the railways, the ultimate responsibility for the industry's costs during the emergency took some time to work out, even though the companies had been asked to submit their proposals for wartime arrangements as far back as the second half of 1937.

The essence of the plan was that the industry's wartime income would be based on recent peacetime results, but one major sticking point was the companies' insistence that the poorly performing year of 1938 ought to be ignored when the calculations were made.

Before agreement could be reached the war had started, and negotiations continued between Government and the companies until a deal was finally announced early in 1940.

Speaking in the House of Commons on 7 February, the Minister of Transport, Conservative Euan Wallace, said:

'The receipts and expenses of the controlled undertakings will be pooled and out of the pool they will be paid annual sums equivalent, in the case of the railway companies, to the average of their net revenues for the years 1935, 1936 and 1937 and, in the case of the London Passenger Transport Board, to its net revenue for the year ended 30 June 1939. The payment of these sums, amounting approximately to £40,000,000, will be guaranteed by the Government.'[4]

This statement revealed that the companies had overcome Government resistance and succeeded in their bid to have the awkward year of 1938 disregarded.

They had also been given a guarantee of minimum net revenues. If traffic had really slumped (a highly unlikely outcome in wartime), they would then have received a Government grant to bring their income up to the minimum.

The division of the pool was based on the financial size of each company. The LMS qualified for 34%, the LNER 23%, the GWR and Southern 16% each, and London Transport 11%.

In fact, there was more on the table than this, because the next £3.5m would also be retained by the five parties in the same proportions. After that, further profits would be divided equally between the Government and the companies until their 'standard revenues' (based on the 1921 Railways Act) were reached.

According to a White Paper published to accompany the announcement in the House of Commons, this financial end of the line for the companies, after which they would be essentially taxed at 100%, was 'approximately' £56m.[5]

Captain Wallace did not escape unscathed. Some MPs were critical of the results of the negotiations on the grounds that they were too generous. One of these was socialist James Maxton, representing Glasgow Bridgeton, who wanted to know about the 'difficulties' that evidently had to be overcome, to judge by the 'very protracted negotiations' that had resulted in an agreement 'so obviously advantageous to the railway shareholders'.

Newspaper advertisement, November 1940.

When Your Train is LATE—

—things may have happened in the night, causing timetable changes and the use of different routes—often at the last minute.

It is frequently impossible to make the changes known to passengers in time or to give reasons for cancelling trains, sending you on roundabout routes or causing you to miss connections.

The Railways are straining every nerve and muscle to maintain regular services and to keep the trains running.

Information services are being augmented at important stations, where details of alterations will be quickly available.

WE'LL BEAT THE BLITZKRIEG BY HELPING ONE ANOTHER

BRITISH RAILWAYS

Captain Wallace's reply curiously anticipated some of the responses made by Ministers in our own time, particularly when they have been pressed to explain the long delay in completing the contract with Siemens to build rolling stock for Thameslink:

'There are, of course, a large number of detailed questions to be dealt with in the settlement, and I was most anxious – and I am sure the House has been most anxious – that we should have a watertight agreement. As regards the rest of the Hon Gentleman's remarks, he seems to be begging a fairly big question.'[6]

Maxton, who was also leader of the breakaway Independent Labour Party and a supporter of Scottish independence, merely retorted (one can imagine a growl): 'I think you are.'

The process must have been watched anxiously by at least some of the 900,000-plus direct holders of railway stock, and one official source pointed out that 'if the number of persons interested in the holdings of railway stocks in the names of insurance companies, building and friendly societies, etc, were added, this would be very much increased'.[7]

Captain Wallace's announcement was therefore of far wider interest than in just Parliament or railway boardrooms, and according to O. S. Nock the possible implications were leaving people 'fraught with some apprehension'.

He continued:

'There were many … who considered that the Railways Act of 1921 … was the first regular step towards nationalisation, and they feared that the agreement of February 1940 could be the second.'[8]

According to Nock, their especial fear was that the agreement could set a precedent for the value of railway assets, should nationalisation be 'raised in definite form later'. As we now know, the railway shareholders of 1940 were quite right to see nationalisation as a future possibility, but there was no prospect of any major change in railway organisation while the war was still in progress.

Although the February 1940 agreement had taken a long time to negotiate, it did not in fact last very long. The Government adjusted the arrangement in October 1941, backdating it to 1 January. The 50% share of net income that had applied between £43.5m and the standard revenues was abolished. Instead, the pool paid to the Big Four plus London Transport was now fixed at £43m, with any surplus going to the state apart from some payments to a Trust Fund intended to cover delayed repairs and renewals.

The new arrangements were linked to a change in the rules of compensation for the results of enemy action. This was originally permitted to be a charge on the revenue pool (with an annual cap of £10m), which would have essentially committed the Government to meeting the full cost up to the cap. From now on the railways were to be treated in the same way as other utilities, and would receive half the cost of any damage.

The *Railway Gazette* described the new deal as 'a very meagre return'[9], and also commented on what would probably now be dubbed a lack of transparency, telling its readers that 'although no figures have been published, it is believed that certain companies have achieved their standard since the outbreak of war'.

The railways would indeed pay large sums to the state before the war was over, but the same article also reflected that the situation could be reversed if there was, 'for example, an invasion of this country or a decline in traffics towards the end of control'.

A German invasion, particularly if it had been followed by occupation, would surely have caused such serious problems for the railways that any notional profit share due to the former British Government would have become irrelevant, but the *Gazette* still had a point: it was true that the new arrangement capped the industry's profits, but it did provide a guaranteed minimum as well.

Fares had been permitted to rise twice during 1940, and were now 16⅔% higher than in 1939.

The first of these increases had come into force on 1 May 1940. When the second was on the horizon, a columnist in the *Daily Mirror* had attempted to voice – or possibly arouse – public resentment, when he wrote:

'On the day in which the 10 per cent increase was announced earlier this year, Great Western ordinary shares jumped from 46½ to 48, LMS were £1 higher at 22½, and preference shares also rose. If the cost of transit rises, then so will the cost of food. Then wages must go up … and the railway companies will need still more money. You see the vicious circle. What is the remedy – nationalisation, subsidy, or restriction of interest *(sic)* on shares?'[10]

Railway shareholders were also unhappy. One of them, a GWR proprietor called Mr Ashley Brown, had commented just after the first wartime control agreement had been announced in February 1940 that a 'section of the press – fortunately small, but with influence on the company's employees [this was probably a reference to the *Daily Mirror*] – had devoted considerable space to the statement that the Government had presented stockholders with something like £100,000,000.'

Never, he supposed, was a statement more misleading or deliberately mischievous. 'Of course [stock] had risen … it had been bought … many years previously at somewhere between 70 and 114. Before agreement had been reached it had fallen to 10 [and] rose during the course of discussions to 20. Could any sane man say that … represented a gain to the holders?'[11]

Thus railway owners confronted railway critics – but their dispute was muted by the all-pervasive threat of German invasion.

Meanwhile, as the *Railway Gazette* had suggested it would, the Government did very well out of the revised control agreement of October 1941, which had been backdated to the start of that year.

In 1943 the companies published their figures for 1940 to 1942, which revealed that the industry had earned some £203m in net receipts over three years, but surrendered £70m of that to the Government – an effective additional tax rate of 35%.

Table 4: Revenue and expenditure, 1940-1942

Year	Total receipts (£m)	Expenditure (£m)	Net revenue (£m)*	Paid to Government (£m)
1940	248.0	203.5	42.7	1.1
1941	293.8	226.6	65.1	22.5
1942	343.5	251.7	89.1	46.8

* includes 'non-pool' revenue, such as earnings from bus companies
Source: 'Facts about British Railways in wartime', British Railways Press Office, 1943

It was not only railway shareholders who wondered if nationalisation was looming. Long before the war was over, the companies were preparing their defences.

In 1943 Sir James Milne of the GWR, who was also Chairman of the Railway General Managers' Conference, contributed a foreword to a collection of articles that had been published by the *Railway Gazette* between June and September.

The reprint of the whole series in booklet form was given the general title of 'A national transport programme', but it was really an overture rather than a definite plan.[12]

In part it formed a response to earlier statements, such as one by the former BBC Director-General Lord Reith who, having served briefly as Minister of Transport in 1940, had launched a motion in the Lords with 'The Public Services' as its subject on 17 June 1942.

Reith, looking ahead to peacetime, had attempted to dissect the nature of public service, saying that 'efficiency is the inevitable and infallible objective and criterion … there are distracting and conflicting objectives and criteria – profits and politics – and profits do not necessarily spell efficiency, as is sometimes held…'

It was a typically Reithian performance, which continued:

'I would rather have private ownership than nationalisation, if nationalisation means the conduct of public services by Government Departments – in private ownership there is often (in the railways, for instance) a high ideal of public service, but the first

TO RAILWAY STOCKHOLDERS

THE net revenue of the four main-line Railways and the London Passenger Transport Board for the year 1942 was £89,000,000. The annual compensation paid by the Government to Railway Stockholders is £43,500,000.

Under the Railways Act of 1921, the 1942 Revenue would have permitted stockholders to retain approximately £56,000,000. The difference between what the stockholders would have received by Statute and what they are receiving is the measure of the sacrifice they are making.

The compensation made by the Government is insufficient to pay any dividend at all upon £78,000,000 worth of L.N.E. stock, in addition to which considerable quantities of other Railway stocks are inadequately remunerated

The Union is pressing for a revision of the agreement between the Government and the Railways in order to ensure more equitable treatment for the junior stockholders now and under post-war conditions.

Stockholders can help this movement by joining the Union and supporting the representations it is making to Parliament.

Write for a copy of the Manifesto amplifying these facts to

BRITISH RAILWAY STOCKHOLDERS UNION, 25, Victoria St., London, S.W.1

The railway proprietors' view, May 1943.

obligation is to shareholders, and I am going to submit that those two obligations are incompatible…'

The author of the *Railway Gazette* articles remained anonymous, but had evidently struggled to understand what Reith was saying:

'Like many others, he advocated a national transport corporation, but he did not say clearly who should own it, or how it should be controlled, or even whether it should be self-supporting.'

The views of another commentator, Labour's Herbert Morrison, were at least easier to grasp. Also an advocate of public corporations, he had made a speech in 1943 declaring that transport was 'ripe – or over-ripe – for public ownership and management'.

Proponents of reform such as Morrison were guaranteed to get a cool reception in the boardrooms of the Big Four. The *Gazette* commented, with barely disguised distaste: 'The words he uses in connection with transport should be considered with great care, otherwise one is apt to get a misleading impression from them.'

One of the chief concerns was to avoid what was seen as the worst of both worlds: private investment funding a publicly controlled organisation:

'If the owners … do not control the management, they continue to take the risk in providing the capital, but they would be unable to protect that capital against risk…'

Although the *Gazette* series tried to convey a judicial approach, it was essentially opposed to nationalisation, pointing out that 'experience of state-owned railways abroad shows that very few pay…'

The series was not bylined, but considering that Milne had provided an approving foreword ('the *Railway Gazette* … has adumbrated a number of constructive long-term proposals') we can reasonably associate him and indeed his colleagues at the General Managers' Conference with the general thrust of the remarks.

It also seems likely that the companies had been in close touch (to put it as moderately as possible) with the *Gazette* while its articles were being prepared.

When the GWR ceased operations, Milne departed as well. His last official appearance, as far as most people were concerned, was in December 1947 on the cover of the final edition of the Great Western Railway staff magazine. The caption was 'Pride in the job'.

Chapter 6

'The fate awaiting investors'

When Labour swept to victory in the General Election of July 1945, supporters of the privately owned railway industry knew that the writing was on the wall.

The party's manifesto had promised 'public ownership of inland transport', asserting that:

'…co-ordination of transport services by rail, road, air and canal cannot be achieved without unification. And unification without public ownership means a steady struggle with sectional interests or the enthronement of a private monopoly, which would be a menace to the rest of industry.'

With Labour firmly in charge (it had won 393 seats, compared with the Conservatives' 213), transport nationalisation appeared to be only a matter of time, but the railway companies did not give up the fight straight away.

They continued to argue in public that nationalisation was not a good idea, although the real priority now was to realise the best return for their shareholders when the state took over.

However, the apparent inevitability of state ownership did not prevent the companies from trying to divert the Government towards some kind of compromise.

The campaign had really started in 1942, when the Railway Companies' Association had decided to pave the way for post-war reorganisation by seizing the initiative and evolving some possible structures. A committee of directors was given the task of refining the possibilities but, inevitably, there were disagreements. The Southern, for example, felt that the companies should be unified, but remain under private ownership.[1]

The LNER, on the other hand, saw scope in allowing a future Government to acquire the railway infrastructure, which would then be leased back to the companies.

Most of these suggestions remained within the walls of the Association, but later on the LNER chose to go public on its own account, as we shall see.

In June 1945, on the eve of the General Election (when nationalisation of transport was still only a possibility), the companies produced a pamphlet that provided some tartly phrased rejoinders in italics to various statements, as this extract demonstrates:

'As a Public Utility service, the railways should be run by the State for the benefit of the people, and any profits should go to improving services or into the Exchequer for the benefit of the taxpayer.

This is a statement of political faith: either you believe it or you do not. It has nothing to do with the efficiency of railway services. It should not be assumed, however, that there would necessarily be profits from state-owned railways. On the contrary, 71% of all state-owned railways in the world (which are not nearly as efficient as British railways) are run at a loss. Under state-ownership the taxpayer is frequently called on to foot the bill…'

This document contained another 43 such 'responses'. One was a bleak assessment of London Transport, which had been created as a public authority in 1933 but still had stockholders:

'The London Passenger Transport Board is an example of how efficiently a public utility can be operated under public ownership.

This statement errs in suggesting that the LPTB is State-Owned. It is neither State-Controlled nor State-Owned. It is privately owned, but the stockholders have no control over their property! It is an example of a bad compromise between private and state-ownership … it was clear some time before the war that the financial position of the LPTB was weak. What will be the outcome after the war cannot be forecast, but … if the Board is an example of a stage on the road to nationalisation of public utilities, it is a warning of the fate awaiting investors and the public.'

It is not very clear why or how the public was threatened by the LPTB structure. Irrespective of the financial returns to stockholders, there are no traceable records of serious public criticism of London Transport in this period, which had actually maintained its services with praiseworthy tenacity during the wartime blitzes.

The LPTB had also made considerable progress with its 1935 New Works programme until the war had called a halt to the construction of more Underground lines, the conversion of tram routes to trolleybuses, and delivery of its newly designed 'RT' diesel buses.

But the Big Four plainly regarded the LPTB as the thin end of the wedge, and their stance in June 1945 reflected the warnings about private owners deprived of effective control that had been expressed by the *Railway Gazette* (almost certainly on the industry's behalf) two years earlier.

The General Election was held in July, and the new Government's intention to nationalise most forms of transport was confirmed in November of the same year. In the event, though, aviation was quietly put on one side.

Another booklet published by the companies entitled *British Railways and the future* followed in 1946. This was mostly devoted to a summary of what the companies had done and intended to achieve, rather than making an outright plea against nationalisation (the introduction went so far as to say that 'the general question of State Ownership versus Private Enterprise is not fully argued here'), but the real purpose was clear enough.

There were really two main issues. One was ownership and the other was the prospect of further amalgamation, which in practice would have meant combining the four companies.

The booklet was quite clear about amalgamation, saying:

'The Companies believe that a complete fusion of the present systems into a single unit would be disastrous, especially at the present time.'

Meanwhile, the question of ownership might not have been 'fully argued', but the companies still maintained that

'...an impartial examination of the results of State Ownership of Railways in other parts of the world shows that the creation of a State Corporation has, in no case, provided the public with as good a service as that provided by British Railways.'

How the companies knew this, or what kind of 'impartial examination' had been carried out – and by whom – was not explained.

The companies then fired an almost despairing shot across the Government's bows, by setting aside the merits or otherwise of nationalisation and simply alleging that reform would, in any case, be too difficult:

'To make such a change today would involve immense administrative and financial dislocation and would obstruct and seriously delay the carrying out of the practical problems of transport.'

In reality, the companies already knew that the winds of change were blowing against them, so this curiously phrased hyperbole ('carrying out of ... problems'?) was largely beside the point.

However, a less abstract theme was pursued separately by the LNER, which was the only member of the Big Four to accept publicly that some form of public ownership was now inevitable. Instead, its directors attempted to limit the damage.

Their proposal has already been referred to briefly.[2] It was labelled 'an alternative to nationalisation', but did in fact propose a partial state takeover, by allowing the nation to purchase the infrastructure while the companies continued as train operators, paying to use the nationalised network.

This proposal, dubbed the 'Landlord and Tenant' scheme, would have resulted in a separation of track and train more than 40 years before it would be required by European law and also be a core element of the 1990s privatisation.

However, there were some aspects of the LNER's proposals that would not be adopted later on.

The financing of the scheme would have involved the granting of long-term leases to the operators (again, an ancestor of today's franchises), but the companies would have continued to maintain the track and signalling, because the LNER felt that making the state responsible for this would have involved 'obvious administrative and financial difficulties'. However obvious these difficulties may have been, no details were given.

Payment for the initial purchase of the infrastructure by the state would have taken the form of interest-bearing government stock. In practice, the 'rent' due from the companies (for which now read 'track access charges') could have been broadly equivalent to the interest on the stock that would otherwise have been payable by the Government.

The avowed aim of this reform was to place the companies on an equal basis with the road haulage industry: both road and rail operators would still be in the private sector, but using 'roadways' owned by the state.

There was probably more to it than that. The LNER proposal could have been intended to satisfy or at least appease those who wanted the state to play a direct part in transport.

True, it would have watered down the Government's manifesto promises, but then these had already been amended to some extent by the omission of aviation from the Transport Bill.

From the companies' point of view they would have survived to fight another day, and indeed would have converted their fixed infrastructure assets into a source of new capital.

This was because the LNER also suggested that some of the interest-bearing stock could be sold by mutual agreement over time to fund such projects as electrification or the purchase of new rolling stock (these were the examples given).

Although the companies would therefore have been able to tap into new capital, they would not, in practice, have had to pay access charges ('rent') because this was broadly covered by the unpaid interest retained by the Government.

As the companies would still have been paying for track maintenance (and, it would appear, enhancements such as electrification), this might have been a reasonable exchange.

A further carrot was that any savings made by the companies could not be retained or converted into dividends. Instead, they would be used to reduce fares and freight charges.

The Government, meanwhile, would have issued considerably less interest-bearing stock than would be needed for a complete takeover of the Big Four.

There are interesting balance sheet implications in some of these arrangements, particularly if a long-life asset, like infrastructure, was ultimately converted into a short-to-medium-life asset, such as new rolling stock.

It is also possible that in the longer term, as units of stock were converted into new assets or perhaps reached maturity, the companies would have found themselves paying increasing track access charges (with real money) into perpetuity – offering a possible gold mine to a cash-strapped Chancellor who would not, unlike

Network Rail, have been responsible for the costs of maintenance.

This is no more than speculation, because the proposal was ignored. Michael Bonavia, who was employed in the Chief General Manager's office of the LNER at the time, has recorded that when the idea was formally submitted to the Minister of Transport, it was 'dismissed by that dignitary in a single sentence'.[3]

The Transport Bill was published in November 1946, and it quickly attracted heated controversy.

One trade magazine[4] spoke of 'incontrovertible evidence of widespread opposition to the Transport Bill', and recorded that by early February 1947 there had been 40 Government amendments and 50 from the Opposition. It also predicted hundreds more.

The Bill was attracting critics from many trades, and this led to some surprising headlines, such as 'Transport Bill will raise drug costs', in the issue of *Commercial Motor* dated 14 February 1947. The story below reported that one wholesale pharmaceutical chemist had been delivering 80% of its orders with a fleet of more than 50 vehicles. The report continued:

'The company estimates that if the carriage of drugs be not exempted from ... the Transport Bill, more than half its goods will have to be sent by rail and outside road transport, and that transport costs will be increased by about 50%.'

In connection with this, the *Manufacturing Chemist* for February 1947 reported that the Wholesale Drug Trade Association was opposing the Bill, and cited eight reasons why the drugs trade should be exempted from its provisions. This is a reminder, of course, that the Bill set out proposals to nationalise transport on a wide scale, and went well beyond railways alone.

A major Commons debate took place on 16 and 17 December 1946, when the Bill received its Second Reading. Bearing in mind that the companies had repeatedly emphasised how many improvements they were planning, it must have been a little galling for them to hear Minister of Transport Alfred Barnes imply that only a state-owned British Transport Commission could rescue the situation:

'Travel in this country is becoming a disagreeable thing, something to be endured in order to get somewhere, rather than a pleasure, as it should be. I depend on this Commission, with its wide powers, radically to alter that state of affairs... The Commission, small, compact, with wide powers, I expect to be sufficiently dynamic in its energies to grapple with problems of that kind. After all, I think that if the structure of this Bill is examined – the Commission as a policy instrument, the Executives to carry out management – it will be seen, quite clearly, that a small body of persons with time to think and plan, and with the vast resources it will have behind it, will work a revolution in the efficiency of the transport system of this country.'[5]

These were brave and indeed optimistic words, which effectively summed up the Government's case for enforcing state control.

The Bill was complicated (it had nine main parts), and opposition MPs had no intention of allowing it to be enacted without placing as many hurdles in the Government's path as possible.

There was also the real rather than political issue of how much the nation should pay for the assets that it was appropriating in the name of the people.

This issue was argued in some detail during the Second Reading debate, led by Alfred Barnes. With the battle to fend off nationalisation evidently lost, the price that should be paid for the railways had become the major point of contention. Now this came to the fore, as Mr Barnes set out to refute opposition claims that the proposed compensation would amount to a loss of capital.

There had apparently been fears that the finances of the wartime controls would create an inconvenient precedent if nationalisation followed (see page 58), and such fears appeared to have some justification when Mr Barnes explained the Government's plans to issue British Transport Stock in exchange for company shares:

'Its terms are to be such as to make it worth, at the time of issue, the amount of the compensation. I would emphasise this as it disposes of any suggestion that the terms of compensation impose loss of capital. Any such loss must have occurred before nationalisation had been announced, because the prices used are in no case less than those ruling shortly before the Election... I do not believe that, in this case, any arbitrator would have been able to find a better and more fair measure of compensation, than is provided by the market assessment...'[6]

As British Transport Stock was to consist of several interest-bearing issues providing fixed returns rather than variable dividends (this would turn out to be a financial millstone for the British Transport Commission), the core of the Government's argument was that the issue of stock worth the equivalent of £25.5m a year rather than, say, £40m was justified because the returns would be guaranteed.

When the Chancellor, Hugh Dalton, took Mr Barnes's place the following day, he described the state of the post-war railway industry in disparaging terms which have continued to arouse intermittent resentment ever since:

'Let us look at the railway system now. It is in very poor shape. Partly that is due to the strain of six years war; partly, but not wholly. Those dingy railway stations, those miserable, unprepossessing restaurants, all the out-of-date apparatus for sleeping and eating, make one ashamed as an Englishman when one is travelling abroad and sees how well the thing is done in Continental Europe, Western Europe, in Sweden and France... I am saying that this railway system of ours is a very poor bag of physical assets. The permanent way is badly worn. The rolling stock is in a state of great dilapidation… It cannot be supposed that the Stock Exchange is seriously undervaluing it, at present terms.'[7]

Dalton has often been pilloried for his remarks, and there was probably some private chuckling within the industry when he felt forced to resign after a misunderstanding led to some details of his November 1947 Budget being published before they had been announced in Parliament, but his railway nationalisation speech should perhaps be considered in context.

As the Chancellor of the Exchequer was essentially the buyer of the railways, he was unlikely to say anything in December 1946 that could conceivably bolster railway shares at such a sensitive time, especially as the benchmark valuation for the purposes of nationalisation was to be based on an average of the Stock Exchange prices that had applied over several days at the start of the previous month.

Any significant rise in the price of railway shares after that would have been inconvenient to the Government, to say the least, because it would not have wished to reopen the argument about how much the railway stockholders should receive in compensation.

The net result was that some £1,065m of 3% British Transport Stock was issued to former railway shareholders and certain other owners, such as the proprietors of road haulage companies.

Three Executives were originally planned as the administrative arms of the parent British Transport Commission. The London Passenger Transport Board was to continue, although under Ministerial direction.

In the event the existing LPTB was dissolved and replaced by an additional Executive. Apart from the railways and London Transport, other Executives took charge of Docks and Inland Waterways, Road Transport and, from an 'appointed day' (which proved to be 1 July 1948), the railway hotels.

Although the Government had to resort to a guillotine to get all its sections through Parliament, the Transport Act received Royal Assent on 6 August 1947, and came into force on 1 January 1948.

Not all the former legal entities in every transport industry affected by the Act needed to be dissolved. In fact, the bus companies that had been jointly owned by the railways and the Tilling Group were placed in a curious position from January 1948, because the directors on their boards who had been placed there by the railways now came from the state-owned Commission, whereas the remaining directors still represented private sector Tilling.

Such a position might have been heralded in a later age as a 'public-private partnership', but it was not to last. Following the passing of the Transport Act, Tilling's own board decided to end that company's century-long adventure with public transport and sold its omnibus interests to the British Transport Commission in November 1948. This infuriated the other major combine, British Electric Traction, which remained stubbornly independent until 1967.

The individual ex-Tilling companies continued to trade under their established names, although their shares had now passed entirely into public ownership. Thus more than 20 bus companies were nationalised by the back door.

Although there was no need to wind up the bus companies, the railway companies had to go because, unlike the buses, their owners included a vast multitude of private investors who could not be legally compelled to surrender their holdings to the state.

As the old railway shares no longer attracted dividends, most of their holders quickly claimed British Transport Stock, but a small office was maintained in London for many years to deal with errant share certificates that continued to turn up in attics and other obscure places.

Now that their last trains had departed, each of the companies held a mournful Final General Meeting at which the directors declared the closing dividends, bid farewell to the former proprietors and usually received their thanks.

However, the shareholders of the LNER petulantly rejected a motion that would have compensated the members of their board for loss of office, and this defeat prevented the departing directors from sharing £63,000.

The directors of the Great Western faced no such humiliation. Uniquely among the Big Four, they gallantly declined to accept any compensation when they reached the end of the line.

Chapter 7

'The unfortunate railway witnesses'

The Transport Act was intended to introduce a new era of integration coordinated by the British Transport Commission or BTC, but the purity of this concept was marred by the fact that some modes would continue to compete with each other. For example, the operators of the Commission's express coach services would continue to advertise that it was 'cheaper by road' – in other words, that their fares were lower than those charged on the BTC's trains.

However, internal competition – whether for passengers or freight – would not be the Commission's main problem.

It was intended that the BTC would concentrate on policy while delegating the details of administration to the underlying 'Executives', but this structure proved to be unwieldy and inefficient. The Commission and its Railway Executive encountered particular difficulties because their respective responsibilities were poorly defined. One rather comic result was that both designed their own logo – or 'totem' – for the newly-unified railway business, and the competing efforts had to be solemnly tried out in turn.

A more fundamental difficulty was caused by the Commission's financial obligations. Section 3 of the Transport Act obliged it to ensure that its revenue was 'not less than sufficient for making provision for the meeting of charges properly chargeable to revenue, taking one year with another'.

There was some flexibility, in that the Commission was permitted to borrow up to £25m with the consent of the Government. It was also allowed to issue more British Transport Stock (again, only with permission) worth up to a further £225m – principally for purposes connected with capital investment. But there was no other way for the BTC to raise funds, and it started life with a legal obligation to service a substantial debt.

There was, inevitably, a honeymoon period. The LMS had produced a staff magazine called *Carry On* since 1939, and readers of the January 1948 edition (now overprinted 'British Railways' and intended for the London Midland Region and Scottish Region) were told:

'The grizzled little porter sat on his truck alongside the solitary passenger awaiting the last train. "Ah well, sir," said the porter soothingly as he summed up their conversation. "We may not be called LMS now but you can still rely on our "Service with a Smile""[1]

There was rather less to smile about when floods devastated the East Coast Main

Official symbols of
state ownership, 1948.

THE TOTEMS.

Competition from
the roads, 1949.
Some of the
member companies
in the Associated
Motorways
consortium were
now owned by the
BTC.

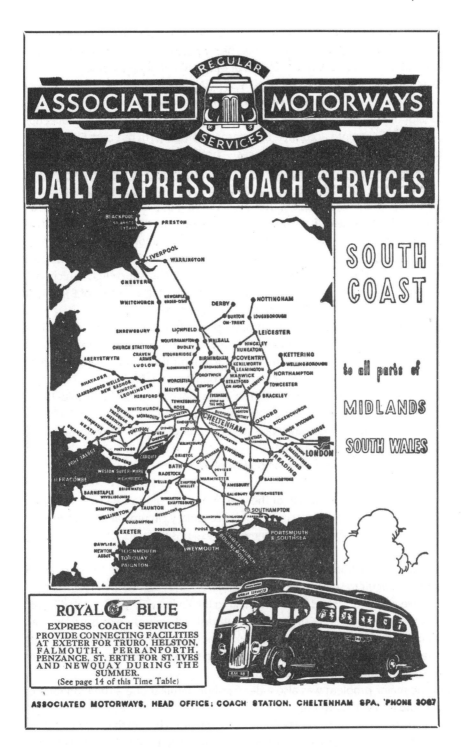

Line during August 1948, and still more reason for gloom when the Commission's first annual results were published in 1949. The railway business had earned £337.3m in 1948, and its net receipts were £26.3m, or barely 8% of gross income.

It was also clear that the BTC was essentially a railway organisation, because these earnings formed 73% of the Commission's total gross income for 'carrying services' and 72% of the net. These percentages took the dire results for BR road collection and delivery services into account – they earned some £8.7m but cost £12.6m.

Fortunately the general road services – both passenger and freight – were profitable, as were London Transport railways. The consolidated net BTC revenue for 1948 was some £45.2m, which included £2.1m from 'non-controlled' companies (mostly buses) and a further £2.1m from 'non-carrying' activities such as property.

If the holders of British Transport Stock had been entitled to dividends rather than fixed interest, it should have been possible (after taxation) to allocate perhaps £15-20m for this purpose and also place at least £5m in the reserves. But the Commission's hands were firmly tied by the 1947 Transport Act, which had authorised several issues of mostly 3% stock. This had a total face value of £1,149.6m by the end of 1948, and the interest due was some £33m.

With other liabilities the total amount payable, together with 'centralised expenditures', came to £46.9m. When some smaller items had also been included – such as the contributions to a long-term 'capital redemption' fund – the total carried forward to 1949 as a deficit on the revenue account was £4.7m.[2]

It has often been recorded that British Railways moved into loss in the mid-1950s, and it is true that the first operating shortfall occurred on the railways in 1956. But although at this stage the railways were still generating a profit, this was more than wiped out by the BTC's other liabilities.

The Commission did its best to be philosophical:

'In relation to turnover, the deficit for the year represents only a small percentage of gross traffic and other revenue receipts, and in ordinary circumstances it might not cause undue concern. The position is, nevertheless, unsatisfactory.'[3]

Indeed it was. The nationalisation experiment was going sour from the start, and it was not too difficult to see why.

There were several factors that were making the Railway Executive's job difficult. One was the run-down state of the railway infrastructure (four express trains had been derailed on plain line in 1946 and 1947, wholly or mainly because of the state of the track), accompanied by a shortage of rolling stock that was keenly felt at times of peak demand, such as holiday periods.

But the major problem was also a depressingly familiar one – the high ratio of capital compared with earnings.

The companies had probably become overcapitalised before the end of the 19th century. At a time when profits appeared to be almost guaranteed (this belief could prove to be an illusion, even in otherwise prosperous periods), new issues of shares had found ready takers. The resulting capital had sometimes been used to overbuild the network, as the more aggressive companies attempted to secure various districts for themselves.

This complex system had proved useful during wartime, but the legacy of too much equity capital invested in assets of doubtful peacetime quality proved to be an enduring handicap that the Commission inherited – thanks to the architects of the 1947 Act.

In fact, the Act made matters worse. In the days of dividends, the companies could at least tailor their coats according to their cloth, with the result that some pre-war shareholders – particularly many of the LNER proprietors – received very little.

Once the equity capital had been converted into interest-bearing guaranteed stock there was no longer any choice in the matter, and the Commission was essentially shackled by a vast pile of quasi-debentures that rested on a doubtful asset base.

Having been bought out against their will, the railways were now expected to service a large proportion of the resulting debt.

Railway earnings were £27m lower in 1948 than the Commission had been hoping. This was particularly disappointing considering that a general revision of rates and charges, lifting them to 55% above pre-war levels, had been authorised in late 1947, but passenger figures dropped from 1,077m to 996m – a fall of 7.5%.

However, the veritable cherry on the Commission's rather unappetising sundae was that it was no more free to set its own rates than the companies had been. Considering the growth of motor transport and the lessons of the 1930s, it might have been expected that the Commission's businesses would have been permitted to charge – at last – what the traffic would bear, especially as the profits would have accrued to the public purse and could have been used to invest in the genuinely useful parts of the system.

However, it was not to be. The railways were no longer part of the private sector and were increasingly confronted by other modes of transport, but they were still treated as a potentially dangerous monopoly – a view that had been out of date since the 1920s.

The old Railway Rates Tribunal had been replaced (under Section 72 of the 1947 Act) by a new Transport Tribunal, but although the name had changed the game was still much the same.

The Commission was also under pressure from sharply rising costs, which led it to lament:

'Unfortunately the trends of traffic receipts and of expenditure in 1949 hold out no hope that the immediate future is likely to show better results, at any rate with the existing levels of fares, rates and charges.'

Three years later, the accumulating effects of the work of the Transport Tribunal would provoke Railway Executive member David Blee to describe the fares and charges deadlock more directly:

'Unlike any other commercial enterprise, British Railways are required by law to define the principles on which their prices are based, to forecast the gross receipts … and to provide estimates of the working expenditure… Moreover, all their customers, through their appropriate organisations, are at liberty to engage counsel to appear before a statutory court to cross-examine the unfortunate railway witnesses and inevitably to attempt to show that the forecasts are wrong and that the prices, or, indeed, the price structure should be different.'[4]

Perhaps Mr Blee felt that these remarks took him to the edge of what a member of a BTC Executive should be saying in public, because he followed this criticism with a repentant

'I do not cavil at this. I merely place it on record and I cannot help wondering sometimes how commercial firms would view the operation of a similar obligation in regard to the selling price of their commodities.'

It seems likely that Mr Blee knew the answer to this question perfectly well.

If the Government was guilty of hampering the Commission's business prospects, it must be said that the Commission itself sometimes appeared to be a willing accessory.

Parts of the railway network were known to be commercially dead wood – some had probably always been so – but the former companies had been very slow to clear this tangled undergrowth, usually relying instead on the time-honoured (but potentially treacherous) principle of cross-subsidy to keep their gardens in some kind of order.

The whole passenger business was a minority partner; it was freight that earned more, which was why lorry competition between the wars had caused the companies so many problems.

Now that the state was in charge, it might have been expected that its transport authority would take swift action as far as unremunerative rail services were concerned, especially as it commanded fleets of buses and lorries that could take on the smaller flows.

But the Commission appeared to accept with good grace that some of its railways would cost more to run than they earned, and it began its explanation reasonably enough:

'In any nation-wide transport undertaking … different services and different methods of transport will show unequal degrees of profitability and will be unable to contribute at a uniform rate to overhead charges…'

So far so good, but what about those services that simply lost money? The Commission had its answer ready:

'Nor indeed is it possible in such an undertaking to avoid the provision of some services which are unremunerative even perhaps in the sense that they do not support their own direct costs of operation. There is nothing new in the acceptance of this principle. Within the main-line railway system itself there are areas of the country, and certain branch lines and perhaps certain traffics, which would not answer to the test of being self-supporting in either sense... The degree to which one form of transport ... can and should be called upon to support another will vary from time to time but, within reasonable limits, bold application of the principle may be essential to any adequate system ... for the country as a whole.'[5]

Various questions were being begged here, not least of which was how would the 'reasonable limits' for the 'bold application' of cross-subsidy be defined (and by whom?), and how a potential breach of those limits would be detected and controlled.

However, the use of the word 'adequate' was probably not accidental, because it appeared in the statutory definition of the Commission's task, as set out in Section 3 of the 1947 Act:

'3.–(1) It shall be the general duty of the Commission so to exercise their powers under this Act as to provide, or secure or promote the provision of, an efficient, adequate, economical and properly integrated system of public inland transport and port facilities within Great Britain for passengers and goods with due regard to safety...'

We have probably come far enough now to see why, financially speaking, the Transport Act of 1947 was unworkable.

It laid a duty on the hapless British Transport Commission to 'provide, or secure or promote' an 'efficient, adequate, economical and properly integrated' transport system, but to help the Commission achieve this its rates and charges were controlled by a statutory court, its ability to borrow was limited (there was no provision for outright grant aid and it started life with no reserves), its ability to withdraw any service depended on the views of Consultative Committees, whose recommendations were then subject to Ministerial approval, and many of the assets in the charge of its Railway Executive were worn out.

It also had a primary duty to service an imposed debt of more than £1,000m, on nearly all of which the annual interest was fixed by law at 3%.

In spite of this, it was supposed to run the business in such a way that its books would balance, 'taking one year with another'.

They did not.

Chapter 8

'A precarious balance'

The early years of transport nationalisation were calculated to bring a grim smile to the face of Wilkins Micawber himself.

As Table 5 (page 83) shows, the British Transport Commission was in deficit on its revenue account for the first three years of its existence – a circumstance that was routinely deprecated in each succeeding annual report ('The trends of traffic receipts and of expenditure in 1949 hold out no hope that the immediate future is likely to show better results' [1948]; 'Only the most strenuous endeavours will bring about a disappearance of the deficit on Net Revenue Account carried forward…' [1949]; 'The opening months of 1951 will necessarily show heavy losses before the position can again be brought into a precarious balance…' [1950]).

The reasons the Commission gave for the continuing deficits were mainly rising costs, coupled with the cumbersome methods it was obliged to adopt, courtesy of the 1947 Act, when it wanted to increase its fares and charges.

Almost two pages of the annual report for 1950 were dedicated to listing increases in costs that had occurred since January 1948. Some of the items highlighted included another £2m for coal and £6m for higher pay, and these had occurred in early 1948, on 1 January and 1 February respectively. Further increases in coal prices – a serious matter for a railway system that relied largely on steam power – had added a further £5.1m by February 1951.

The logical response to these and many other increases in expenditure – ranging from higher National Insurance rates to the prices of petrol and softwood – would have been to adjust fares and charges to keep the books in balance, as the law required.

But this was more easily said than done. The Commission was soon all too aware of the problems presented by the Transport Tribunal process, to judge by this comment in the 1949 annual report (page 38): 'The charges made by the Commission for the bulk of transport services provided can be altered only after formal and public hearings which involve preparation and investigation over a considerable period of time, and experience has shown that deficiencies of revenue can amount to a serious sum before balance is restored.'

The later remarks of Railway Executive member David Blee on the same topic have already been quoted.

The 1950 General Election had slashed the previously ample Labour majority to just five. This fragile position prompted another election in October the following

Encouraging passenger traffic, 1950.

The way to enjoy a change of scene

Out into the country . . . down to the sea . . . your railway station is the gateway to wherever your fancy roams. And if you've an eye to your purse as well as your pleasure, how doubly gratifying to find that British Railways will often take you there and back at single fare. There are many attractive day excursions just now. Ask at your station or at any travel agency.

BRITISH RAILWAYS

year, when Winston Churchill led the Conservatives to victory with a majority of 17. Labour would now be out of office until 1964.

In the meantime, the Commission felt that a general increase in fares was no longer avoidable. These would be the first major revisions since nationalisation.

Accordingly, it applied to the Transport Tribunal for a new charges scheme (including provincial buses and London Transport as well as British Railways) in April 1951. The scheme affected discounted fares, such as cheap day returns and season tickets. The mileage basis for ordinary Third Class fares was not changed, but as most passengers travelled by one form of reduced fare or another the proposals caused an extraordinary degree of deliberation and debate, including a public inquiry.

The heat of growing dissatisfaction spread through the press and eventually reached the Cabinet. In the meantime, the Tribunal gave its provisional blessing to the increases (subject to a minor limitation on the basis of fares) on 17 January 1952, confirming them just over a month later.

Nine months had already elapsed since the BTC had submitted its scheme, but by now the fat was well and truly in the fire.

On 6 March a Cabinet meeting heard the Prime Minister Winston Churchill declare that he had been 'disturbed by the *sudden* announcement of increased passenger fares on the railways and road transport undertakings [author's italics]. Would it not have been possible to give the public longer notice of these increases, and to explain that they were made on the authority, not of the Government, but of the Transport Tribunal?'[1]

The notes go on to record, with a detectable note of restrained exasperation, that 'the Cabinet were informed that the Transport Tribunal had been considering this matter for nearly a year'.

The discussion then moved on to 'the powers of the corporations responsible for the management of the socialised undertakings of transport, gas and electricity', and a suggestion 'that the relations between these corporations and Ministers were not in all respects satisfactory and needed examination'.

This was probably another masterpiece of understatement by the civil service, but it highlighted an extremely important point of potential misunderstanding and contention where nationalised industries were concerned.

These industries, including of course the British Transport Commission, were created by Acts of Parliament as individual corporations owned by the state.

In theory, then, their shareholders were the people, but in practice it was the elected representatives of the people who were in a position to call the managers of such industries to account.

This was not always particularly helpful, because it was virtually impossible for a Minister, however dedicated, to gain the same level of knowledge and understanding as a senior manager within the industry involved, particularly when the Minister was always at the mercy of the next Cabinet reshuffle and might soon be called upon to make snap decisions about, say, the conduct of a war rather than the price of cheap day returns on British Railways.

In this particular case Churchill's Government was principally concerned, as are all governments, with its own survival and the survival of its party, and by March the London increases had become an issue in the forthcoming local elections.

The Central Transport Consultative Committee turned up the metaphorical gas a little further in early April by endorsing the Tribunal's approval of the provincial increases, but Churchill was now provoked and could not resist intervention, evidently heedless of the wider economic realities.

The issue was sensitive, and caused divisions at the highest levels. On 10 April the Cabinet returned to the topic. After a discussion the Minister of Transport, John Maclay, was 'invited' to use his powers to direct the Commission.

It appears that Maclay was not convinced, and it is certainly true that he left the Government in early May, when he was replaced by Alex Lennox-Boyd. Even so, on 15 April he ordered the Commission not to make the announcement of provincial fare rises on British Railways that had been due the following day.

The ace of trumps had been slapped down on the Commission's table in the cause of political expedience.

It was not a first offence, because the previous Labour administration had already intervened more than once. It delayed a rise in freight charges in 1949-50, which the Commission later estimated cost it £11m in lost revenue, while on the other side of the accounts the Railway Executive had been virtually instructed to improve a wages offer in early 1951, to avoid a potential strike.

At least that instruction was based on a concern that industrial action could have caused disproportionate damage to the national economy, but the later intervention authorised by Churchill appears to have had a purely (if that is the word) political motive.

We have already seen that there were various collars and chains that had restricted the Commission from the beginning, but in fact the situation was even less favourable when outright meddling by Ministers had to be taken into account.

The Commission was responsible for balancing its books as provided by statute, but this was not complemented in reality by the freedom to take the actions necessary to achieve this goal.

Instead, Governments from both left and right appeared to be saying, in effect, 'It's your job to make ends meet and we don't intend to bail you out, but if your activities are causing us inconvenience we will step in and tell you what to do. If that leaves you with new problems, tough luck.'

The Commission's report for 1951 was presumably being drafted while the fares brouhaha was at its height in early 1952 (the report was published on 11 July of that year), and this comment in it may have been prompted by current developments:

'Passenger travel … is now being provided at a level of fare which is substantially less than pre-war, when changes in the value of money are taken into account.

Whether this position can continue is open to doubt.'[2]

This was just another gentlemanly understatement, because the Commission must have known quite well that it could not.

It was possible, therefore, to argue that some aspects of the Commission's proposals were tactless, but by now the BTC was not merely on the back foot over the whole question of fares and charges but deeply entangled in the contradictory meshes of the 1947 Act.

This undignified posture allowed the recently elected Conservative Government to assume the role of the White Knight, and ride gallantly to the rescue of the nation's persecuted passengers.

What this fairy tale did not include was any form of relief for the BTC's tottering profit and loss account. As before, the Commission simply had to grin and bear it.

There were occasional signs that there was some understanding of the Commission's position, as when Chancellor 'Rab' Butler had warned the Cabinet on 16 April that although the fare rises had been suspended,

'…he hoped that the increases to be made in rail fares would be finally determined and applied without avoidable delay. Although it had been right to step in and prevent the unreasonable increases which would otherwise have taken place outside London on 1 May, the railways would have a serious financial deficit if fares were not adjusted soon to reflect increases in costs.'[3]

This was an interesting use of the future conditional tense. The Commission as a whole had already been incurring a 'serious financial deficit' by any reasonable measure since 1948, and the real question was how much worse this deficit might now become as the result of the Government's interference.

Revised fares were announced in June, and came into effect later in the summer. The London element included yet another revision of the increases that had been approved in the previous March, and the former bus fare stages were restored.

Many rail travellers such as anglers, mariners and music hall artistes could also celebrate, because their discounted fares survived.

While the negotiations with the Commission were still in progress, the Cabinet was advised on 10 June that the price of simply modifying the increases in concessionary fares for these 'special classes of passengers' had been estimated at £1,902,000 a year, and the total cost of the accumulated delays was later put at more than £8m.[4]

There was, however, no accompanying simplification of tariffs.

The fares crisis marked a low point between the Commission and the Government in this period (the tone of the BTC's 1952 annual report was later described in the Commons as 'querulous'[5]), but it was also almost the end of the old regime, because the Conservatives were already sketching out transport reforms.

Paradoxically, the 1952 results were the best since nationalisation, notwithstanding the protracted bickering over fares. The accounts showed a net surplus of £8m, of which a healthy share was contributed by the railways, as Table 5 shows. But the Commission was still handicapped by its accumulated deficits, and the reserves available for capital investment were non-existent.

Although London Transport railways were reasonably modern on the whole, thanks to sustained investment before the war, the same could not be said of a large part of British Railways.

There were complaints in the Commons about dirty trains[6], and indeed the railways were still patently run-down. A radical solution would have to be found if the system was to recover, and the Commission could not achieve this with its own resources.

Even if the trains were not particularly inviting, efforts were still made to sell unused off-peak capacity for leisure travel, particularly in London and the South East, where the 'problem of the peaks' was greatest. When revenue was discussed by one railway staff society in March 1951, it was suggested that there should be 'more attractive day excursions, even if this involves the collection of passengers from street corners'[7]. This raised the novel concept of sparing railway customers the wearisome task of actually getting to the station, but sadly (perhaps) it was not put into effect.

Table 5: Revenue and journeys, 1948-1952

Year	BR passenger totals (m)	BR receipts		All BTC receipts	
		Gross (£m)	Net (£m)	Net (£m)	Surplus (£m)
1948	996.1	344.8	22.3	45.2	(4.7)
1949	992.8	334.1	29.0	31.3	(20.8)
1950	981.7	351.3	25.2	35.2	(14.1)
1951	1001.0	384.9	33.3	46.0	0.1
1952	1017.0*	416.3	38.7	52.9	8.0

* Break in series as a result of change in methods
Figures in brackets are deficits
Source: British Transport Commission Annual Reports

It is worth bearing in mind that as freight was still the senior partner on BR (it earned almost £179m in 1949, compared with £114m from passengers), improvements in passenger revenue would not necessarily balance the books. Even so, because increases were usually delayed while they worked their way through the Tribunal and Committee (and sometimes the Cabinet as well), the forced continuation of lower fares was seen as a serious disadvantage.

But were these delays really such a major drain on the Commission's revenues?

The implications were considered later by Stewart Joy, who was the British Railways Board's Chief Economist for several years in the later 1960s after he had previously acted as an adviser to Minister of Transport Barbara Castle.

In his account of the industry's money problems, *The train that ran away*[8], the hawkish Dr Joy had little sympathy for the BTC, because he believed it had been disastrously out of touch with the realities of the industry – financial, technical and administrative.

He suggested that rates restrained by the lengthy tribunal process might have been expected to attract some traffic from other modes – but went on to point out that such a shift did not occur, commenting that this had 'most dangerous implications'.[9]

The reasons for this sluggishness are actually not clear, and it is possible to speculate that some new traffic was gained, only to be balanced by other losses, but the Commission was probably still likely to lose some revenue unless its rates could be adjusted promptly.

Joy was not only doubtful in retrospect about the true effects of tribunal delays on the Commission's earnings; he was also dismissive of the alleged merits of cross-subsidy.

This had been defended by the Commission in 1948[10], which regarded it (then, at least) as a means of painlessly maintaining 'adequate' services, but Dr Joy condemned the use of profits to support losses elsewhere as 'a tax on some users, for the benefit of others', because he claimed that 'many of the users they were "taxing" would eventually rebel and buy their own transport facilities'.

This conclusion seems to rest on some assumptions, particularly that the 'taxed' users of profitable routes would necessarily be discontent with the price they were being charged. Neither could they know (and if they did, would they care?) that a proportion of their payments was being used to support other services. Even British Railways found such calculations extremely difficult.

It is no doubt true, however, that cross-subsidy is not a universal panacea, and it falls to the ground when the well of profitable services runs dry, for whatever reason.

The point at which cross-subsidy ceases to be admissible (if it is allowed at all) must be calculated with great care, and even then it will depend on whether the primary aim is to provide as many services as possible or the maximum financial return.

Joy was one of a group of analysts (Dr Beeching was another) who maintained that there were really two railways, namely a viable group of routes and services at the core, surrounded by a distracting layer of loss-makers.

These loss-makers, it was argued, had to be stripped away to move the industry towards profit.

In these circumstances, the highest possible direct financial returns (or lowest possible subsidies) are king, and all other factors – such as the effects on the wider economy or the social implications – become more or less irrelevant.

(After Dr Joy left the BRB and returned to his native Australia, his views remained unchanged. In 1977, when he had become a senior bank executive, he recommended wholesale reductions of the railways in the State of Victoria, alleging that they were trying to do too many jobs and had too many unproductive staff.[11])

In spite of its supporters, the truth of the 'core viability' theory has continued to be debated vigorously down the years.

Later on, in the early 1980s, the Serpell Committee would identify a vestigial 'core' that it thought could be profitable, but even then only with the help of freight.[12]

The perceived size of the 'ideal' railway network was to change repeatedly between the 1950s and 1980s – now smaller, now larger – before it settled down.

As we will also see later on, the most severe Serpell option was only a little more extreme than the official visions of a sustainable network that had been evolving since well before the Beeching period, even if those visions were kept behind tactfully closed doors.

Although the Commission had moved into surplus (just) in 1951, it was still failing to comply with the provisions of the 1947 Act. This required it to meet the costs that were properly chargeable to revenue, 'taking one year with another', but the balance sheet remained sullied with the deficits that had been carried forward. These amounted to £31.5m at the end of 1952, even after the surpluses that had been achieved in the past two years.

The Commission had reported after the 1951 results that with 'one exception, all the major branches of the Commission's undertaking contributed to the improvement'.

The exception was London Transport, which the Commission claimed was a victim of the delayed fares rise.

It was also keen to justify itself in other ways, pointing out that the accumulated deficit (£39.5m at that time) was 'less than the surplus profit accruing to the Government in any single one of the later years of the war'[13]. We cannot know if this ingenious argument appealed to the Chancellor of the Exchequer – although we can guess – but at least the arithmetic was undeniable.

In the meantime, 'central charges' continued to erode the net returns, largely because of the continuing need to pay interest on British Transport Stock. The BTC's total capital liabilities rose from £1,217m at the end of 1948 to £1,259m in 1950. By 1955 they would be more than £1,444m.[14] Nearly all these liabilities related to British Transport Stock mostly paying 3%.

The annual totals rose partly because the issue of more stock was the Commission's main method of raising capital in the early years, and also because tranches of new stock were sometimes used to finance acquisitions.

For example, the Tilling Group had received stock worth £24.8m in late 1948 in exchange for its shares in bus companies.[15] The interest payable then inflated the Commission's central charges by a further £744,000 a year.

In other words, the Commission was buying undertakings on credit, although its balance sheet would be theoretically in order so long as the value of the additional assets and the net profits they earned matched or preferably exceeded the value of the new stock issued plus annual interest and allowance for depreciation (another controversial matter).

At the same time as the Commission was issuing stock and paying interest to its holders, it was also making annual payments into a Capital Redemption Fund, which further increased the 'central charges'. The amounts were intended to be enough, as the result of the accumulation of compound interest, to repay the face value of the stock after 90 years had elapsed.

Because the Commission had been unable to accumulate any reserves, it was forced to tread delicately when new liabilities arose. One example of these was an outstanding balance of £27m due to the Treasury-owned Railway Finance Corporation, which had supported guaranteed borrowings by the former companies for capital projects in 1936.

The Commission paid off this debt when it became due in 1951, but only by using part of £60m that it raised in turn from the resoundingly named Commissioners for the Reduction of the National Debt.

This new injection of funds was equivalent to almost 10% of the Commission's annual turnover and was achieved by a special issue of British Transport Stock to the Commissioners at 1¾%, due for redemption in December 1952. When the time came, the repayment was only achieved by refinancing the debt elsewhere.

In short, when the BTC admitted to the 'precarious balance' of its affairs, this was an alarmingly accurate description. Of course, the essential question was how much longer Peter could go on paying Paul – and get away with it.

Chapter 9

'War to the knife'

In many respects time was indeed running out for the Commission, as it was originally conceived, by the start of 1953.

The recent change of government would soon trigger a change of structure, although regrettably no major financial improvements would follow.

In fact, the Commission would go on to discover that a theoretical lifeline intended to help it transform the worn-out railways was also a potential bear trap. Later on this trap was duly sprung, and the consequences for the industry, although not wholly bad, would prove to be largely irreversible.

The Tory manifesto for the 1951 election had claimed that 'nationalisation has proved itself a failure which has resulted in heavy losses to the taxpayer or the consumer, or both'.

It went on to promise that publicly owned rail and road transport would be 'reorganised into regional groups of workable size'. Future ownership of the railways was left unspecified, but private road hauliers were promised 'the chance to return to business'.

The Conservatives had opposed nationalisation after the war, and now the question had to be whether they would attempt a wholesale reversal of the 1947 Act.

Such a winding back might have been considered briefly, but the administrative and financial implications of restoring the Big Four would have been vast, and in any case quite impractical.

By issuing British Transport Stock the Government had guaranteed its holders a rate of return. It would have been possible to form new companies, but the owners of BTC stock could hardly be forced to exchange their secure holdings for equity shares once again.

It is true that the restored companies could have been floated like any other business, but the markets were unlikely to rejoice, particularly if road haulage was to be returned to private ownership and freed from most of its current restrictions, which is what actually happened.

It is perhaps conceivable that the revived companies could have been 'given' the railway assets of the British Transport Commission at a knockdown price, but such a transaction would probably have been very difficult to achieve unless a form of long-term purchase could have been negotiated with a reluctant Treasury.

To make matters worse, although they might have been able to meet day-to-day costs for a while (the railway account had been in profit from 1948 until its share of the Commission's 'central charges' had been deducted), the revived companies' underlying financial position would have been weak. Although we can only speculate about the share structure in these circumstances, they might have found it difficult to raise new, cost-effective capital.

This would have been a rather different situation from their former position of tending to be overcapitalised, but nonetheless it would have been very difficult for them to survive without public support.

In the meantime, the Government would still have been obliged to pay the interest due on British Transport Stock, but now without the assistance of railway revenues.

In short, the 1947 Act had involved a journey down a one-way street, and there could be no fundamental retracing of steps.

(When the railways were eventually privatised in the 1990s the proposition and resulting structure were very different, as we shall see. After some trials and tribulations, the result today is a hybrid industry in which the private sector is largely responsible for operations [with the significant exceptions of infrastructure management and train regulation], but owns relatively few of the assets.)

Meanwhile, the incoming Conservative Government of 1951 was convinced that over-centralisation lay at the heart of the BTC's troubles. This belief, accompanied by the manifesto pledge to denationalise road haulage, formed the foundations of a Transport Act that received Royal Assent in 1953.

Before the necessary Bill was unveiled, a White Paper had been published to set the scene for reform. An early draft of this document was presented to the Cabinet on 18 April 1952, where the railways' destiny was set out in these terms:

'11. The present excessive centralisation of the railways will be reduced by giving greater autonomy to areas which may follow the general pattern of the present regions. Scotland will be a separate area. The areas will together continue to constitute a single entity for financial purposes and for the control of charges.
12. The existence of these separate areas should encourage a healthy rivalry between them, and give greater scope for initiative than is possible under a single centralised administration.'[1]

It was not clear how the railway Regions could really develop an effective 'rivalry' with each other, healthy or otherwise, when their rates and charges were to remain controlled, while road haulage was to be freed of most restrictions, but there was no mention in the White Paper that this bold new era of managerial initiative would be accompanied, indeed encouraged, by the abolition of all the Executives with the exception of London Transport.

In the event, the Commission would be given direct responsibility for those remaining administrative tasks that could not be devolved to the railway Regions or returned to the private sector.

The wording of the White Paper was not only rather vague, but may also have been felt, on reflection, to be somewhat brusque as well.

Certainly the revised draft, which was submitted for consideration by the Cabinet on 23 April, now included a distinctly softer preamble, although the core message remained:

'11. The railways are a national asset. They must remain an essential element in transport, and cannot be allowed to fall into decay. The present excessive centralisation of the railways must, however, be reduced by giving greater autonomy to areas which may follow the general pattern of the present regions…'[2]

The Bill that followed this White Paper also went through some changes during the drafting stage, before it began its official progress through Parliament.

In particular, one section in the original Bill had made the BTC Chairman responsible for keeping the Minister of Transport 'informed on the Commission's activities'.

However, on 28 October 1952 the Cabinet was told that this requirement had been reconsidered by the Transport Policy Committee:

'The object … was to establish a proper statutory relationship … between the Commission and the Minister. On reflection, however, the Committee think that the provision – which has no parallel in the other nationalised industries – is better omitted.'[3]

It very probably was. A legal obligation to effectively justify the Commission's decisions to the Minister at frequent intervals would have been a daunting prospect for the most sanguine of chairmen.

Another provision – which did survive – allowed the BTC to make an interim application to the Transport Tribunal for an increase in fares or freight rates of up to 10%. A full hearing would still follow, but the new charges could be applied in the meantime. The Commission's repeated complaints that Tribunal delays were costing it dearly had evidently found a receptive ear at last.

The 1953 Act had two main strands. One was to return most road haulage to the private sector, and the other was to decentralise the railways so that, in theory, they would be freed of some controls and be better able to mimic the former companies. But the business remained state-owned. Regional managers would report to the Commission, not shareholders.

The Big Four had also become the Big Six, because the former LNER territory had been the responsibility of three Regions since nationalisation. One of these – the Scottish Region – also included the ex-LMS lines north of the border.

The boundaries that had been redrawn following the creation of six regions from four company territories in 1948 were never wholly satisfactory. The Executive and later the Commission were perceptibly uncomfortable with them, rather like someone who breakfasts in bed but is irritated by the resulting crumbs, so they kept trying to brush them away by making adjustments.

After some preliminary reforms there had been one particularly detailed round of such changes in 1950, which included the transfer of large swathes of the Southern Region in the far south-west of England to the Western instead, but only for 'commercial' purposes.

This made the successor of the Great Western Railway responsible for such unlikely places as Halwill Junction, although the lines affected – all in north Devon or Cornwall – continued to be worked by the Southern Region and included in its public timetable books.

(In 1958 this territory would be transferred back wholly to the Southern, but only until 1963 when the Western regained it once more, this time in all respects. By 1968 most of the routes affected by this parlour game had been closed, a development that could have been regarded as Paddington's ultimate revenge on its traditional foe at Waterloo. If so, it would have been an unfortunate example of the 'healthy rivalry' envisaged by the architects of the 1953 Act.)

The Great Central main line was another victim of this regional uncertainty. As an LNER route it became part of the Eastern Region at nationalisation, but during the 1950s was transferred somewhat haphazardly between the Eastern and London Midland, while even the Western Region gained the London end for a time. (The London Midland Region eventually took over entirely, but was then prompted by the BRB to withdraw all passenger services north of Aylesbury and close most of the route. Even Marylebone barely survived.)

As it made its way through the Committee stage in December 1952, the Transport Bill was greeted with a good deal of scepticism by Opposition MPs, who could see their vision of integrated transport being seriously eroded.

Future Labour Prime Minister James Callaghan, representing Cardiff South East, spelled out a grim prospect for transport:

'From the moment this Bill becomes law, it is war to the knife. There will be no co-operation between road and rail. The services that are now together will be torn apart. They will be fighting each other for every piece of trade, for every piece of merchandise, for every job on the roads. We shall be back to the days that existed before, which hon. Gentlemen opposite have conveniently forgotten, when their own Government were forced to introduce measures to restrict the unrestricted war to the knife that had been raging on the roads and railways.

'This is the task to which the railways have to return. They will have 12 months in which to do this job and they will have to do it quickly. Yet the Parliamentary Secretary says that at the same time as they are putting themselves in a proper state to meet the battle with the road hauliers which they will have to face, they must get ahead with re-organising themselves, get rid of the Railway Executive, get down to the big internal administrative job of overhauling the entire machine. This is typical of the Minister. It is exactly in line with everything he does; he holds all the balance on the side of the road hauliers and seizes every opportunity of doing down the Transport Commission.'[4]

It was to be expected that the Opposition would defend their legislation, which had come into force less than five years earlier, but the Conservatives were having none of it. Later in the same debate, the Minister of Transport, Alan Lennox-Boyd (later Viscount Boyd of Merton), who represented Mid Bedfordshire, set out the principal intentions of the Government:

'There should be a clear line of authority and responsibility from the Commission to the regions for the railways, as some may prefer to hear them called again … in respect of matters that are reserved for central control. Here let me say that I am very anxious that in the field where there has been a good result from central control nothing should be done to dissipate that valuable achievement. Second, there should be a clear division between such matters and those which will be the direct responsibility of the regions … we believe there should be a clear chain of responsibility from the officer responsible to the general manager of that particular region. There are also, of course, many issues which must be centrally controlled – investment policy, for instance, and the question of charges … but in general … the field of central control should be reduced rather than increased.'[5]

The question of charges must have been something of a red rag to the BTC, which was surely still smarting over recent events, and Mr Lennox-Boyd was keen to make it clear that here, too, the Commission could look forward to a novel – although as yet unspecified – era of commercial adventuring:

'The Bill provides for a re-organisation scheme which shall reserve to the Commission the general control of charges, but a scheme which may also provide for a substantial measure of elasticity in regard to detailed control, and I think it would be very unwise of me to attempt at this stage to tie the hands of the Commission in this field. But interesting possibilities, not without hope in some parts of the United Kingdom, may spring through this new freedom.'[6]

Another interesting possibility that had become clear by now was that the Government proposed to make the Commission directly responsible for British Railways, with no intervening Executive. This prompted Percy Collick, Labour member for Birkenhead, to observe that he was 'astonished' by this revelation, and that 'I suppose there has been no Bill before this House of Commons for a very long time which has had a worse reception than this one'.[7]

What also emerged at this time was that the friction between the Railway

Executive and the Commission had continued, and that there had been a good deal of confidential discussion about the Railway Executive's fate between the Commission and the Government with a result that was probably inevitable, given that the Commission was evidently heartily tired of being kept in the dark by its unruly junior partner and that Ministers were simultaneously intent on giving the Regions new 'freedoms'. (As early as April 1948 the Commission's Chairman, Sir Cyril Hurcomb, had lamented in a letter to Railway Executive Chairman Sir Eustace Missenden in connection with a diesel plan inherited from the former LNER that 'The Commission would, I think, like to know whether it is the fact that this scheme has now been shelved…'[8])

Some light was also shed on the efficiency or otherwise of the Executive, when former railway solicitor Geoffrey Wilson, Conservative member for Truro, recounted an occasion at Paddington during which no fewer than seven members of the station management had been asked by Executive representatives how many fire extinguishers were installed on the platforms.

Mr Wilson observed:

'Each particular functionary at the executive level had thought that this question applied to him and therefore to his corresponding number on the railways. I am sure that such a situation must have happened in other matters.'[9]

We know that 1953 produced 'change and stress' for the Commission, because those words appear in that year's annual report. The new Transport Act became law on 6 May, and all the Executives, apart from London Transport, were abolished on 1 October.

This was followed by an immediate move for the Commission's staff from their headquarters at 55 Broadway in Westminster to 222 Marylebone Road, near Baker Street station. This rambling building, originally the Great Central Railway's London hotel, had been the home of several Executives, including that for railways. (It later became the headquarters of the British Railways Board but is now a hotel once again – although no longer in railway ownership.)

The 1953 Act also changed the Commission's primary objective. In 1948 this had been the provision of an 'efficient, adequate, economical and properly integrated' transport service.

The new Act required the Commission to provide services outside London that 'appear to the Commission to be expedient', but 'due regard' was to be paid to 'efficiency, economy and safety' and the 'needs of the public, agriculture, commerce and industry'.

In the London Passenger Transport Area, in contrast, passenger services were to be 'adequate and properly co-ordinated', and this duty would fall in practice on the London Transport Executive.[10]

The word that was now missing outside the capital was 'integrated'. This had fallen out of favour, much as governments of our time seem determined not to mention nationalisation.

Instead, 'decentralisation' of the railways was the approved way forward, so new 'areas' and 'authorities' were to be set up 'as may be specified', although the Commission was to retain 'general financial control' and 'general control of charges'.

This requirement for a continuing central responsibility for controlling charges amounted to a virtual admission that the 'healthy rivalry' predicted in the White Paper was little more than hopeful twaddle, having perhaps been drafted by someone who had vague recollections of the famous railway 'Races to the North' on the East and West Coast lines more than half a century earlier.

Quite apart from the continuing presence of a theoretically watchful Commission, the time had long gone since individual parts of the railway could have usefully or sensibly competed with each other for freight or passenger traffic, because the real threat to them all was rumbling or racing along the roads of every county.

Meanwhile, the Labour victory in 1945 had reshaped the political landscape fundamentally, and this was accompanied by a major change to the railway industry and how it was regarded.

Before the war, it had been the right wing that had defended Government support for the railway companies, on the grounds that they provided a 'great public service'.

The left typically viewed such support, even if it was limited to assisting capital projects, as an underhand way of converting taxpayers' money into dividends.

After nationalisation the wind changed direction. Labour had succeeded in transferring the railways to the public sector, and now it was the Conservatives who resisted further cash injections.

The main consequence was the unfortunate 1953 Act, which damaged the already struggling Commission still further by depriving it of a major portion of the profits that it had been receiving from road haulage, notwithstanding that hauliers were now liable to contribute towards a 'transport levy'. This, however, was only intended to compensate the Commission for the direct costs and losses incurred associated with the disposal of road haulage assets.

The temporary existence of this levy (it ended in 1956) did nothing to reduce the effect of the newly liberated hauliers gnawing at the railways' primary source of revenue in the 'war to the knife' that had been predicted by James Callaghan, and the result was that the 1953 Act had the unsought effect of helping to tilt the railway operating account into deficit, a position from which it never truly recovered.

In the free market economy favoured by the traditional right there was no place for losers, and an industry that could not even cover its costs (much less show a return on capital invested) was, in their eyes, *ipso facto* redundant.

If the railways were to survive unscathed in such circumstances, they had to return to profit. But as the 1950s advanced, it became increasingly clear that this was something they could not do.

Part 2:

'The pressures being exerted'

Chapter 10

'A thoroughly modern system'

On 21 December 1954 the Minister of Transport, the Rt Hon. J. A. Boyd-Carpenter MP, received an unusual Christmas card.

In fact, it was not so much a message of greeting as a begging letter, because when opened it proved to be a suggestion from the British Transport Commission that it should be allowed to spend some £1.2bn of taxpayers' money modernising the railway system.

The Commission attempted to soften the impact by setting out a 15-year timetable for its plan, and also cunningly pointed out that almost £600m would have to be spent over that period in any case, just to maintain a 'present basis', steady-state railway.

Even these bare statements begged some essential questions, such as how much railway did the nation really need, steady-state or otherwise, and what transport ends would be best served by such a major investment?

BR economist Stewart Joy later described the BTC Modernisation Plan as 'the greatest shopping spree in railway history'[1] – but then he was writing in the days before the creation of Railtrack, which would go on to test new heights of unwise expenditure in its ill-fated attempt to modernise the West Coast Main Line in the later 1990s.

Almost four decades before Railtrack would be launched on its uncertain path, a group of British Transport Commission officers from Headquarters and the Regions had been summoned to join a special Planning Committee in May 1954. Their brief was to research the technical details of a modernisation project that would rescue the railways from their semi-moribund post-war state and return them to profitability.

In fact, the Modernisation Plan was the second attempt that had been made in this period to devise an upgrade of the system.

In the last few months before it was disbanded in the autumn of 1953, the Railway Executive had devoted some of its final hours to the compilation of a modernisation plan of its own – 'A development scheme for British Railways'[2].

It appears to have been a rushed job, the work of railway officers who knew there was practically no chance of their ideas being adopted *nem. con.*, but it did sound a clarion call for electrification, which may have set the stage for the Commission's own proposals.

In fact, as far as main-line electrification was concerned the BTC plan was less ambitious than the Railway Executive had been. For example, the BTC envisaged electrification of the West Coast route to Birmingham, Manchester and Liverpool, but the Executive had thought the wires should continue to Glasgow.

Other sections of route that are only now (2015) being dealt with also figured in the Executive's stillborn plans, particularly the Great Western Main Line to South Wales and the Midland Main Line, although the MML project was temporarily 'paused' by the Government in June 2015 on cost grounds. When it eventually happens, this scheme will take electrification to Sheffield and very probably onwards to Doncaster and Leeds, but in 1953 the Executive was proposing to include the now severed former Midland line to Manchester as well.

Similarly, the Commission recommended East Coast electrification to Leeds and was willing to consider York, whereas the Executive had looked further north, as far as Newcastle.

The 'real' Modernisation Plan[3] submitted to the Minister of Transport in December 1954 went much further than electrification alone, which together with new electric or diesel locomotives accounted for £345m of the proposed budget.

Another £210m was allocated to improving track and signalling (including more power boxes and colour lights), £285m for electric or diesel multiple units and upgrading stations and parcels depots, and £365m for modernising freight services.

A further £25m would be for 'sundry items', including staff welfare, improvements at packet ports and 'office mechanisms', with a final £10m for research and development.

These items came to a total of £1,240m, which the Commission rather airily reduced to 'say, £1,200m' in its proposals, evidently assuming that a mere £40m could probably be saved somewhere along the way.

The plan had two distinct aims, although the achievement of the first was being claimed to make the second more likely.

The railways were suffering, as we have already seen, from a serious backlog of maintenance and renewals, partly because of the recent war (some larger stations such as London Cannon Street still had skeletal roofs at this time, unrepaired since the attentions of the Luftwaffe) but also because there had been a post-war clampdown on capital spending, so that the British Transport Commission had started life with no reserves and strict limitations on capital-raising powers.

One aim was to recover these arrears, then proceed to make some overdue technical progress, such as abolishing steam. Even this was not straightforward, because the Commission did not appear to be really questioning – minor closures aside – whether the network as a whole was worth mending. (In fact, there was another side to this story, but it would remain under cover for a while.)

The second aim – and this would have been of greater interest to the Treasury – was to return the railway to profit, which the Commission claimed would be a principal benefit of modernisation.

The problem was that no one could know how much traffic had been lost to the railway simply because the network was run-down and inefficient, and how much would have transferred in any case to other modes of transport – particularly the private car and lorry. Conversely, therefore, it was also difficult to assess how much potential business existed that a modern system could attract.

However, it is true that there were some improvements embedded in the plan that were calculated to encourage passenger growth, as later experience confirmed. Electrification of main lines would allow significant accelerations, and shorter journey times win customers from other, slower modes, as was later proved by 'Pendolinos' on the West Coast route and the opening of HS1 from London to the continent.

A desire for electrification and faster intercity services would not raise eyebrows today, and the Commission was obviously right to include these ambitions, although it should have been pursuing them from 1948, resources permitting. Instead, the wayward Railway Executive designed and built fleets of new steam locomotives that were essentially obsolete before they had even left the works.

It was probably not a coincidence that the committee responsible for the Commission's plan had been convened as recently as the spring of 1954, not long after the Railway Executive had been disbanded.

However, although it is hard to fault the Commission's wish to improve its intercity services (except, perhaps, that the proposals were not ambitious enough), the same could not be said of the plan as a whole, because it included the promise to Government – and this was plainly the unique selling proposition – that the railways could be returned to profit by about 1962.

The suggestion that this was even possible without a radical reappraisal of the industry seems to have been based on a combination of wishful thinking and an ostrich-like disregard, for which the Ministry of Transport must share some responsibility.

But before the chill draughts of reality could blow down the long corridors at 222 Marylebone Road, the Commission had invested in hundreds of new diesel units for local services that could not cover their direct costs, much less contribute to general overheads.

Even worse, because at least the diesel units could be used elsewhere, vast new marshalling yards would be built with 'modernisation' money to cater for the declining wagon-load business. Some of these yards were hardly used before they closed – grim monuments to the Commission's lack of judgement.

The problem was that diesel units could and did encourage more traffic on branch lines, but not always enough of it. This was not necessarily clear at the outset and seems to have led the Commission down some blind alleys.

For example, 22 four-wheel railbuses of various types were ordered for a number of local lines in England and Scotland, including Gleneagles-Crieff-Comrie, Witham-Braintree, Bedford-Hitchin and Bedford-Northampton.

Most of these lines later disappeared, but some new halts were sometimes added together with the railbuses in a final bid to boost business, such as at platform-less Strageath and Pittenzie on the Comrie line, where 'retractable steps' were needed.[4]

Installing additional halts in the 1950s does not seem to have made much difference to revenue, and it seems likely that in the motor age most people living some distance from established stations had long since made other arrangements that they were unlikely to overturn.

Railway geography was part of the problem as it had been after the First World War, when railway companies building belated halts to combat the new rural motor buses were handicapped because they could do nothing about the fact that country lines had often been built some distance from local settlements, following contour lines in the name of economy.

Buses, on the other hand, could go right into village centres and even set people down at their gates. Once private cars became more widely available, a halt some distance away across the fields was probably even less inviting.

The performance of any business depends on income and also on controlling costs, but the Commission persisted in running the railway to Victorian standards, with thousands of small goods yards (5,804 stations were still handling freight at the end of 1959, just 142 fewer than a year earlier, while there were also 878 marshalling yards[5]), a maze of underused lines and far too many employees who were a relic, in a sense, of the long-gone days of cheap labour.

Although the Commission protested periodically that it was introducing more efficient working methods, the picturesque little terminus at Moretonhampstead, on the edge of Dartmoor, still employed seven staff on the day that the branch closed in 1959.[6]

Supporters of rural routes like the Moretonhampstead line have since speculated that more of them could have survived if they had been converted much earlier to 'basic' railways, with minimal staffing and the simplest of track layouts, but this was not tried until after the unlamented Commission had been replaced. A pioneer of this strategy, most of the East Suffolk line, is still in business today.

As things were, it has been said that until 1960 the London Midland Region would not countenance unstaffed stations at all.[7]

However, it would not be true to say that the Commission, and indeed the Railway Executive before it, made no attempts to rationalise the system. In fact, a special committee had been created after nationalisation to examine the issue of 'unremunerative lines'.

Given that evaluation of each line took time, and that each closure proposal affecting passenger services was scrutinised by the Consultative Committees before being submitted to the Minister, perhaps it would have been unreasonable to expect very much in the early years.

However, by the end of 1953 only 671km of route had closed completely, which represented just over 2% of the 1948 network.[8]

The withdrawal of passenger services was more vigorous, and the total length of route served had shrunk by 1,878km during the same period. (The difference between the two figures is explained by the fact that freight trains continued to use the rest.)

However, the Railway Executive had been constrained by several factors. One was the laborious process of submission to the committees and the Minister, but another was the almost guaranteed wave of opposition that greeted proposed withdrawals of passenger services.

This trend led to a major inquiry into the future of the railways on the Isle of Wight in the summer of 1953, which was told by the Railway Executive that the island lines were losing £271,000 annually. This claim was denied by various vocal opponents, who included the Railway Development Association as well as the Isle of Wight County Council.

They alleged that the Executive was exaggerating both the costs of maintaining the island's railways and the savings that would be realised by their closure.

Briefed for the Council, Melford Stevenson QC claimed that

'...the [Executive's] figures have now been demonstrated beyond any doubt as quite wrong. If the same form of accountancy as has been applied to the Island were used for the whole of British Railways, their 1951 profit of £34m would be turned into a loss of £40m.'[9]

Whether that was strictly true or not, by the time its modernisation plans appeared the Commission was rapidly coming off the rails.

Piecemeal closures had been nibbling away at the fringes of the problem, but there was no visible national plan setting out the shape and size of the ideal network, 'modernisation' notwithstanding, probably because neither the Commission nor the Government knew what that ideal was.

All the Commission could say in 1955 was that its aim was to produce 'a thoroughly modern system', although it should also have been questioning whether its approach to running the existing network was sufficiently cost-conscious, as well as thinking twice before investing precious capital in new trains for minor branch lines.

Its early adventures with diesels for main lines were also unfortunate. The multiple units bought for local services mostly worked well (the real failures in this department proved to be the small railbuses), but the same could not be said of the locomotives.

The Commission spent a substantial slice of modernisation money on a wide range of types from various manufacturers, with mixed success. In retrospect it is clear that the Commission cast its new locomotive net too widely, although it still declined to deal with most foreign manufacturers, particularly those in the USA, where firms like General Motors had been accumulating valuable experience with diesels since well before the Second World War.

This misplaced patriotism may have cost the country dear, while the upheavals accompanying nationalisation had also, to coin an appropriate phrase, put a spoke in the traction wheel.

In July 1947 the LNER Board had approved in principle a plan to upgrade its East Coast express services by replacing 32 'Pacific' steam locomotives with 25 diesel-electrics. The LNER had taken a long hard look at US practice, although its directors were warned that loading-gauge differences would be a factor if American designs were to be adapted for service in Britain.

This scheme did not find favour with the Railway Executive, but the LNER was not alone. Even as nationalisation was looming, the LMS had ordered two diesel-electric main-line locomotives from English Electric (the first of these was driven triumphantly out of the Derby works just weeks before the state took over), while the GWR had unveiled its preliminary designs for a gas turbine main-line locomotive in 1946. Construction of two types of these machines began in the following year, one of them in Switzerland.

Further traction experiments of this kind were frozen at nationalisation, to be followed by the inevitable appointment of a Railway Executive committee to reconsider the whole question. The pace was leisurely: the Committee's terms of reference emerged in April 1948 but its members were only appointed in December and the resulting internal report was not completed until October 1951.

The Committee conceded that diesels were more economical in most circumstances – the relative costs of coal and fuel oil were strongly in the diesels' favour – and also, where local services were concerned, that railcars were more attractive to passengers.

But it also claimed that diesel railcars had a working life of 20 years, while steam locomotives could be expected to last twice as long. (There have been plenty of examples since then of diesels remaining in service into their fourth decade.)

The conclusion was cautiously worded:

'It seems reasonably clear ... that increasing reliance will have to be placed on motive power other than steam. At the present stage of technical progress, this would seem to mean electric or diesel traction. Yet, for obvious reasons, steam must provide a considerable proportion of the traction for many years to come. Any decision to go forward with new types of motive power should not therefore be taken at the expense of a neglect to continue to develop the steam locomotive.'[10]

This was hardly a wholehearted endorsement of the alternatives, although the Committee also recommended wide-scale trials of more recent technologies and admitted that steam locomotives possessed 'inherent limitations'.

Even so, a booklet produced to welcome new employees to British Railways in 1949 included a sketch of steam locomotives but no diesels, gas turbines or even a humble Southern Region electric multiple unit. Plainly, this was still a steam railway.

The internal report was written less than four years before the Commission's Modernisation Plan would present a determined case for newer forms of power, demonstrating one of the many differences of opinion that had existed between

Commission and Executive.

Even as the Modernisation Plan was pushing the former Executive's affection for steam firmly aside (Parliament having already done much the same thing to the Executive itself), new managerial chasms were appearing within the Commission's restructured railway empire.

This was partly because the 1953 Transport Act had given the Regions a greater degree of autonomy, but the justification for this reform was dubious.

However desirable (or even possible) it may have appeared to be from the political viewpoint at Westminster, the reality was that the Regions were not, and could not be, the companies reborn.

In spite of the creation of new 'area authorities' for each Region, they were still components of the state-owned BTC, which was answerable to the Minister and presented a single set of accounts to Parliament.

One result of this enhanced devolution was that some managers were able to enjoy themselves for a few years while they played at reviving pre-nationalisation days.

But even as the Western Region, in particular, basked in the rosy glow of nostalgia – complete with chocolate and cream coaches, copper-capped chimneys and

BRITISH TRANSPORT COMMISSION

BRITISH RAILWAYS

2491A/168

XXXXXXXXXX XXXXXXXXX

SOUTHERN REGION

H. C. LANG
Regional Staff Officer
G. R. ROBINSON
Assistant Regional Staff Officer
Telephone : WATERLOO 5151
Extension
IN YOUR REPLY PLEASE
QUOTE THIS REFERENCE

W.339/2/123
Yr : 200/456/2

REGIONAL STAFF OFFICER

WATERLOO STATION

LONDON, S.E.1

11th January, 1954.

A.C. PARKER, ESQ.

**APPLICATION FOR OUTDOOR MACHINERY
ALLOWANCE - CARPENTER H.W. CROSS,
C.E. DEPARTMENT, CATHAYS.**

    With reference to your letter of
12th December, on this Region Carpenters
in the Civil Engineer's Department
performing work for the Outdoor Machinery
Section are not paid the Outdoor Machinery
Differential and I am in agreement with
the attitude adopted by the Western Region
in this matter.

LEFT: This was the Railway
Executive's conception of motive
power, as shown in a booklet for new
employees produced in 1949.

THIS PAGE: The continuing autonomy
of the Regions, which increased after
1953, may well have added to the costs
of administration and reduced the
theoretical advantages of unification.

103

precious symbols such as Brunel's walking stick (solemnly bequeathed to each regional civil engineer on appointment) – back at Marylebone Road the losses were mounting.

The brutal truth was that these seemingly harmless pleasantries were irrelevant while traffic stagnated, deficits increased and millions of people fell in love with the motor car.

Chapter 11

'A disgrace which ought not to be permitted'

During the second half of the 1950s the British Transport Commission was busily engaged in digging a deep hole that would eventually engulf it, even though it had succeeded in its bid to invest £1.2bn or more of public money in the railways.

The BTC Modernisation Plan would fail in two fundamental respects. One was that the network had only been upgraded rather patchily by 1970, the year that should have marked completion. Steam lingered until 1968, while by 1970 other factors were threatening to ignite a new and possibly terminal crisis, as we shall see.

The other failure would spell doom for the Commission itself much earlier, because far from heading towards the profit that had been promised by 1962, the industry was incurring ever greater losses each year. This was partly because so much modernisation money had been wasted on vast marshalling yards and other fruitless projects, rather than invested in more economical ways of working that would, for example, have reduced the need for so many expensively staffed mechanical signal boxes.

This was the important point. A loss-making nationalised industry diving further and further into debt with no recovery in sight was calculated to furrow brows at the Treasury.

Some observers have tended to blame the problems of this period on a blatant anti-rail political conspiracy involving a vigorous road lobby, which led in the end to Beeching. But pleas and propaganda from lorry owners and motorway builders might have been less effective if the railways had behaved themselves.

As things were, the industry had become the naughty child of transport, demanding more and more pocket money from governments. They, however, became increasingly uncertain whether the price was actually worth paying.

The results for 1954, the first full year following the abolition of the Railway Executive, still showed a railway surplus – but at £16.4 million this was less than half the profit of the year before. Passenger journeys were up by five million to 1,020m, and gross receipts had risen by more than £14m.

For the Commission as a whole the picture was more sombre: when all its activities were taken into account the result was the first deficit since 1950, amounting to £11.9m. This included capital charges of £43.2m payable on British Transport Stock.

The Commission explained that fares and charges were lagging behind expenses, especially as there had been 'further and substantial increases in wages'[1]. In short, it was the old, old story. In a bid to close the liquidity gap, a further issue of British Transport Stock worth £80m had been made in February.

The report also recorded that 'there is no remedy except withdrawal' for the many stopping trains that 'fail to cover their direct costs by many millions of pounds', but commented morosely that 'local opposition to this process is still however very great'.

1954 had also been notable for the start of a reorganisation of British Railways following the reforms of the Transport Act, and a further White Paper had been published on 13 July that paved the way for the creation of the new 'area authorities'.

These were seen to sit within the management structure between the Commission and the general managers, but the White Paper also conceded that 'it is common sense that direct contact should exist between ... British Transport Commission headquarters and executive management in the person of the Chief Regional Manager in the Region.'[2]

So the new area authorities were not to be in the direct line of command. Indeed, 'they are not intended to be executive organs of day-to-day management, nor will they be suitably composed for that purpose. In this they resemble the boards of the former railway companies.'

In this phrase, the Government revealed once again its yearning to turn back the clock to the days before 1948. As that was not possible, the area authorities would act as pseudo-boards and apparently assist the Commission (for which there was no pre-1948 peacetime equivalent) in the formulation of policy.

Since this arrangement was not a true restoration of the former company structures, it might strike the reader that here was a new potential source of conflict, much as there had been between the Commission and the Executive.

When the reorganisation was debated in the House of Commons in November 1954, it became plain that James Callaghan, speaking for Labour, had similar reservations, particularly because the boards would theoretically control large budgets:

'This Scheme of divided authority ... is sinning against the cardinal principle of organisational administration, that there should be a clear chain of command... The area boards have been tucked in half way down the scale to satisfy the Government's back benchers. We shall have this discussion continuously going on about where the level of responsibility lies, who is responsible, and how the responsibility is to be carried out, just because the Minister has sacrificed good administration to party dogma and prejudice... If the Minister tells us that the area board is no more than a façade and a sham under which the regional manager will do the job for the Commission, I understand. That means that he has tossed another bone to the back benchers... If he is telling me that these part-time gentlemen ... are to be responsible for spending £446 million, I reply that it is a disgrace which ought not to be permitted.'[3]

In the event, the BTC did not prove to be willing to be confined to matters of broad policy. Instead the Commission's new Chairman, General Sir Brian Robertson, followed military practice and created a 'General Staff' at headquarters that would more or less supervise and coordinate the Regions.

Later on this precedent would be enshrined in the 1962 Transport Act, which by creating the British Railways Board effectively gave full executive authority to the General Staff.

Of course, bickerings about the details of organisation concealed a much greater weakness that the Commission was about to confront – in theory – with its £1.2bn plan for the railways.

But, as we have seen, the plan failed to include a thorough review of the industry of the kind that Beeching would undertake within a few years, so failure was all but inevitable.

However, there was much more awareness behind the scenes of the industry's plight than was reflected in the public modernisation plan or indeed the Commission's annual reports, apart from its vague references to stopping trains that failed to cover their costs.

An internal report drawn up in 1955 in preparation for the abolition of steam on part of the Western Region also included details of the performance of minor routes in the area. It would have made grim reading for branch-line supporters – had they been allowed to see it.[4]

Although this document was mainly concerned with complete conversion from steam to diesel west of Newton Abbot, it also set out proposals to close nearly all the Region's branches in south Devon and Cornwall to passenger traffic, with only the Par-Newquay and Truro-Falmouth lines keeping some summer services.

The statistics that accompanied this analysis demonstrated clearly how the traditional style of railway management and staffing, inherited from Victorian times, was now utterly inappropriate in the second half of the 20th century.

The South West was perhaps an extreme case, with its sharp peaks of holiday traffic requiring extra facilities and resources that were unnecessary for the rest of the year, but it tended to demonstrate how BR had lost its way.

None of the services examined came anywhere near covering even their direct costs, and at this time there was no form of subsidy available from national or local government.

The mainly single-line 32km Par-Newquay branch had no fewer than nine crossing places as well as four longer double-track sections. All five intermediate stations were staffed, including the diminutive Quintrel Downs Platform, and at least three train sets were needed, regulated by signalmen in ten boxes along the route.

Yet the normal timetable offered just nine or ten services each way, carrying around 100 passengers between them outside the summer season. (The line now has two crossing places, and one unit provides seven local services on an average day. Apart from a summer presence at Newquay, which is still reached by intercity trains, there are no station staff and, although the line has kept its mechanical signalling for now, only two of the boxes remain.)

Excessive provision of resources was not confined to the far South West, although too many people on the payroll not only inflated current wage costs but also made the Commission even more vulnerable to the effects of pay increases. It attempted to restrain wages for some years until this particular dam burst in 1960. By the time it did, the Commission was already up to its neck.

Table 6: Revenues and journeys, 1953-1962

Year	BR passenger journeys (m)	BR receipts Gross (£m)	Net (£m)	BTC receipts (all Executives) Net (£m)	Surplus/ deficit (£m)
1953	1,015	434.7	34.6	55.7	4.2
1954	1,020	449.3	16.4	40.4	(11.9)
1955	994	453.9	1.8	24.2	(30.6)
1956	1,029	481.0	(16.5)	2.1	(54.4)
1957	1,101	501.4	(27.1)	(6.5)	(63.5)
1958	1,090	471.6	(48.1)	(30.8)	(89.0)
1959	1,069	457.4	(42.0)	(15.4)	(73.9)
1960	1,037	478.6	(67.7)	(39.2)	(100.9)
1961	1,025	474.7	(86.9)	(56.6)	(122.0)
1962	998	465.1	(104.0)	(72.8)	(143.7)

Figures in brackets are deficits

Source: British Transport Commission Annual Report

At the end of 1959 British Railways still employed 519,000 staff, down from 649,000 in 1948, and 4,705 of these were 'stationmasters, yardmasters, goods agents, etc.'[5]

Just a few of them were listed in a Bristol area timetable booklet, and a close look might cause the reader to wonder what people like Mr Coggins and his staff at Flax Bourton did with their day.

This station was served by just nine up passenger trains and 10 down, and the intervals between them mostly ran into hours rather than minutes. There was perhaps a brief bustle in the early evening, when two down trains from Bristol arrived just 13 minutes apart, but that was the high point of the timetable. Even so, the station possessed a three-ton crane to handle goods, and could also deal with horse boxes and 'prize cattle' vans. Flax Bourton was listed by Beeching in March 1963, and closed to passengers before the end of the year.

The population of Flax Bourton is well under a thousand even now, but as with many other former stations there have been suggestions that it could reopen (see, for example, Flax Bourton Parish Council's parish plan for 2004).

New housing may justify restoration one day, particularly as the village is only 9km from Bristol, but any future installation need not be equipped to deal with horse

LIST OF STATIONS, TELEPHONE NUMBERS AND STATION MASTERS

Station	Telephone	Station Master
Ashley Hill	Bristol 46195	Mr. H. P. Hole
Avoncliff Halt	Bradford-on-Avon 3216 ...	Mr. T. J. Bunce
Avonmouth Dock	Avonmouth 2445	Mr. R. W. B. Thomas
Bath Spa	Bath 5451	Mr. A. E. Stowe
Bathampton	Bath 8-8107	Mr. S. L. Plummer
Bathford Halt	Bath 8-8107	Mr. S. L. Plummer
Bedminster	Bristol 21001	Mr. R. C. Price
Black Dog Halt	Calne 3386	Mr. P. Gleed
Bleadon & Uphill	Bleadon 227	Mr. G. L. Richings
Box	Box 311	Mr. W. Clothier
Box (Mill Lane)	Box 311	Mr. W. Clothier
Bradford-on-Avon	Bradford-on-Avon 3216 ...	Mr. T. J. Bunce
Bradford Peverell	Maiden Newton 218 ...	Mr. W. E. Rattenbury
Brent Knoll	Highbridge	Mr. W. V. Edwards
Bridgwater	Bridgwater 2721	Mr. A. Perkins
Bridport	Bridport 3310	Mr. G. W. H. Gover
Bristol (Temple Meads) ...	Bristol 93451	Mr. R. J. Parks (Passenger Agent)
Bruton	Bruton 2114	Mr. R. J. Gould
Calne	Calne 3386	Mr. P. Gleed
Castle Cary	Castle Cary 319	Mr. R. G. Hopkins
Cattistock Halt	Maiden Newton 218 ...	Mr. W. E. Rattenbury
Chetnole Halt	Yetminster 256	Mr. H. J. Perry
Chippenham	Chippenham 2252	Mr. W. J. E. Ellwood
Chittening Platform ...	Avonmouth 2445	Mr. R. W. B. Thomas
Christian Malford Halt... ...	Bradenstoke 242	Mr. S. Rawle
Clevedon	Clevedon 2223	Mr. J. W. Hankey
Clifton Down	Bristol 33417	Mr. W. G. Beale
Corsham	Corsham 3255	Mr. R. M. Ludgate
Creech St. Michael Halt ...	Henlode 235	Mr. D. F. H. Atkins
Cross Hands Halt	Pilning 206	Mr. W. A. J. Pike
Dauntsey	Bradenstoke 242	Mr. S. Rawle
Dilton Marsh Halt	Warminster 2002	Mr. J. R. Lane
Dorchester West	Dorchester 24	Mr. W. R. Channon
Dunball	Puriton 238	Mr. A. Perkins
Durston	North Curry 219	Mr. D. F. H. Atkins
Evershot	Evershot 233	Mr. H. J. Perry
Filton Junction	Filton 2016	Mr. T. L. Powell
Flax Bourton	Flax Bourton 38	Mr. A. Coggins
Freshford	Limpley Stoke 3146 ...	Mr. W. S. E. Humphries
Frome	Frome 2482	Mr. H. H. Soper
Grimstone & Frampton ...	Dorchester 572	Mr. W. E. Rattenbury
Henbury	Bristol 62-1608	Mr. L. H. Mogridge
Highbridge for Burnham-on-Sea	Highbridge 374	Mr. W. V. Edwards
Holt Junction	North Trowbridge 241 ...	Mr. E. A. Russell
Horfield	Filton 2016	Mr. T. L. Powell
Keynsham & Somerdale ...	Keynsham 3278	Mr. N. R. Bartrum
Lacock Halt	Corsham 3255	Mr. R. H. Ludgate
Lawrence Hill	Bristol 21001. Ext. 465 ...	Mr. F. J. Jenkins
Limpley Stoke	Limpley Stoke 2244 ...	Mr. W. S. E. Humphries
Maiden Newton	Maiden Newton 218 ...	Mr. W. E. Rattenbury
Marston Magna	Marston Magna 234 ...	Mr. E. W. J. Shapley
Melksham	Melksham 2200	Mr. D. R. Widdows
Montpelier	Bristol 4-3022	Mr. W. G. Beale
Nailsea & Backwell	Nailsea 44	Mr. S. F. Veal
New Passage Halt	Pilning 210	—
North Filton Platform	Filton 2016	Mr. T. L. Powell
Oldfield Park	Bath 5451	Mr. A. E. Stowe

Stationmasters on parade, 1959.

boxes. Had this station been run more economically in the 1950s, it might still be open now.

Transport commentator David St John Thomas pointed out in 1963 that the railways were often fighting a losing battle:

'It is far harder than realised by most people opposing branch line closures to bring traffic back to the railways once it has been lost. The possibility of raising the revenue of many lines sufficiently to cover the cost of one signal box is remote … the reduction of expenditure offers infinitely greater scope. It is in failing to prevent needless waste that British Railways have sorely jeopardised their future.'[6]

Efforts to reduce railway expenditure by closing lines and withdrawing services had begun in 1949 and would pick up speed after Beeching's report in 1963. Rarely did these withdrawals appear to have much lasting effect on BR's profit and loss account.

As St John Thomas had said, costs might have been saved on the overstaffed and overequipped minor lines where expenditure could have been cut, while retaining most of the revenue.

Outright closure, however, threw away the local business and probably weakened the network, because wistful suggestions that people would then obediently catch buses to the nearest railhead (Beeching would embrace this notion) proved to be largely illusory.

It was, of course, the growth in car ownership that caused much of the decline in the railway's passenger business for several decades after the war, although there was a brief upturn in rail's favour when the Suez crisis of 1957 forced a temporary return to petrol rationing.

The statistics for that year as reported in the annual reports and accounts of the BTC tell their own story: for the first time since the war the annual total of passenger journeys on British Railways exceeded 1,100m. Unfortunately when fuel rationing ceased this spurt in business began to die away, and the lower 1958 total represented the start of a new retreat.

Although closures continued, by the end of the 1950s modernisation had yet to improve much of the surviving BR system significantly, and in this respect it was increasingly out of step with the wider world.

Sainsbury's had opened the first of a series of 'self-service' shops – the forerunners of today's supermarkets – in Croydon in June 1950, while food rationing was gradually eased and then finally abolished in 1954 after a dismal period of continuing austerity during which it must have seemed that wartime restrictions would never be lifted.

Commercial television was launched in London in September 1955 and the second channel was soon available to millions of people in the provinces as well, eroding cinema revenues and also the demand for off-peak public transport, because fewer people sought evening entertainment outside their homes, and those

TRAIN SERVICE ECONOMIES

The following trains from this Station will be discontinued on and from **MONDAY, 30th JUNE, 1958.**

WEEKDAYS

to SOUTHAMPTON TERMINUS

to DIDCOT

to NEWBURY and DIDCOT

For details of alternative services or other information apply at the Ticket Office.

Railway economies (station staff added the departure time details by hand).

who did were increasingly using private transport to reach it.

Popular music was given a boost in 1957 by the arrival of rock 'n' roll from the United States, and on the new ITV stations Lady Isobel Barnett was bringing her well-exploited patrician techniques to bear by endorsing another novelty ('For a long time I've thought that the only civilised way to make tea was with Tetley tea bags…').

By now a British prime minister was able to proclaim in all seriousness that 'most of our people have never had it so good', but while the tides of exciting modernity lapped ever higher the railways had become a more or less charming anachronism, with their puffing steam engines and peak-capped porters. More importantly, they were increasingly beside the point.

In case it is thought that the author is exaggerating, the official 116-page guide to one Cornish holiday resort for 1959 gave no clue that the town was served by train at all, apart from the inclusion of the station on an enclosed street map. However, car park charges were carefully quoted and 'motor and omnibus services' explained in some detail, while a local coach operator had a full-page advertisement.

No doubt the good people of Bude belatedly raised their voices when their branch line was listed by Beeching four years later. As in many other places, their protests would come too late.

Rail passenger traffic rose when petrol rationing was imposed during the Suez crisis of 1957, but the improvement proved to be temporary.

Chapter 12

'Effort and sacrifices'

The British Transport Commission was faced with increasing deficits in the second half of the 1950s, although it was also spending considerable amounts of new capital in a bid to modernise the railway system.

The results, however, could hardly have been less encouraging. Passenger figures on British Railways resumed their retreat after the brief and artificial peak of 1957, while goods traffic also fell.

Only the deficits rose. For BR itself, the first working loss had occurred in 1956, when a modest surplus in the previous year of £1.8m had become a loss of £16.5m.

The shortfall had leapt alarmingly to £48.1m by 1958, and the Commission's deficit as a whole in that year was almost £89m when 'central charges' (mainly interest on BT stock) had been added.

However, a thin coat of entirely fictitious reassurance was applied when the accumulated railway deficits began to be transferred to a handy 'Special Account' from 1956.

This arrangement was given statutory authority by the 1957 Transport (Railway Finances) Act, which not only extended the BTC's borrowing powers for a second time (the first increase since the 1953 Act had been in 1955) but also allowed both Commission and Government to paper over the persistent cracks by removing the Commission's railway deficits from its final 'results'. This measure was intended, in part, to compensate for continuing restraint by the Government of both passenger and freight rates.

With its help, the 1958 railway deficit of £90.1m (which included the 'central charges' applicable to British Railways as well as BR's actual revenue account deficit of £48m) was miraculously transformed into a 'surplus' for the BTC as a whole of £1.1m, but only because the railway losses had been tucked away out of sight.

This sort of wishful thinking only concealed the deferred deficits, which had reached £308.2m by the end of 1958.

The justification for such a strategy was dubious, although at this stage the Government seemed willing to accept the Commission's claims that viability would return after modernisation.

Meanwhile, yet another proposed extension of the BTC's borrowing powers was debated in the House of Commons on 11 December 1958.

The Bill was passed, but this continued deepening of the Commission's liabilities was inevitably a one-way street and the journey would end in tears. Labour MP Ernest Davies, representing Enfield East, pointed out that the position of BTC Chairman Sir Brian Robertson was becoming increasingly vulnerable:

"This is the season of largesse, although I admit that the Minister does not look exactly like Father Christmas. Coming here today presenting the Bill to the House, he has in effect been presenting a Christmas Box to the Commission, but in fact he has robbed little Brian's money box in order to fill his stocking with these 150 million golden sovereigns. When poor Brian grows up and ceases to believe in Santa Claus there is a nasty shock awaiting him. He will find that Uncle Harold wants them back – and with interest."[1]

Although the BTC's spiralling debts – which were attributable both to direct borrowing and also to the ominous annual increases in the special account – might appear to have been bad enough, worse was to follow. The Commission's railway revenues remained sluggish for several reasons, including a fall in heavy freight traffic, and the only realistic alternative was to reduce expenses.

Unfortunately the Commission and the Regions had been timid, maintaining too many routes littered with generously staffed small stations and goods yards. Partly because of this, the fulsome financial predictions of the Modernisation Plan were still as far off as ever.

Growing unease in Whitehall prompted the BTC to produce a 'reappraisal' of its modernisation plan in 1958, which was published as a White Paper.[2]

One particularly tricky point was how to explain convincingly why the financial situation of British Railways was still getting worse, in spite of the substantial investment that had been made since 1955. The reappraisal had its answer ready:

'A large part of the investment in modernisation has of necessity been devoted to major schemes which take some years to carry out, many of which will come to fruition during the next five-year period.'

In other words, hang on chaps. This will take a little longer, that's all.

Unfortunately for the BTC, the predictions it made in the reappraisal were still too optimistic. They rested on assurances that there would be a recovery of traffic and therefore an increase in revenue, which did not come about.

Stewart Joy later commented that the Commission was now in an embarrassing situation: if it had admitted that the original plan was wrong, that would have amounted to an admission that its officers were 'either knaves or fools, or a bit of both. So they tried to brazen it out...'.[3]

The reappraisal was probably the last chance for the British Transport Commission but, as Stewart Joy implied, it had painted itself into a corner. The road that would lead to Beeching was now clearly signposted, and the journey had begun.

Meanwhile staff costs were about to become another major problem for the BTC. They had been contained to some extent for a number of years by restraining wage increases, but this strategy created increasing tensions with the unions, which had observed pay rates in other industries moving ahead of average railway earnings.

To see the root cause of these tensions we need to go back to July 1953, when wage increases of up to 15% had been demanded. The Commission had estimated that such increases would add £50m a year to its costs, and said that it could not agree to them, citing its 'financial position' in justification.[4]

The claims were then referred to the Railway Staff National Tribunal, which on 3 December recommended rises for male adults of four shillings a week, although women and 'juniors' were entitled to less. All three unions rejected the offer, and the Executive Committee of the National Union of Railwaymen – the NUR – called a strike from midnight on 20 December.

The Cabinet discussed the situation at its meeting on the evening of 14 December, when the railway pay dispute formed the first item on the agenda. Minister of Labour Sir Walter Monckton told his colleagues that the increase awarded by the Tribunal had been 'unexpectedly low', although the Commission was 'ready to implement it'. There was also a small carrot at the end of the Commission's stick, because 'if the Unions accept this position, the Commission will be ready to examine the whole of the wage and salary structure of the railways with a view to removing anomalies and providing further incentives, where these are necessary.'[5]

However, this was unlikely to placate the NUR by 20 December, so the problem 'was now one of finding a means of modifying the suggested statement in such a way as to make it acceptable to the NUR, without saying anything which would undermine the authority of the Tribunal or involve the Commission in immediate wage increases.'

The consequences of a railway strike over Christmas could have been serious, and the meeting was warned that emergency powers would have to be sought. Parliament might have to be recalled and members of the forces required to help, with dire effects on leave arrangements, while the Christmas mails would be disrupted. It was also noted that farm labourers had just been awarded another six shillings a week, and that there could be some 'public sympathy' for the NUR strikers, because 'it was widely recognised that the rates of the lowest grades of railwaymen had failed to keep pace with the general movement of wages'.

The result was an improved offer two days later, which averted the stoppage. This included the immediate four shilling rise plus the promise of a further increase to follow. This turned out to be another three shillings a week, applicable from February 1954.

Although industrial disruption had been avoided, the Commission's finances were inevitably damaged. When increases for other BTC employees in London Transport, Inland Waterways and Docks were added, the total cost was another £7.63m a year.

Although the 1953-54 settlements had staved off a potentially damaging strike, peace did not reign for long. Further demands followed in 1954 and 1955, and further strikes were called. Most were cancelled, but members of the drivers' main union ASLEF walked out for 17 days from 28 May 1955, costing the Commission £12m.

The Commission, which described this particular stoppage as 'disastrous'[6], was reeling by now under the effects of successive wage increases within its various businesses.

It calculated that various increases that took effect between October 1954 and January 1956 would cost a total of £45m annually. Even so, after the improvements of 1953-56, general wages in British Railways began to lag behind the levels paid in other industries once again, and the 1955 annual report recorded that a shortage of labour was now also starting to cause concern.

The Commission concluded that the answer was twofold. In the short term increased efforts would be made to recruit more staff, particularly young people, while the longer-term answer had to be better productivity. Higher pay was not mentioned.

The result, in May 1955, was the creation of a British Railways Productivity Council with 18 members, nine of whom came from the unions, and which first met in July.

Although this body became a useful link between management and unions, particularly in connection with productivity, it is hard not to see its best efforts as a prolonged tinkering with a much deeper problem.

Even if the staff in the thousands of country goods yards that still survived at the end of the 1950s could have become more productive, this would not overcome the fundamental error: most of them, and the yards they ran, should not have been there at all.

This burden became even more acute after yet another official inquiry into wages and productivity. It was by no means the first such body to be appointed during the 1950s, but its effect was much greater than that of its predecessors, and it provided one of the final nails for the Commission's coffin.

It was led by Claude William Guillebaud, Emeritus University Reader in Economics at Cambridge, who had already produced a landmark report examining the cost of the National Health Service in 1956. Following this achievement, he was commissioned by the BTC to investigate railway pay in August 1958, and provide comparisons with staff conditions in the other nationalised industries.

The Commission's annual report for 1958 predicted that this work would take 'some months to complete', but in the event this proved, rather like some of the BTC's financial projections, to be far too optimistic. The 1959 report recorded that the inquiry was continuing, and that its conclusions could be expected in 1960.

Although the Guillebaud inquiry had been set up only after full discussions with the unions, their patience began to fray and the NUR submitted a 'substantial' pay claim on 1 April 1959.

This was met, probably inevitably, with a refusal from the BTC representatives on the Railway Staff Joint Council in May, and the union then referred its claim to the Railway Staff National Council. This, in turn, rejected it in December 1959.

The stage was now set for a new conflict. The Commission urged the NUR to wait for Guillebaud's findings to be published, but the membership was becoming increasingly impatient. The NUR therefore pushed forward to the next negotiating level, which was a submission to the Railway Staff National Tribunal.

While these manoeuvrings were in progress Guillebaud was approaching its conclusion, but before publication the NUR continued to push for an immediate increase, although the Commission had promised to backdate any settlement that resulted.

The NUR then turned the screws a little more by calling a strike from 15 February, but although Guillebaud then promised that his report would appear at the end of the month, the union stayed firm.

After a tense period of further negotiations, and just three days before the strike was to have started, the Commission improved its offer to an 'interim' 5%, backdated to 11 January. This proved to be enough. The NUR cancelled the strike and withdrew its submission to the Tribunal.

Now everyone was waiting for Guillebaud's Railway Pay Committee of Inquiry to reveal its findings.

Guillebaud had made detailed comparisons between railway workers and those in other industries, and the headline conclusion was that most railway staff (workshop employees were outside Guillebaud's scope) should receive an 8% increase, while those on salaried grades had fallen behind their contemporaries by 10%.

This verdict delighted the unions, who saw it as a vindication of the claims they had been pursuing, but it proved to be a body blow that the Commission could not survive.

Stewart Joy later calculated that the BTC had been understating its potential liabilities for some years, partly by assuming that wages could be artificially restrained almost indefinitely.

When the Modernisation Plan had appeared, five years earlier, the Commission had predicted that its books would be roughly in balance by 1961, and in surplus by some £50m a year by 1970.

This fantasy depended on several assumptions, which not only included a disregard for real wages growth but also complete freedom in respect of fares and freight rates. This, as we have seen, the Government was not willing to allow. Joy went on to suggest that if 'real' wages were taken into account, the Commission would still have been in the red by £48m in 1968.[7] In short, the Commission's financial forecasts were built on sand.

The increasingly unimpressed Ministry of Transport began to tighten its grip. In February 1960 it quietly placed a spending limit of £250,000 on the Commission's capital projects, so that more expensive schemes now had to be cleared by the Minister.[8]

Meanwhile, the first public confirmation that the BTC was living on borrowed time was a Commons statement by Prime Minister Harold Macmillan on 10 March, just six days after Guillebaud had reported.

The Cabinet had heard on 8 March that the cost of Guillebaud to the Commission would be in the region of £40m to £45m, including the interim increase of 5%.

Chancellor Heathcote Amory told his Cabinet colleagues he had always envisaged that the Guillebaud conclusions would be 'implemented by degrees over a considerable period, and that a higher wage structure would only apply to an industry that had been reduced considerably below the size of the present railway system'.[9]

Meanwhile, in what must have been a difficult meeting, BTC Chairman Sir Brian Robertson had advised Minister of Transport Ernest Marples that it would be 'unwise' to count on obtaining more than £5m from increases in fares and charges.

The shadow of the axe over the railways was becoming larger. Macmillan, who had been a director of the Great Western Railway, told the House on 10 March that the Commission's total deficit had 'increased very rapidly over the last five years and now amounts to some £350m', adding that 'it breaks one's heart to see an industry piling up deficits year after year'.

The 1960 shortfall was estimated to be another £80m, while the interest due on the deficit borrowing added £15m more.

He set out what the Government proposed to do:

'First, the industry must be of a size and pattern suited to modern conditions and prospects. In particular, the railway system must be remodelled to meet current needs, and the modernisation plan must be adapted to this new shape. Those working in the industry must accept this. This is the only way of bringing about conditions in which a fair reward, not only in terms of money, but of satisfaction with their job, can be secured. Secondly, the public must accept the need for changes in the size and pattern of the industry. This will involve certain sacrifices of convenience, for example, in the reduction of uneconomic services.'[10]

By now the BTC's total liabilities stood at more than £2,400m. By the end of 1959 the Commission had borrowed roundly £602m. In addition, the Special Account stood at nearly £418m and the total value of British Transport Stock was almost £1,444m. Against these liabilities, the Capital Redemption Fund, intended to repay stockholders after 90 years, stood at a mere £41m.

This was the background when Chancellor Heathcoat Amory announced in his Budget speech on 4 April that there would be no further 'advances' of the type that had been made several times since 1955. Instead, he proposed to make a straight revenue grant of £90m to the Commission for the year 1960.

This, the Chancellor said, was 'a sharp reminder of the harsh realities of a disturbing situation'.[11]

At this point, the Government was determined to accelerate the process of railway rationalisation. Accordingly, it recruited Sir Ivan Stedeford, an industrialist friend of Macmillan, to chair a new advisory group examining British Transport.

Formally set up on 6 April, it became known (inaccurately) as the Stedeford Committee. Stedeford himself had risen to prominence particularly through his career with Tube Investments, where he had become chairman and managing director.

He was joined by the joint managing director of Courtaulds, Frank Kearton, and Henry Benson, a partner in the accountants Coopers.

The fourth man invited to take part was Sir Frank Ewart Smith, who had just retired from his post as deputy chairman at ICI. He declined, instead recommending one of ICI's younger rising stars, a metallurgist who was now the company's technical director. His name was Dr Richard Beeching.

The Government refused to reveal what advice it was given by Stedeford and his colleagues. On 25 January 1961 Government transport spokesman John Hay resisted calls in the Commons for the group's main conclusions to be made public, saying, 'We made it perfectly clear that the advice of the group would be confidential.' However, it is now known that the four soon divided into two pairs with differing views. The result was that the Government was presented with options rather than a consensus.

One pair was Stedeford himself and Kearton, who were opposed by Beeching and Benson. In particular, the amount of 'decentralisation' or devolution that was desirable within the railway industry proved to be an unresolvable point of contention.

It will be recalled that the role of the Regions had been strengthened by the 1953 Act, with mixed results, but Stedeford and Kearton continued to support this in principle, urging the creation of a holding company, a British Transport Corporation, which would not, however, have over-riding executive authority.

Under this would be a British Railways Board to maintain the railways as 'an effective entity', but its Regions would be incorporated as individual business with the 'maximum degree of autonomy'.

Beeching and Benson, on the other hand, preferred an advisory Transport Council, while the various parts of the Commission that had been Executives until 1953 would be re-separated into a number of autonomous bodies, each directly answerable to the Government. One of these would again be a British Railways Board, but this Board's Regions would possess less power, being supervised by the BRB.

The main Board would also keep control of such system-wide matters as budgets, pay and fares.

The four members of the Stedeford group recognised that they should present a united front, but this fundamental difference of opinion defeated them. As a result, both structures survived as options within one of the eight main recommendations presented to Marples on 7 October. Other points dealt with by the Group included the financial position of the BTC and how its accumulated deficits might be dealt with, as well as the outlook for major schemes in the Modernisation Plan. It felt the size of the network needed to be reduced together with the number of employees, while the remaining statutory restrictions should be removed, so that the Commission could, for example, do more to develop its property estate.

In short, the future Commission (or Board) should be a leaner, more efficient beast, no longer shackled by outdated restrictions and therefore free to behave in a commercial manner.

However, the future structure of the industry was not the only point of contention. Beeching proved to be dubious about the benefits of intercity electrification, preferring diesels. (After he had taken over at the new BRB, he almost halted the scheme to electrify the West Coast route south of Crewe, and also set his face against proposals to extend the scheme from Weaver Junction to Glasgow.)

With the advice and conclusions of the Stedeford group now in the Government's hands, the pace of change began to quicken as 1960 drew to a close.

A White Paper, 'Reorganisation of the nationalised transport undertakings', followed shortly before Christmas, but pressure on Parliamentary time meant that it could not be debated in full until the end of January.

The introduction pulled no punches:

'Sweeping changes will be needed. Effort and sacrifices will be required from all. The public will have to be prepared to face changes in the extent and nature of the services provided and, where necessary, in the prices charged for them... The heart of the problem is the railways... The railways are now in a grave financial plight.'[12]

The proposals in the White Paper spelled the end for the British Transport Commission, and the creation of a series of statutory authorities including a new British Railways Board, reporting directly to the Minister.

There would also be a Nationalised Transport Advisory Council. Beeching and Benson had won the day.

Also just before Christmas, Marples decided to replace Sir Brian Robertson with a new chairman, who would manage the transition from Commission to Railways Board.

His choice was one of the Stedeford 'winners' – Dr Richard Beeching.

Chapter 13

'Purposeful slimming'

As the New Year dawned, the reconstruction of the British Transport Commission remained a priority on the Minister of Transport's agenda.

1960 had mainly been a year of assessment followed by broad statements of policy, but 1961 would see the start of major reforms.

The BTC's finances continued to worsen, adding to the sense of urgency. The railways proved to have lost £112.7m in 1960, up by £25.7m from 1959, and although a comparatively small profit of £11.8m from other activities helped a little, the total BTC deficit for the year was still £100.9m.

Neither could 'central charges' be singled out for special blame any longer, because the working deficit alone for BR was a record £67.7m, partly because of the fallout from Guillebaud but also because of a rise in the price of coal – still a significant factor. In spite of fare increases in late 1959 and again in May and June 1960, the nation's railways were now bleeding £1.3m a week, even before any interest payments were taken into account.

As before, all the railway losses were scooped up into the now-bulging Special Account, leaving the Commission with a quite fictitious 'surplus' of £11.8m.

These figures had yet to be published when the House of Commons debated the reorganisation White Paper on 30 January, but the totals revealed by Minister of Transport Ernest Marples on that occasion were quite bad enough.

He told the House that the Commission had capital liabilities of £2,000m, of which £1,600m was attributable to the railways. Just £400m spent on modernisation was believed to be 'sound'. Of the rest, £400m was 'bad' and would be written off, while another £800m was 'doubtful' and would be placed in a suspense account.

The final £400m of 'sound' railway deficits would remain on the books as a capital liability. This was to be inherited by the British Railways Board at the start of 1963, once again saddling a new organisation with old debts.

However, the BRB would not take over just yet. Mr Marples continued:

'Over the next two years, even allowing for reduced interest charges, large sums will have to be provided from the Exchequer to meet current deficits. The object, which is formidable, is to place the railways in a position where they will have a real hope of achieving solvency and the resolution to attain it.'[1]

It is interesting that a truly commercial railway was still thought to be possible, in spite of the fact that all the trends pointed in the other direction and had been doing so since before nationalisation. However, it was becoming clear that the railway of tomorrow would have to endure a 'purposeful slimming', to quote Mr Marples.

He could also see newer forms of transport becoming more important, asking, 'What will happen in ten years' time with internal aircraft flying, say, between London and Manchester?'

Down on the ground, another new influence and source of railway competition would be provided by the motorways:

'It is not only a question of the air. What will happen when the motorway network of the country has been completed? What has been the effect of M.1, between Birmingham and London, on the railways, and what will be the effect when there is a complete network?'[2]

It is worth comparing this view from a Minister who had spent much of his life in the road construction industry with that of Dr Beeching three years later, when he would tell a reporter:

'People who can afford to choose won't motor between the main centres of population. They don't now and they won't in the future.'[3]

This remarkable claim, worthy of the British Transport Commission in its most wildly optimistic moments, stands alongside another of Beeching's misjudgements, which was that branch line users would happily clamber on board buses to the nearest railhead when their trains had disappeared. In the event, many of them chose to 'motor between the main centres of population' instead.

In retrospect, it is clear that Marples's questions were very much to the point, because both motorways and aviation would become major contenders for the railway's intercity passenger business during the following decades. Happily, even if it was rather late in the day, BR played the electrification card with considerable success from the 1960s onwards, but it would still not be an easy ride.

We can only speculate what might have been the result if a major programme of electrification, together with many more 'fully fitted' vehicles with continuous brakes for fast main line freight as well as the rationalisation of overstaffed branch lines, could have been pursued with vigour by the Railway Executive from 1948.

Instead, as we have seen, both Executive and Commission only tinkered with the issue of staff numbers, while obsolete steam locomotives continued to be built until the end of the 1950s. Meanwhile, the vast marshalling yards laid out in this period were at least supposed to be part of 'modernisation', but all too often they catered for the needs of the past rather than the realities of the future.

These failings, coupled with restraints on fares and charges, the almost unachievable financial targets in the 1947 Act and the devastating follow-on of the 1953 legislation, spelled inevitable doom.

Had the Commission managed to keep its head even approximately above water in its first decade, the subsequent course of events might have been very different. But in January 1961, with its losses now exceeding £100m annually and capital liabilities of at least £2,000m, much of which were 'bad' or 'doubtful', there was no longer any chance that it would be allowed to continue.

The necessary powers to dissolve the BTC and create its successors were included in a Transport Bill, which was debated at its Second Reading in the House of Commons on 20 November 1961.

The Bill followed the broad proposals in the White Paper, and Mr Marples told the House: 'The Railways Board will be required to put itself in a position to pay its way as soon as possible.'[4]

He also revealed that the new Board would have to inherit a greater share of the Commission's losses than before, because 'All the figures that I have given are the result of more precise calculation than was possible in the White Paper, which was based on the 1959 position. But they are still only approximate.'

The capital debt of the Commission was now revealed to be £2,450m, and of that the BRB would have to shoulder a burden of £900m (more than twice as much as originally planned), which would 'bear interest and be repayable'.

There were some compensatory changes, including the removal of statutory controls on fares and charges (except in the London area) as well as the abolition of the outdated 'common carrier' obligation, which meant that the railway would finally be free to refuse traffic that was not worth having. These changes were sensible but also desperately overdue, and for that delay successive governments had been responsible.

By now, Beeching was poised to move centre stage. He joined the BTC on 15 March 1961 as a part-time member and became Chairman on 1 June, for a contract term of five years.

His salary of £24,000 (originally it was to be £25,000) was intended to maintain parity with his post as Technical Director at ICI, but the difference between this and the salary of the outgoing Sir Brian Robertson, which had been a comparatively miserly £10,000, was calculated to attract critical headlines.

It was during Beeching's preliminary tenure as a part-time member of the Commission that a major census of railway traffic was conducted during one week in April 1961.

This census, particularly its timing, would be the subject of considerable argument and debate after Beeching's 'Reshaping' report had appeared in 1963, but that was almost two years in the future. For now, the new Chairman's priority was to ease the railway's transition from Commission to Board.

It had become clear that the Commission was on the final stretch ever since Macmillan's reorganisation speech on 10 March 1960, which had been followed by the deliberations of Stedeford and the White Paper in December.

The BTC annual report for 1960, which would be Sir Brian Robertson's last, contained a remarkable claim: 'Looking back over the first thirteen years of the

Commission's existence it may be said that over the first eight years, 1948 to 1955, the finances were broadly in balance.' The Commission had accumulated a total deficit of £69.8m during those eight years, five of which had been loss-making. Indeed, even one of the profitable years, 1951, had shown a slender surplus of just £0.1m, on a turnover of £616.5m.[5]

Although the ever-present millstone of 'central charges' was admittedly a major part of the problem, the fact that the BTC could seriously describe accumulated deficits of almost £70m as 'broadly in balance' only demonstrated how detached from reality 222 Marylebone Road had become.

One BTC officer provided independent confirmation of this curious stance when he wrote his own account of the post-nationalisation period.

A. J. Pearson's experience had included assisting 'the Railway Executive to design and introduce the new organisation', then helping to 'implement the Transport Act of 1953'. He also worked on the Modernisation Plan and chaired the supply and contracts committee. In 1958 he transferred to the operational railway by becoming Assistant General Manager of the London Midland Region.

Such an observer would presumably have seen what was happening at the highest levels of the BTC, yet after Beeching's 'Reshaping' report had appeared in 1963 he wrote that as the railways 'were heavily losing money (through no fault of their own) it was also decided in one dramatic document to close a large part of the railway system…'[6]

It is true that the BTC had been shackled by a number of factors outside its control, but it had also failed to rationalise the railways or use its modernisation capital effectively. In short, 'through no fault of their own' is a revealing indicator of the attitudes that had evidently existed and quite possibly prevailed at senior levels within the Commission.

Another persistent cause of BTC deficits had been an unwillingness to accept that its statutory duties had been changed by the 1953 Act, which no longer obliged it to provide 'an adequate and properly co-ordinated system of passenger transport', with the exception of the London area.

Instead, the BTC now had a modified duty merely 'to provide railway services' for the rest of the nation.

It does not seem that this dilution of legal obligations made much difference in practice. The Commission's annual report for 1953 did acknowledge the change, saying that it 'must of course affect the extent to which the Commission can be expected to maintain facilities'.

But in spite of this acknowledgement, the reductions were not noticeably accelerated in the years that followed.

By 1956, although the Modernisation Plan was starting to take effect, the Commission was complaining that it felt 'considerably hampered' by the delay in affording it 'the greater freedom' for the commercial management of its affairs that had been 'promised' in the 1953 Act, and, as we have seen, the financial skies darkened steadily during the rest of the 1950s.

But the 84,000km of track (including sidings) that British Railways possessed in 1948 had only come down by just over 1,400km at the end of 1955, while the number of passenger and freight stations had fallen from 8,359 to 7,899. These reductions, of 1.7% and 5.5% respectively, hardly indicated wholehearted rationalisation.

The problem was partly caused by the word 'adequate'. This term had not been defined in 1947, so it was left to the Commission to decide what it meant, at least until 1953.

Chairman Sir Brian Robertson later admitted to a Select Committee in 1960 that, notwithstanding the 1953 changes, the BTC had continued to aim for the provision of an 'adequate' level of service.

However, when he was asked to define the term he could only say that it 'conveys a certain expression in my mind. I feel I know roughly what is meant, but I could not go further than that.'

Stewart Joy was rather derisory about this response[7], but Sir Brian was not wholly to blame. If the legislators could not explain what they wanted, how could the BTC be expected to do any better?

This was probably just another example of how the Commission had been hampered from the start by poorly drafted legislation, but by 1961 the Acts of 1947 and 1953 were both about to become irrelevant, together with the BTC itself.

The man who would take the railways into their new era was Dr Beeching, who spent his first year at Marylebone Road finding out how the wheels went round.

The 1962 Transport Act received Royal Assent on 1 August. It set out the duties of the new British Railways Board in simple terms: the Board was 'to provide railway services'. There was a residual obligation to coordinate the BRB's operations with those of the new London Transport Board, but no attempt to say how much railway there should be, and certainly not whether it had to be 'adequate'.

The BRB took over officially on 1 January 1963, but its grand entrance, so far as most people were concerned, did not occur until 27 March. On that day (to pursue the theatrical metaphor) there was a cloud of smoke in the wings, from which leapt a demon king.

The demon was Beeching, and in his hand he brandished a twin-bladed sword of retribution – two slim blue volumes entitled *The Reshaping of British Railways*.

Chapter 14

'A great emotional upsurge'

Although unsigned, it is said that the 'Reshaping' report was largely drafted by Beeching himself. Now at last, for the price of £1, the public could find out what the man from ICI thought of their railways.

His prognosis was by no means all bad. Beeching saw a good future for intercity passenger services and trainload freight, the types of transport that railways were well suited to provide, he thought. He also introduced the concept of 'liner trains', which were to evolve into BR's Freightliner services, and it was during his tenure that the brand 'British Rail' was introduced, along with the double-arrow logo that survived the abolition of the Board and is still used today.

He believed the weak points that were largely responsible for railway losses included stopping passenger services, underused minor lines and the high proportion of goods traffic that went as single wagon loads or in even smaller quantities from a multiplicity of local depots and sidings.

The April 1961 census had been followed by traffic studies in July. These surveys had revealed that 36% of the 28,695km route network was handling fewer than 3,200 passenger kilometres a week, and that 42% conveyed fewer than 5,000 'ton miles' of freight (8000 tonne/km).

Most of this lightly used network was to go – some 8,000 route kilometres and 2,363 stations were set to lose their passenger services (235 of those listed had already been closed).

The report predicted that if its proposals were 'implemented with vigour', then 'much (although not necessarily all) of the Railways' deficit should be eliminated by 1970'.

But, in hindsight, the Beeching report is almost as interesting for what it did not say.

For example, it gave no consideration to trimming costs on lines rather than closing them. Beeching, who, after all, had spent little more than 18 months learning about the railway almost from scratch from existing senior officers, either chose not to consider economies, or was genuinely not aware that they could be possible without widespread line closures.

We already know that the traditional BTC approach had tended to be 'all or nothing', so that unstaffed stations ('halts') only formed a small part of the railway estate. (There are just over 2,500 stations on National Rail now. Roughly half are unstaffed.)

The succeeding Board's similarly inflexible policy was unconsciously revealed in such statements as: 'As on branch lines, the presence of a stopping service on a main line adds appreciably to the system cost, by complicating the signalling, and by necessitating the provision *and manning* of small stations.' (Author's italics)

It is not very clear why signalling would be 'complicated' significantly, if at all, by the existence of a minor stopping place. Stopping trains do reduce route capacity, because they inevitably occupy each section longer than a fast express, but this only becomes important if capacity is under pressure.

The real giveaway, though, is the reference to 'manning', which the author of this statement appeared to think was inescapable.

A similar glimpse was provided when the report turned to possible ways of improving the economics of local passenger services.

It considered, and dismissed, such strategies as lower fares ('if fares were halved, traffic would have to increase at least fourfold to cover direct costs…'), higher fares ('to cover the costs of many services, fares would have to be increased to eight or ten times their present level … [traffic] would, of course, disappear completely'), railbuses ('ignores the high cost of providing the route itself'), or fewer trains and stations ('thinning out the trains or the stations would not make a route self-supporting').

The possible economies offered by reducing the complexity of track layouts, simplifying the signalling and removing station staff were not mentioned. Route costs were fixed.

Meanwhile, the value to BR of each station was measured in the report by the total revenue it earned, and this proved to be another point of contention.

In particular, seaside towns tended to attract visitors from big cities who would almost invariably buy discounted returns. Beeching's methods allocated all the credit for such journeys to London Waterloo or Birmingham New Street, and nothing to resorts like Swanage or Aberystwyth, although if the resort stations had not existed it was at least questionable whether the journeys would have been made at all. (Carrying out a major traffic survey in April had also tended to undervalue the traffic on holiday lines.)

Even the report betrayed a little unease about this, saying:

'Whilst passenger receipts are not necessarily a true measure of the contribution each station makes, because some receive more traffic than they originate, they can be regarded as a reasonable guide.'

This half-admission may have concealed Beeching's apparent belief that closing a branch would not mean the loss of all the associated 'contributory' revenue, because buses would provide connections to the junction instead. For example, the report acknowledged that the Thetford-Swaffham line in Norfolk was earning £16,000 a year in 'contributory revenue'. But it went on to predict that just £1,700 of this would be lost after the line was closed.

This kind of calculation was based on what proved to be some unwarranted assumptions, probably summed up in an airy dismissal of any possible objection to 'bustitution' (on page 18 of the report), which read: 'It is not immediately apparent … why it is thought that rail buses would give a better standard of service than a road bus…'

Such a suggestion could only have been made by someone who had little experience of either, and who had presumably not tried to travel by bus when laden with the kind of luggage carried by long-distance travellers. Indeed, the entrance to single-decker buses of the period with underfloor engines usually involved a couple of steep steps.

However, many lines were closed after 1963 only on condition that buses were available.

The one major advantage of road vehicles is their flexibility of route, but many railway replacement buses doggedly reflected the former pattern, even trundling down country lanes to call at remote and disused stations. At the other extreme, David St John Thomas cited so-called 'rail replacement' buses, subsidised by the railway, which dumped their passengers at a town centre bus station a good 15 minutes' walk from the railhead.[1]

Although buses could provide better local links, they were a weaker alternative for through passengers, particularly if they ran less frequently than the former trains.

Their very existence was often poorly publicised, being reduced to brief references in railway timetables, which gave no details about connections, while guidance about the existence of through ticketing was also scant.

(The Winter 1963 edition of the Western Region timetable informed its users that the Brent to Kingsbridge branch in south Devon had just closed, and that 'road services are operated in the area by the Western National Omnibus Co Ltd'. This was true in a general sense, but useless to passengers alighting at Brent for a connecting Western National bus to Kingsbridge. As far as the author can discover, the last one had run in September 1939.)

Through travellers forced on to connecting buses usually faced longer, less comfortable journeys, particularly when traffic congestion worsened, while the longer-distance passenger was also discouraged by the ominous and frequent note: 'Heavy Luggage Not Conveyed'.

After the branch line to Fowey in Cornwall was closed to passengers in 1965, a replacement bus timetable was introduced that almost halved the number of journeys from a workable nine to a sparse five, and some of these took fully twice as long to reach the main line junction at Lostwithiel.

Even though much better road links to Fowey were already available from nearby Par, British Rail was obliged to subsidise the Lostwithiel bus service for some years, although it is long gone now. While they continued to run their largely pointless course, buses like these would have made their own, unwelcome contribution to the railway deficit, but as they had no statutory protection, unlike trains, most rail replacement road services from the Beeching era soon disappeared.

Bus services that existed independently of railway requirements could be more useful but, although both the railways and most bus operators were nationalised until 1986, there were few signs of practical cooperation, and David St John Thomas could write as late as 1981 that connections remained 'a disgrace'.

He recounted how one bus no longer offered a practical interchange at Totnes, the railhead for Kingsbridge, because although the train concerned had been retimed the bus had not.[2]

One alternative route to Kingsbridge, recommended in BR timetables, involved a protracted tour of south Devon by train, ferry and bus via Paignton, Kingswear and Dartmouth, which lengthened the through journey by two hours.

The causes of such nonsenses may have been numerous (they were certainly obscure), but if they discouraged the use of public transport this did not appear to distress the nationalised operators, local authorities or central government to any great extent.

Only those passengers who could not use cars were inconvenienced. The resulting losses were shouldered by the taxpayers who unknowingly subsidised road and rail, but the cost to them was not so evident.

Reactions to the Beeching plan were swift and emphatic. Broadsheet newspapers devoted double-page spreads to many of the details, which were closely set in small type under such banner headlines as 'Is your station on this list?'

Although it is often suggested otherwise, Beeching did not close a single passenger railway himself, because he had no power to do so. The procedure (which had been established at the time of nationalisation) was for BR to propose a closure, which was then considered by the relevant Area Transport Users' Consultative Committee and, if necessary, the Central (in other words, national) Transport Consultative Committee, before being passed to the Minister for a decision.

However, the 1962 Act reduced the role of the committees in two ways. They were now barred from considering fares and charges and, more to the point where closures were concerned, 'not to consider any question relating to the discontinuance or reduction of railway services'[3] with the exception of potential 'hardship'.

If written objections were received (which almost invariably they were), the Area Committee was obliged to consider whether hardship was likely, taking oral evidence if necessary, and to make recommendations accordingly. The Minister was supposed to take these into account, but was not bound by them.

These rather cumbersome steps on the administrative ladder accounted for the time taken to achieve some closures – indeed, the discussions could last for many months.

The process was still more protracted if a public hearing was involved at the area level, and before 1962 this could assume the full panoply of a formal court case, particularly if objectors decided to instruct counsel.

This is what had happened on the Isle of Wight in 1953, when the Commission's financial justifications for several closures were rigorously dissected (see Chapter 10).

Such dissections were evidently regarded as an inconvenient distraction in the Beeching era, and the chairmen of the Consultative Committees were now bound by the narrower role set out for them in the 1962 Act. This meant in practice that objectors could no longer challenge a case for closure, only the extent of its consequences.

(In some cases, and certainly in later years, closure suggestions often originated with the Department, which made its wish known to the Board so that the Board could formally 'propose' it, before solemnly submitting the idea back to the Department for a decision.)

A quarter of a century after Beeching, one industry commentator would note: 'The closures procedures [were] blatantly rigged so as to discourage rational and informed debate.'[4]

Beeching himself was philosophical about the wave of disapproval. He told a press conference: 'In general, there's a great emotional upsurge every time we intend to cancel a service, and the week after the service is discontinued the whole thing dies away.'[5]

His report was inevitably welcomed by the Government, and the pace of closures began to pick up later in 1963 (the first specifically 'Beeching' closure took place in October).

Was Beeching on the right lines? This is not a simple question, even with the benefit of more than half a century of hindsight.

Economist Stewart Joy, who would play his own part in proposing further rationalisation of the post-Beeching network in the early 1970s (see Chapter 17), commented that the Reshaping plan lacked 'arithmetic, logic and a sense of priorities'[6].

Indeed, although Joy would prove to be willing to relinquish 'unprofitable' routes himself, he queried whether Beeching's axe, wielded with 'an obvious relish', would ever have yielded more than 'negligible returns'. Instead, he felt the Board should have concentrated on more fruitful reforms, such as charging market-rate fares on high-quality intercity services, improving productivity and carrying out a fundamental analysis of railfreight.

The fundamental problem as Joy saw it was how to define the 'commercial' railway, although he would do his best to do so while he was Chief Economist at the BRB. But he also pointed out that there was a risk that various elements were leaning on each other, so that taking away parts of the railway weakened the rest.

This was (and is) a powerful argument in favour of the 'contributory revenue' school of thought, which even Beeching acknowledged, although he was led astray by his belief that much of this revenue could be retained when a local train service had been replaced by buses.

The difficulty was not confined to branch lines. Joy gave the specific example of Edinburgh Waverley, which had given rise to a debate about whether the 'Waverley

Route' (closed in 1969 and partially reopened in 2015 as the Borders Railway) should be expected to bear any of the costs of the main Edinburgh station, considering that so few Waverley Route trains used it.

Joy pointed out that the only profitable services using Edinburgh were the intercity trains. If they had to bear all the terminal costs, as well as those of other stations on their route such as Darlington and York, then they would become loss-makers too.

In short, although Joy still apparently believed that there was a profitable business lurking somewhere at the core of the railway network, the example of Edinburgh suggests otherwise.

This may go some way to explain why Beeching's plan manifestly failed to rescue the railway's finances. Most of his closure proposals were carried through (and more were added later on), but in 1970, the year when much ('although not necessarily all') of the deficit should have been eliminated, it stood at roundly £64m.

At first sight, this looked better than in the worst years of the old British Transport Commission, but it was still a very long way from the Government's vision of a 'commercial' railway. Although the Board was supposed to service £900m of inherited debt, it had been relieved of the obligation to pay interest on £1,400m of British Transport Stock. Instead, this was now costing the Treasury at least another £40m a year under the terms of the 1939 National Loans Act.

As in the days of the BTC's notorious Special Account, even £64m was not the official headline result, which was ingeniously reported as a 'working surplus' of £9.5m. What this total blandly concealed was that the Board had received some £73.6m in grants from the Government in 1970 alone.

If the Treasury's payments of interest on the old BT stock were included, the railway industry had still cost the country at least £100m in 1970, but, thanks to Marples and Beeching, the nation was now getting a lot less railway for its money.

Meanwhile the grant-aided railway had arrived, thanks to the 1968 Transport Act (see Chapter 16), but one awkward question remained. What would happen to BR if the grants were to be withdrawn?

As we shall see, after Beeching had departed the Board would be grappling with exactly that possibility.

Chapter 15

'The pressures being exerted'

The Beeching 'Reshaping' report had been presented in March 1963 as a solution, but in spite of optimistic statements about deficits being more or less eliminated within a few years, there can be little doubt that behind the scenes Beeching and his Board were rather less confident.

A second report, *The development of the major railway trunk routes*, was published almost two years later, in February 1965.[1]

This proved to be the last of Beeching's major public assessments of the industry's prospects, because he left the BRB at the end of May.

This report was noticeably more conciliatory than its predecessor of 1963, emphasising that the future of those routes not earmarked 'for development' was undecided.

'It should be recognised that the purpose of this study is to select routes for future intensive use, not to select lines for closure, and many of the lines not placed in category 1 ['clearly sound'] will remain in category 2 ['judgment must be suspended … future usefulness remains questionable'] until their future prospects are seen more clearly.'

Category 3, inevitably, was a doleful collection of routes that were 'unsound now and never likely to be sound in future'.

These definitions may have provided a useful guide to the Board's (at the time, Beeching's) thinking, but its usefulness was distinctly limited unless the real status of each route was also disclosed. This, with the exception of category 1, the 'trunk routes' report was careful not to do.

This did not mean that decisions had not been taken in private, and more than one contemporary observer described the process in broad terms.

Geoffrey Freeman Allen, when discussing the evolution of the 1965 'trunk routes' report, said:

'A first draft circulated internally took a very draconian line and spelled out a schedule of definite closures in some detail. The Regions are said to have protested vehemently…'[2]

There is support for this from one of the Regional General Managers of the time, G. F. ('Gerry') Fiennes, who had taken charge of the Western Region during the Beeching era, on 3 October 1963.

Fiennes recalled that he was summoned to a presentation about the shape of the future railway. He wrote:

'Back in the office, I sat forlornly in front of my authorised version. No railway west of Plymouth. No Exeter-Salisbury. No Taunton-Westbury-Reading. In a while I rallied…'

He then describes how

'…the Doctor wanted publication, and he got it. In the teeth of the General Managers and a majority of the Board he published it. The scythes and pitchforks came out all over the West Country…

'I had at least saved a little. West of Plymouth; Exeter-Salisbury; Taunton-Westbury-Reading were in as grey "routes not for development". Naturally it was with some suspicion but not overt hostility that MPs began to arrive…'[3]

This can only be a reference to the 1965 'trunk routes' report: there was no other publication of this type in Beeching's time containing the phrase 'routes not for development'.

The Board had modified the public version of the second Beeching plan, and the result, as hoped, was 'not overt hostility'.

But behind the scenes the intentions were quite different – more 'draconian' – to quote Geoffrey Freeman Allen.

Until now no confirmation of any details has come to light: Fiennes gives only two or three titbits. (Even these brief details may have been one of the indiscretions that allegedly annoyed the BRB sufficiently to dismiss him after his book had been published.)

Table 7: Revenue, journeys and network route lengths, 1963-1967

Year end	Passenger totals (m)	Passenger receipts (£m)	Freight receipts (£m)	Misc receipts (£m)	Net receipts (£m)	Route length (km)
1963	938.43	161.80	292.84	8.45	(81.56)	27,330
1964	927.62	167.22	291.55	9.48	(67.48)	25,725
1965	865.07	172.96	283.89	9.34	(73.09)	24,011
1966	834.96	179.43	275.24	9.11	(71.65)	22,101
1967	837.35	179.70	250.32	8.70	(90.45)	21,218

Figures in brackets are deficits
Freight totals include parcels and mail
Route lengths include freight-only lines
Source: British Railways Board Annual Reports

Beeching's successor from June 1965 at the BRB was Stanley Raymond (he was knighted in the 1967 New Year Honours). But Beeching's departure did not change the policy of the BRB towards 'unremunerative' lines, because it was still struggling with major deficits and urgent demands from Government for improvement.

Although no copy of the original 'draconian' internal draft has been traced, two sets of internal British Rail maps issued in November 1965 and early 1966 became available to the author in 2012 accompanied by some related private memoranda, and together they shed a great deal of light on what was really happening.[4]

Certainly, many of the details inside the orange covers of the 1965 edition are compatible with those that were modified for public consumption in 'trunk routes', as Gerry Fiennes had recorded, suggesting that 'not for development' indeed meant closure.

These internal maps divide the lines operated by the BRB into three categories: trunk routes, feeder lines, and 'other lines'.

The 'other lines' are marked with a figure – 5, 10, 15 or 20 – which 'indicate the maximum period in years for which the continued usefulness of these lines can be foreseen.'

Those given a maximum of 10 years were further classified as 'short term'. All the rest were 'long term', but that was not necessarily the equivalent of 'permanent' or 'indefinite', because the 'long term' lines included the 15- and 20-year routes.

Among the many casualties are most of the routes mentioned by Fiennes as those he had 'saved' – Taunton-Newbury, Exeter-Salisbury and west of Plymouth. In fact, had the proposals been carried out in full, Devon would have lost everything except the main line serving Exeter and Plymouth, and there would have been no railways in Cornwall at all.

Many other parts of the network faced similar retrenchment. Most routes would have closed in Norfolk, with the exception of the main line to Norwich and the line between King's Lynn, Ely, Newmarket and Haughley, where it joins the main line between Ipswich and Norwich. However, as the section between Ely and Cambridge was to be closed, this route was presumably retained only for freight (the maps do not make this clear).

Both Norwich and Cambridge would have become simple termini (services between King's Cross and Cambridge would have disappeared because the line between Royston and Cambridge was to be closed).

Similarly, nearly all lines in the Highlands of Scotland were considered redundant, apart from the East Coast route to Aberdeen. Other towns that would have lost their trains included Harrogate, Aberystwyth, Oban, North Berwick, Skipton, Whitby and Stratford-upon-Avon, while even the Midland Main Line south of Market Harborough would have been downgraded to 'feeder' status, with intercity trains from Sheffield and Nottingham apparently diverted via the now-closed line from Market Harborough to Northampton, then presumably onward to Euston. This may have been related to plans – which were seriously considered by BR in the

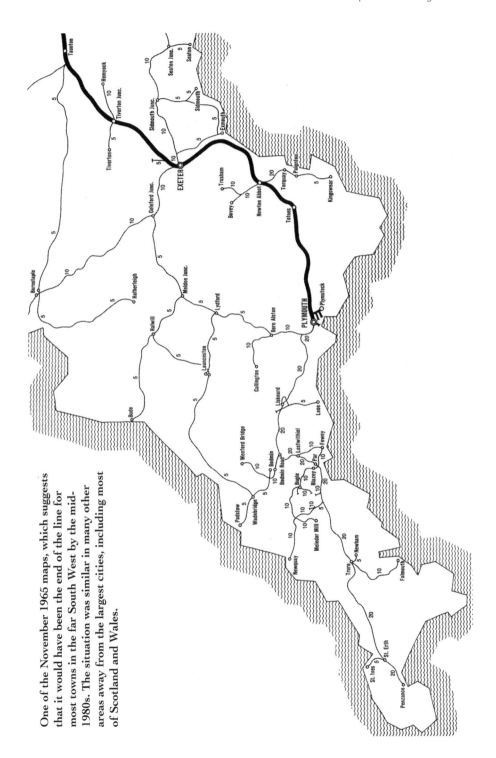

One of the November 1965 maps, which suggests that it would have been the end of the line for most towns in the far South West by the mid-1980s. The situation was similar in many other areas away from the largest cities, including most of Scotland and Wales.

BELOW and BOTTOM: The soothing preamble of the 1965 public 'trunk routes' report, compared with an internal BRB memo at the end of the same year that includes the phrase 'every attempt will be made to reduce the size of the network in the shortest practicable time'.

It should be recognised that the purpose of this study is to select routes for future intensive use, not to select lines for closure, and many of the lines not placed firmly in category 1 will remain in category 2 until their future prospects are seen more clearly.

The publication of this report is not a prelude to precipitate action on a broad front. It is, rather, the exposure of ideas about the way in which the trunk route system should be shaped, and is made for four important reasons:—

(i) Firstly, so that the selection of trunk routes can be subjected to constructive criticism,

(ii) Secondly, so that the next phase of development expenditure can be well planned,

(iii) Thirdly, so that any future proposals for trunk line closure, or diminutions of line utilisation, can be seen in a broader context,

(iv) Fourthly, so that commercial policies can be properly developed and customers be given a clearer view of the future.

Following a conversation I had on the 21st December with Mr. Ratter, I enclose for your private information a copy, of Map No. 13, of the Railway Route System Maps which has been agreed with the six Regional General Managers. It will be appreciated that the lives shown are more an indication of priorities than an absolute time scale.

In the light of the pressures which are at present being exerted because of our financial position every attempt will be made to reduce the size of the network in the shortest practicable time. As a rough guide therefore, the system may be divided into long and short term lines. The long term network will comprise approximately all trunk routes, feeder lines and all other lines shown as having a life of up to 15 and 20 years; the short term network will be those lines having a maximum life of up to 10 years.

Where changes have already been agreed it will be seen that the appropriate maps have been amended.

Early next year I hope to be in a position to give you a further series of maps which will depict the railway system as a long and short term network and which will break-down the short term network into passenger lines, freight lines whose closure is imminent and freight lines whose closure although in the short term, may take a few years to close because of collieries and other declining industries at present situated on them. You will appreciate that the maps are highly confidential and apart from yourself and Mr. Woodbridge and Mr. Butland they have only been released to the six Regional General Managers. Mr. Ratter is aware of the fact that I have released these extra copies.

1960s – to close St Pancras and transfer other remaining Midland services to King's Cross.

The senior officers responsible for these maps, which appear to have been based on Beeching's real policies, were obviously aware that they were political and social dynamite.

Each set was individually numbered, and it seems that only a handful were distributed.

One privileged recipient was warned in an attached memorandum dated 29 December 1965 that 'you will appreciate that the maps are highly confidential'.

This document also recorded that they had been agreed by the six Regional General Managers, then went on to sound an ominous note: 'In the light of the pressures which are at present being exerted because of our financial position every attempt will be made to reduce the size of the network in the shortest practicable time.'

The length of time left for each threatened line was not precise, but rather an 'indication of priorities'. Indeed, some routes might have had even shorter lifetimes than the maps suggested.

The maps provide a highly revealing glimpse of the network as the Board envisaged it from about 1985, and make an interesting comparison with the intentionally gentler 'trunk routes' report.

There had been a tremendous furore after Beeching had revealed his hand (or at least, some of the cards in it) in 1963 by publishing detailed lists of proposed closures, so the following trunk routes analysis concentrated instead on development.

Even so, the internal and external versions were essentially telling the same story in 1965, and the clues were there for those who could read between the lines, so to speak.

Stewart Joy, who was soon to become BRB Chief Economist and later chronicled his experiences[5], emphasises the positive aspects of 'trunk routes'. He gives no hint that in 1965 the Board was planning major route closures that went far beyond the public Beeching proposals (indeed, he may not have been aware of the real position, as he was not with BR at the time).

We know that a copy of the November 1965 'confidential' maps was approved for release to a senior Board officer on 29 December 1965. It is possible that this was the last copy to be provided to a new recipient, because Barbara Castle had taken over from Tom Fraser as Minister of Transport just a week earlier, and her appointment was to mark a change of direction at the Ministry.

Fraser had not been an ardent supporter of the railway industry, and his cool attitude probably contributed to the Board's alarm. He was the Labour member for Hamilton and had become Minister of Transport in Harold Wilson's first government in October 1964. He had inherited the programme of closures initiated by Beeching in 1963, under the previous Conservative administration.

Fraser made a statement in the Commons about railway closures on 4 November

1964[6], when he had been faced not only by BRB deficits but also a manifesto pledge that read:

'Labour will draw up a national plan for transport covering the national networks of road, rail and canal communications, properly co-ordinated with air, coastal shipping and port services. The new regional authorities will be asked to draw up transport plans for their own areas. While these are being prepared, major rail closures will be halted.'[7]

This implied promise proved difficult to keep after the election, and as he told the Cabinet ruefully on 9 March 1965, 'everyone regards his own line as "major"'.

He had told the Commons that no closure that seemed likely to damage the new regional transport plans would be approved, and that in other cases track would be left in position 'except where I found that this was an unnecessary precaution'.

But pressure from backbenchers to halt all closures continued, and on 9 March he told the Cabinet:

'This pressure, I am convinced, is based largely on a misunderstanding of our policy and of the place of railways in a modern, co-ordinated transport system. I recommend that it should be resisted.'[8]

Barbara Castle was not impressed by the man who had preceded her at Transport; she had noted on 22 March 1965 that he had been 'completely negative' about proposals to extend the types of equipment being manufactured in BR workshops. When she took Fraser's place at the end of December she began a reassessment of railway policy, although it must have been an uphill task to encourage a more positive view at the Ministry.

Although her diary makes it clear that she would not try to force people to use railways, that did not mean she was unsympathetic, saying, 'We had to decide what size railway system we wanted in the new situation, how to subsidise it and how to get more traffic from road to rail.'

By early February 1966 she had decided that she 'wasn't happy just to continue Beeching with some minor refusals' in spite of the fact that her officials were 'closure mad'.[9]

Meanwhile, the BRB needed to find out what the new Minister was thinking, and the process probably began when Castle met the Chairman on 4 January. She recorded: 'Raymond was friendly and we got on well.'

Castle would go on to separate the profitable and loss-making railways as far as possible, so that necessary passenger services that did not cover their costs could be given direct grants. The process became active after her Transport Act had been passed in 1968.

But this was some way ahead. The first priority for the Board at the start of 1966 was to acquaint the new Minister with work in progress. So far as rationalisation was concerned, the real (as opposed to public) state of play had been represented by the November 1965 maps, but it seems that a new version was now required.

A second edition was deployed in some haste (a loose-leaf addition setting out some closure statistics is dated 11 February).

References to the Board's internal rationalisation maps of this period in existing sources are mostly brief or vague, but we get one clue from Gourvish, in which he writes:

'When Castle was first shown British Rail's "watershed" map in February 1966, which divided lines into those marked black (main – for retention), red (others – for retention) and green (for immediate closure), she remarked that there were "at least a few [lines] which we would regard at first glance as very doubtful starters".[10]

Castle spent most of 16 February 1966 discussing railway policy, and this is indeed the day that gave rise to her reference to 'doubtful starters'.

Her own note of that day does not mention a map as such, but she does report that 'existing closure policy' was 'demonstrated'.

We do not know exactly why the Board redrew its existing maps for Mrs Castle – the categories of individual routes did not seem to change – but the detailed assessments of between five and 20 years of 'foreseeable use' were deleted, to be replaced by much broader colour codes.

The 1965 maps[11] do not figure in previous commentaries, so far as the author has been able to discover, and seem to have been unknown until, as already mentioned, an errant set came to light in 2012 (it is now in the National Archive). It is possible that the rest were recovered from the senior officers involved and tactfully destroyed, so that they could not distract Mrs Castle.

The British Railways Board had inherited major problems, including substantial debts from the British Transport Commission, continuing annual deficits and a high level of hostility from the civil servants at the Ministry of Transport.

Since many lines were unremunerative, it may have seemed logical to follow the process that Beeching had started and continue to shed the losers.

What was less clear was how much railway could usefully be kept. Certainly the November 1965 maps set out a far more radical retrenchment than Beeching had admitted in public, although there was a clue on page 19 of his original 'Reshaping' report of March 1963, which had warned:

'Decision with regard to the remaining stopping services will be reserved for the present, until the most hopelessly uneconomic ones have been dealt with, but they will then be reviewed and should they be found to be uneconomic they will be dealt with similarly.'

In other words, although it had been tempting to regard the 1963 report as complete in itself, coupled with brave statements about abolishing much 'though not necessarily all' of the deficit by 1970, it was actually only the start of a continuing process. Indeed, it was admitted that the plan it set out had not been carried 'to the stage where it purports to answer the question "How much of the railway can ultimately be made to pay?"'

The confidential maps of November 1965 seem likely to have been the results of a further 'review', as predicted in 1963. Since the picture they drew would have been politically and socially unacceptable, it is hardly surprising that they almost gained the status of state secrets, and were even concealed (it would seem) from transport ministers.

What was also unclear was how much railway the Government really wanted. Happily, the new Minister of Transport was willing to approach the question with an open mind.

Chapter 16

'An economic or social role'

The years of Barbara Castle's reign at the Ministry of Transport continued the period of close attention that the Government had been paying to railways since at least 1960, but now the mood was not solely destructive.

Her arrival at the end of December 1965 showed her to be unprepared, but very far from incapable. She noted, 'I practically had to build a transport policy from scratch.'[1]

It should be noted that the railway had not gained an all-out advocate, and this was probably a good thing. Such an advocate would probably have only flared briefly in the heavens of government before, like the firework it resembled, plunging to the ground in smoking submission.

What the railway did not need was unthinking, uncritical support – because the industry would then have remained wide open to the corrosive influence of hostile civil servants, particularly in the Treasury.

Indeed, although Castle suspected that Beeching's bleak prescription was not the only way forward (unlike her predecessor at the Ministry, Tom Fraser) neither was she willing to give the railway a free ride:

'It was no use trying to turn back the clock. I refused to be a King Canute, trying to force people on to railways which could not take them where they wanted to go. If the private car had brought the boon of mobility to millions of people … that boon should be available to everyone. We must then collectively face the consequences …'[2]

Her historical analogy might not have been perfect, but it was plain that this Minister would not attempt to restore the railway to its former supremacy. Instead, she would go on to introduce a new economic structure for the industry that still has relevance today.

Until Castle moved to Transport, the view had persisted in Government circles that the railway industry should be self-supporting, and preferably profitable.

Efforts to revive such a mythical beast would continue after she had left the Ministry (see Chapter 17), but her memorial is that she succeeded in establishing the principle that the country should be prepared to support 'socially necessary' railway services that did not, in themselves, pay their way.

Before such an ideal could be achieved, it was necessary to define the qualifying services. Some of Beeching's closure proposals were justified, and had the British Transport Commission been willing or able to pay dispassionate attention many of the lines in his 1963 report would have been abandoned long before.

We have already seen that Castle met BRB Chairman Stanley Raymond at the start of January, and began what seemed to be a promising relationship.

One result of her meeting with Raymond was the establishment of a Joint Steering Group, which was to consider how the 1962 Transport Act should be amended. It would also discuss possible changes to the Board's management structure and take a fresh look at railway finances.

Before this could make much progress, the spectre of a new railway strike was now haunting the industry, because the National Union of Railwaymen had called a walkout that was to start on 14 February. Railways might have come down the national transport agenda from their previously pre-eminent position, but questions were still asked in Parliament a few days earlier about the possible consequences of such a strike.[3]

The root of this dispute was a Price & Incomes Board report, which had concluded that railway pay in the 'conciliation grades' – in other words, most uniformed staff – was keeping up with general industrial earnings, although clerical staff had fallen behind their counterparts elsewhere.

The NUR rejected the prices board's conclusions on the grounds that the efforts of its members to improve productivity were appearing to be set aside. Talks were arranged at the highest level, although this episode was tainted by allegations that the NUR was being influenced by Communists – a possibility that was taken seriously enough to be discussed by the Cabinet after it had received a report from an MI5 officer.

As a result of the negotiations, a 3.5% increase was brought forward to September, as well as the reduction of the working week to 40 hours from March and an additional one-day holiday for staff with more than ten years' service.

This offer was accepted by a narrow NUR majority and the strike was called off, but the results could only put a new strain on the already uncertain finances of the British Railways Board.

Labour survived a second General Election in April, which returned Harold Wilson with an increased majority. Castle stayed where she was, and continued to reset the direction of railway and other transport policy. One of the first tangible results of this was a White Paper published on 27 July 1966.[4]

One of the Government's aims, said the White Paper, was a 'fundamental review' of transport, and the document also revealed that work was under way on defining a fresh 'basic network', which should have the result of giving some stability to the businesses of the British Railways Board.

The White Paper received a mixed response, and Castle wondered in retrospect whether her first major policy document should have spelled out that it was not a detailed transport plan but 'merely' the basic decisions:

'I outlined the general direction of my policies: the need to come to terms with the motor car without allowing it to ruin our environment. This, I argued, meant an expanded road programme ... the preservation of an adequate rail network with subsidies for non-paying but socially necessary lines; the diversion of freight traffic from road to rail; and the encouragement of public transport, particularly in urban areas.'[5]

Among the future developments set out in this White Paper were 'comprehensive transport authorities' for urban areas, which would prove after 1968 to be the new Passenger Transport Authorities and Executives in the largest provincial cities. Their responsibilities would include the developing of interchanges as well as 'new rail tracks, rapid transit facilities and so on'.

Meanwhile, the Joint Steering Group was continuing to develop the best way forward for the BRB, which was still expected to break even as soon as possible. However, it was now clear that it could never do so if it was also required to retain loss-making lines to meet social need.

Consideration of all the options evidently took some time, because the first interim report from the Group did not appear until the start of 1967. This considered the 'scope and form of grants' for unremunerative railway services.

After a further pause, a second report was published in July. A headline conclusion was that the 'best estimate' of the costs of supporting socially necessary lines would have been no more than £40m a year in 1969 and £35m in 1974. Both these totals excluded interest, while grants would be fixed for periods of three years.

This had the inevitable counterpoint of preparing for a time when the Board would no longer be in deficit, because the Government would then be compensating it fully for the loss-makers while the rest of the network was paying its way.

Another topic was rationalisation of the network, which did not refer in this instance to closures but to reducing the capacity of routes that were to survive, theoretically matching their capacity to predicted demand.

This involved singling some double-track lines or sections, or reducing some quadrupled sections to three tracks or two. This work also cost money, and the Steering Group estimated that the total would be around £15m a year in 1969, with the aim of reducing it to zero by 1974, by which date the Board 'should have received savings of about the same order'.

(This kind of trimming has often been regretted more recently, and some of it has now been reversed.)

Meanwhile, the extent of the future 'basic network' had also been revealed, when a supposedly definitive map was published in March 1967.[6]

This network consisted of some 17,700km, which the introduction compared to the 'drastically reduced system which would result if the Board were to continue to operate under its existing terms of reference'.

The map was signed by Barbara Castle and BRB Chairman Sir Stanley Raymond, provided for in the 1974 Railways Act, in compliance with European law.

Labour was still in power when the BRB complied with another section of the 1968 Act by producing a report on its organisation, which was published in December 1969.[9]

This set out some proposed reforms, by appointing a chief executive for each railway business and moving the main Board to a broadly non-executive position.

The Joint Steering Group had recommended that a post of 'Chief General Manager' should be created, with 'responsibility for controlling and co-ordinating all aspects of the day-to-day running of the railways'.

The Board's response was to create a new post of Chief Executive, underpinned by a series of Executive Directors. The 'businesses' they were to run should not be confused with the later Sectors of the 1980s. Instead, their departments were defined as Passenger Services Planning and Marketing, Freight Services Planning and Marketing, System and Operations, Finance, and Personnel.

The Regions were to continue, although the 1968 Act had ended the legal requirement to maintain Regional Boards. However, the BRB decided to keep them in existence in an 'advisory' capacity.

So the BRB prepared itself for the challenges of the 1970s, ready to put the days of deficits behind it – hopefully for good.

being kept confidential, although there had been substantial clues in Beeching's valedictory 'trunk routes' report in 1965.

After Beeching's departure, Barbara Castle had changed the direction of railway policy and went on to promote the 1968 Act, but she was replaced as Minister of Transport by Richard Marsh in that year. He, in turn, would play an unlikely double role by leaving the Ministry in 1969 and later becoming Chairman of the British Railways Board in 1971.

While this game of political musical chairs was under way, the Board had been settling down to the new regime of grant-aided services introduced by Castle.

At first the results looked encouraging, with a deficit of some £83m in 1968 becoming a 'profit' of more than £48m in 1969, although this total included grants for the first time, amounting to almost £62m to support passenger services alone.

Much of the rest of this seemingly remarkable turnaround was achieved by a financial restructuring, which could not be repeated.

But over the next two or three years the picture slowly darkened again. Passenger figures remained sluggish (they would dive in 1972, probably as a reflection of perturbations in the national economy), and by 1971 the Board's railway surplus, including grant income, had fallen back to £26m.

Some other indicators were also telling a worrying tale. Freight income remained volatile and, more significantly, the relationship between freight and passenger revenues changed for good in 1971. Freight was now earning less than passenger services for the first time, even before grant aid was taken into account.

As grants of more than £63m were received in 1971, the underlying result in that year was a loss approaching £40m, which was an improvement on the early 1960s but fell distinctly short of Beeching's prediction in 1963 that his 'Reshaping' plan would account for 'most, if not all' of the deficit by 1970.

It was true that not quite all his recommended closures as set out in 1963 had come to pass, but even so something, somewhere, was going wrong (see Table 8 over).

This was the background when the BRB launched its highly confidential research to combat the civil servants in May 1971.

Entitled 'Special Study No 1', it was the preliminary to a full study intended 'to discover if there are any railway systems which would be financially self supporting in the long run within the framework of existing legislation'.

Existing legislation was primarily the Transport Acts of 1962 and 1968 but, as we have seen, the support from the latter was limited and the shrinking surpluses were not calculated to encourage confidence at the Department of the Environment or the Treasury.

Indeed, the text of Special Study No 1 reveals that the Board was only too well aware that the Department (the DoE or 'D. of E.') was once again sharpening its railway axe, by producing its own lists of 'tentative' withdrawal proposals:

Table 8: British Rail results, 1968-1972 (excluding ancillary businesses)

Year end	Passenger totals (m)	Passenger receipts (£m)	Grants (£m)	Freight receipts (£m)	Misc receipts (£m)	Net receipts (£m)	Route length (km)
1968	831.07	185.16		262.39	8.98	(83.46)	20,051
1969	805.24	205.42	61.61	255.55	10.61	48.60	19,470
1970	823.87	227.77	61.68	270.63	11.40	47.42	19,989
1971	815.51	260.99	63.1	258.90	12.30	26.16	18,738
1972	753.61	274.06	68.2	251.99	38.15	17.83	18,567

Figures in brackets are deficits
Freight totals include parcels and mail
Route lengths include freight-only lines
Source: British Railways Board Annual Reports

'In the absence of adequate criteria … some simplifying assumptions will be made. (1) For London and the South East, a single statement of the service network will be used. Most existing services will be shown continuing. (2) For other remunerative services, two options will be considered for the situation at 1976. The first is that services would be withdrawn in line with D. of E.'s tentative proposals, i.e. 10 in the first year 1972 and 20 in each subsequent year. The order of withdrawal would be in line with expectations which would not necessarily be the least damaging for B.R.'

It is clear from this extract that the Board was nervous, but if this was not bad enough, the alternative was worse:

'The second option would correspond to the complete withdrawal of grant aid including that in P.T.E. areas.'

This sombre sentence would have amounted to a 'Beeching 2' of unprecedented severity. It also suggests that the network map agreed with Government as recently as 1967 was already not worth the paper it was printed on.

The Board's group was hampered by the fact that it was working in the dark in several important respects, not least that, in spite of more than two decades of developing traffic costing techniques since nationalisation, it was still not apparently possible to say how each service was really performing. (This suggested in turn that the allegedly careful calculations that accompanied grant aid applications were also questionable, to say the least.)

The Board would not have cared to see such an admission given publicity, but within the covers of the confidential Special Report the emperor's clothes were revealed to be a sham:

'We do not have practicable techniques for showing precisely the effect on overall profit of adding or subtracting particular services. We cannot therefore work towards an optimum situation in an ideal iterative manner. We shall therefore postulate a series of service networks of which the range in size is likely to embrace the optimum which is sought.'

This was quite bad enough, taken as an indication of how a nationalised industry was organising its affairs, but the note of philosophical resignation then became all but despairing: 'The precise definition of "optimum" can be difficult.'

So although the members of the Special Study Group were attempting to retrieve a going concern, they could not say exactly where or what it might be. Resorting by default to the pursuit of an 'optimum', they were still hardly any nearer to reaching a valid conclusion because, rather like the fabled Snark in Lewis Carroll's poem, the target kept evading its hunters.

The reader may recall that the principal problem facing the characters in this poem was that if the Snark proved to be a Boojum, it was the hapless hunter who would 'softly and suddenly vanish away', again rather like the Study Group's elusive and unspecified optimum.

Nonetheless the task had to be attempted, and the initial result in October 1971 was a series of six networks that purported to show the effects of various contractions – to be achieved within five years – and their financial consequences.

As we shall see, these original proposals were not seen to be enough, and an updated report in May 1972 added another five possibilities, one of which included 123 withdrawals of grant-aided services – roughly two-thirds of such routes then existing.

So that some analysis could be attempted, the Study Group had been presented with some basic choices by two senior officers. These were the Executive Director (Finance), A. W. Tait, and Chief Economist Stewart Joy. Tait's approach, potentially the less draconian of the two, was described in the minutes as the 'break-down' method. Joy preferred an alternative, dubbed 'build-up'.

These labels need some explanation. Tait's assessment started with the Board's forecast Rail Plan for 1976. From that starting point, 'by a process of judgement, areas of activity and services least likely to contribute to overall profitability will then be peeled off'.

Joy, however, wanted to begin with a core network of intercity services that 'would attract over 85% of the intercity passenger revenue in current plans'.

Other services and routes would then be progressively added to this core 'in ways which should improve the overall profitability of the system'. Any line or service that did not satisfy this criterion would evidently be thrown to the wolves.

The test of what should be 'peeled off' under the Tait rules also seemed to be less severe ('services least likely to contribute to overall profitability') than Joy's view that lines should be added to the core network 'in ways which should improve the overall profitability'.

In short, because it was aware of the increasing official unease, the Board was attempting to head off the axe-wielding civil servants by producing its own proposals, rather than being faced with a challenge from Whitehall that might be even less informed and more radical still.

Later on, however, the DoE joined in and a degree of cooperation became evident.

But the Board's proposals were inevitably compounded by the difficulties of identifying where many losses were occurring, quite apart from the further hurdle of attempting to adjust its network to comply with an 'optimum', which itself could only be guessed at.

However, one surely safe assumption was that the Government would accept a 'no-loss' railway, requiring no state aid.

Beeching had attempted to launch the process of defining such a network in 1963, but it is self-evident that he knew his first 'Reshaping' plan would not be enough, hence the 'trunk routes' sequel and indeed the internal maps of 1964-65.

The evolution of the first Special Study proposals took some months, and these were reproduced in a second 'strictly confidential' document entitled 'Preliminary study on size of service network' in October 1971.

This suggested six options, ranging from the Board's existing 1976 plan (17,703 route kilometres, 210,000 staff, 1,970 stations, £52m in grants, gross surplus before interest £64m) to the most severe Option 1, which like 2 and 3 assumed no grant aid.

Option 1 envisaged just 6,116 route kilometres, 940 stations and a surplus before interest of £29m. Interestingly, even this option still included 110,000 staff – some 20,000 more than are employed by train operators and Network Rail today. (However, exact comparisons are difficult because the Board had more businesses then, such as workshops and shipping services.)

Although Option 1 provided a much smaller railway, the financial results were not necessarily very much better. The forecast surplus before interest of £29m had been selected from a range between a surplus of £58m and a deficit of £21m.

The freight outlook under Option 1 was particularly bleak, with both trainload and wagonload traffic completely lost. Only Freightliner container trains would continue, moving an unimpressive 11m tons annually, compared with 206m tons by all types of train in 1970. (The railfreight total for 2013-14 was 116.6m tonnes, according to the ORR. The reduction between 1970 and now is almost entirely accounted for by the absence of wagonload traffic.)

Option 1 included 27 billion passenger kilometres, compared with 30.6 billion in 1970 (and the 59.2 billion which were actually recorded in 2013). The relatively small fall for Option 1 would presumably have been accounted for by retention of the busiest commuter and intercity services.

A BRB meeting on 3 December 1971 was told that the first conclusions had been discussed with 'the Minister' (either Minister for Transport Industries John Peyton or possibly DoE secretary Peter Walker), who wanted a railway policy paper for the Cabinet.

This meeting had been followed by discussions with DoE staff to map out what needed to be done, but the minutes recorded, rather gloomily, that 'after three meetings this was still not entirely clear'.

The BRB meeting was also told that 'a slightly smaller railway might be slightly more profitable but that a much smaller network would definitely not be'.

There was still concern at the Board that if a faction within the DoE had its way, many local train services would be replaced by cheaper buses, and this concern was almost certainly heightened by a suggestion at the last DoE discussion that grants could be withdrawn from 150 services – three out of four grant-aided lines.

The meeting also heard that there was a 'real danger' of conditioning both BR managers and DoE civil servants into the belief that anything smaller would necessarily be better, and that the Department still regarded unremunerative passenger services and wagonload freight as 'suspect areas of railway activity'.

On the other hand, the first report 'could not be underwritten by any department'. It was 'very unlikely that 75 services could be withdrawn, let alone 150, having regard to public reaction', and for this reason 'the publication of lists of closures had been deferred'.

The almost inevitable result of these deliberations was yet another report in May 1972, which has already been referred to. This was still 'strictly confidential' and was described as the 'second stage'.

Five more network options were added, but the Special Study Group had failed to discover a truly profitable railway – of any size – so attention now turned to at least reducing railway deficits by shedding the worst loss-makers.

This meant that many local lines were still at risk, because this version included a list of 123 services that could have been withdrawn in stages over the coming eight years.

By 1980, such routes as Cambridge-Ipswich, Norwich-Lowestoft, Glasgow-Dumfries-Carlisle and Plymouth-Penzance (with its branches) could all have been closed, together with more than 100 others. The railway would have become a shadow of its former self.

These proposals formed the basis of a Railway Policy Review that began in mid-1972, but the contents of a leaked draft copy became public knowledge in early October of that year, first appearing in the *Sunday Times*. This leak was followed by a police investigation, but no charges were brought.

The controversy was deepened by allegations of illegal phone-tapping, but on 4 July 1973 the Minister for Transport Industries, John Peyton, told the House of

Commons that 'draconian cuts of the kind at one time rumoured following the escape of a regrettably mobile document are not, in the view of the Government, the answer to the industry's or the nation's problems'.[1]

Even so it was, in retrospect, a close-run thing.

The Board achieved an operating profit of £24.9m in 1972, but this was £5.3m less than in 1971, although fare increases during the year had contributed some £12m. This profit, of which the core railway business provided almost £18m, was more than wiped out by interest charges, and the result was a deficit of £26.2m, in spite of grants for loss-making services worth £68.2m.

The loss was covered by a special grant of £27m. (Because the Board was supposed to balance its books since the passing of the 1968 Transport Act, a special Act of Parliament was needed to make such a grant lawful.) The position was plainly unsustainable, and goes some way to account for the DoE hawks who wanted many railway services to be replaced by buses.

British Rail Chairman Richard Marsh struck a (probably unintentional) note of irony in his introduction to the Board's 1972 annual report, when he commented that 'BR is in business today as never before'.

In a sense he was right, because most businesses struggling with a 12-month deficit of more than £26m could not have relied on a strategic Act of Parliament to stave off the receivers.

Unfortunately, there was worse to come in 1973 – a troubled year of galloping inflation and industrial strife (particularly in the coal industry), which culminated in the introduction of a three-day working week on 31 December, intended to save electricity.

The already fragile finances of the Board reeled under the impact of so many economic stresses, and the result was an operating loss for the core railway business of just over £5m, while the 1972 overall loss of £26.2m had virtually doubled, to £51.6m.

The 1973 report lacked a Chairman's introduction, perhaps because Richard Marsh preferred not to attach his signature to the Review of the Year that appeared at the front.

As the Board seemed to have tired of trying to second-guess plotting civil servants, and evidently relying on the dictum that attack is the best form of defence, the introduction pulled no punches.

After pointing out that 'no major industry relying on the custom of the community for its business can emerge unscathed from a year of unprecedented inflation, industrial unrest, the recession ... and an energy crisis,' it then claimed that the year had still been marked by some 'notable achievements', including a rise in the passenger business, 'many new freight contracts' and the start of 'important new development projects'.

It continued:

'The search for a long-term solution to Rail problems with a co-ordinated transport policy, begun in July 1972 and advanced a stage further in November 1973, continued into 1974.'

(This statement prudently overlooked the existence of the Special Study Group, which had started work in May 1971.)

Having warned that the results for 1974 would be worse than 1973, it said, 'The Board still suffers from and is bound to suffer in perpetuity from the effects of past price restraint,' a comment that had been a familiar theme of the former British Transport Commission. The uncertainty of the Board's position was emphasised by a reference to a railway investment fund of £891m, which had been agreed for the next five years. Within weeks of this decision, the amount had been reduced by 20% as part of a 'general cutback in the public sector'.

The Board evidently felt ill-treated, to judge by such a statement as 'no organisation can cope efficiently with such abrupt and frequent changes of policy', which again could have been written by the Commission more than 20 years earlier. It concluded with a warning: 'If the nation wills the ends it must provide the means.'

So the stage was set. But wider changes in the world were also about to have their effect on the future railway.

Chapter 18

'Opportunity for change'

The changing political landscape of the 1970s could not fail to influence the railways. The second General Election of 1974 – a troubled year – had resulted in a narrow victory for Labour, led by Harold Wilson. He resigned 18 months later, and was replaced by James Callaghan.

The United Kingdom had joined the European Community in 1973, and one consequence was the 1974 Railways Act, which had changed both the method of paying for the railway and also the amount it was receiving. The structure of line-by-line grants set out in the 1968 Transport Act was replaced after 1974 by a block payment, known as the Public Service Obligation (or PSO), in accordance with European law.

The PSO meant that BR no longer needed to calculate the expenses of every grant-aided service as it had before, but one unsought effect was that the amount payable rose sharply, so that the old-style grant aid in 1970 of £75m had risen to more than £400m by 1975.[1]

There were underlying reasons for this, and one was the familiar millstone of restraint on fares and charges. It was not always unjustified, but had tended to hamper the railway at various times ever since the days of the 19th century Railway & Canal Traffic Acts. The effect of such restraint had been worsened during the first half of the 1970s by a period of rapid inflation.

The British Railways Board summarised the problem by pointing out that direct comparisons were highly misleading. When the amounts were adjusted for inflation and stated at 1969 values, the level of support in 1975 was really worth £179m, as compared with £61m in 1969.

This was still a large increase, but the greatest leap by far had occurred between 1974 (£95m at 1969 prices) and 1975. The Board's fares had been restrained as part of the Government's Prices & Incomes policy (itself intended to control inflation) until November 1974, when the railways were given the freedom to increase their fares to a realistic level.

But, as the Board pointed out, 'By that time the base was so low that the market could not take the increase needed. The result: costs rose by 33% and we were enabled to increase prices by 16%.'[2]

The same report also fired a subdued shot across the bows of the railway unions:

'The year of 1974 has been a very difficult one and 1975 will be no easier. But with the help of every Railway employee we could still emerge from this difficult times with a first-rate Railway – one of which the nation can be proud. But we do need that co-operation: if we do not get it we may find we have not got a future for the Railway as we know it today.'

Appeals of this kind did not prove to be sufficient. As the 1980s dawned the industry would be riven by almost catastrophic industrial strife.

However, that was still several years in the future when BR's new Chairman Peter Parker arrived in 1976, to take over from Richard Marsh. (It was Parker's second chance at BR: he had already been offered the Chairman's post by Barbara Castle, but on that occasion they had been unable to come to terms.)

One of Parker's first remarks on arriving at his new office in September was 'we need a few victories', and he had arrived ready to fight a battle.

He was hot on the heels of his opponent, which took the form of a consultation document called 'Transport Policy', published in April. The Board had already produced a robust response in July, essentially Marsh's parting shot, entitled 'An Opportunity for Change'.

The consultation paper, which was the responsibility of the Environment Secretary, Anthony Crosland, had contrived to make the Board's financial position worse than it really was by quoting grants of £75m in 1970 and 'over £400m' in 1975 without qualifying them to take account of inflation.

The Board had responded vigorously by criticising the 'inadequacies and inconsistencies of ... rail transport policies [of successive governments] which failed to take account of the changing economic, industrial and social climate.'[3]

Not long after this, Parker arrived to pick up the baton that had been relinquished by Marsh. Soon afterwards, he told the BR workforce:

'We must win the debate on transport policy which the consultation document has begun ... we have to convince the doubters – all of us – that railways are a vital part of the national scene.'[4]

Parker was in no doubt that long-term planning was essential. He continued:

'The life of a government is five years, and the thinking of most politicians is geared to that fact. But in transport terms, implementing major changes takes much longer than this, and the policy-maker needs to know what the demand for transport will be in 1990 – and beyond...'

He also made it clear that he would have no truck with slanted official statistics:

'Don't let the government's freight figures confuse you. They include the mileage of milk floats, dustcarts and the like, and tend to upset the percentage of trunk haul road traffic that can be won to rail. Indeed, when assessing figures, like for like, the potential freight traffic to be won from the roads could cut the number of long distance lorries by over one third.'

Thus Parker wielded the railway sword. The second half the 1970s saw major changes. The first Intercity 125 High Speed Trains came into service, initially on the Western Region, and trials of their intended successor, the Advanced Passenger Train, were also under way.

The rest of the decade saw very few passenger closures, and the beginnings of a revived Channel Tunnel scheme (an earlier project had been stopped by Wilson's Government in 1974) were seen, although the initial proposal for a single bore, built to the constricted British loading gauge and nicknamed 'the Mousehole', was happily superseded by a much grander structure before anything came off the drawing board.

Parker was later able to describe 1979 as a 'year of harsh success, but frustrating too'.[5] The Board's finances were under control – there had been an operating surplus of £70.2m after PSO had been taken into account – but he also warned that 'fare levels are high by European standards and the strains of short term success are showing through'.

The real problem, as Parker saw it, was that 'we are meeting our financial targets and falling short of fulfilling our capability. The prospects for railways have never been better, but under present financial stringencies, we may be forced to contract in an expanding market.'

A period of unstable government came to an end in 1979. The slim Labour majority had evaporated, and on 28 March 1979 Jim Callaghan faced a motion of 'no confidence' from the Leader of the Opposition. It was passed by a majority of just one vote.

The resulting General Election on 3 May gave the Conservatives a majority of 44 seats, and the post of Prime Minister to their leader, Margaret Thatcher.

The following decade posed many challenges for British Rail. One was the inquiry into railway costs, chaired by David Serpell (see Chapter 19). Once again the members of the Serpell Committee attempted to retrieve a profitable railway, but were forced to conclude that if it existed at all, it would be a very small one.

Industrial relations reached a perilously low level at the start of the 1980s, as efforts continued to improve productivity and also trim the size of the workforce still further. (In 1976, Peter Parker had set out plans to reduce the headcount by 8,000 a year over the following five years, largely by natural wastage.)

Although the unions routinely (and understandably) opposed redundancies, it was the productivity measures – set out in a BR document called 'The Challenge of the Eighties' – that caused greater anger.

Parker told the National Union of Railwaymen that more jobs would have to go unless changes were accepted:

'The Corporate Plan envisaged a net reduction of 38,000 posts – posts not people –

in the rail business over five years, 1981-85 – a calculation based on current conditions of service. Changing conditions of service by eliminating systematic overtime, making Sunday part of the working week, and moving to continental rostering, will mean new jobs can be created by modernising the railway.'[6]

He also gave an example of how costs could be cut:

'When instead of two to two-and-a-half men on each freight train shift, we come down to one, and when instead of three sets of men per train journey we could come down to two, and we reduce the backup (Shed, Spare, Relief, Road Learning, etc.) for each set actually working … we could achieve a 10% reduction in cost – easily.'

These logical arguments were not enough on their own.

The two conflicts that gained by far the greatest attention and opposition in the early 1980s were flexible rostering and DOO – driver-only operation.

The DOO flashpoint was ignited when trains arrived for the newly electrified Midland suburban services between London St Pancras and Bedford – which had gained the irresistible nickname of the BedPan Line.

They were designed for driver-only operation, with no guard's position or door controls within the train. As a result, although ready in 1981 they were declared 'black', and stayed unmoving in sidings at Cricklewood and Bedford for a year while passengers rattled by in the decrepit diesel units that the new trains were intended to replace.

This was the industrial climate of the early 1980s, and it may even have endangered the very existence of British Rail. Certainly senior managers believed so.

An all-out stoppage was declared on 31 August 1981, but peace was declared after further talks. Any celebrations proved to be premature, because the temperature rose again later in the year.

The sticking point was the largest union – the National Union of Railwaymen – which called for an all-out strike in May 1982.

By mid-June the crisis was at its most acute. Parker wrote to 225,000 people on 16 June, including the 170,000 who worked for BR and 55,000 in subsidiary companies.

He told them: 'Make no mistake – if there is a strike, there will be no pay increase, no job to come back to for many, no prospect of investment in electrification.' A further letter, addressed to 'Dear Member of Staff', said: 'It is now one minute to midnight… I am asking you to follow your own interests. I am asking you not to strike.'

Surely no manager in the British railway industry had ever addressed his staff in such terms before.

Strikes followed, nonetheless, and Parker then took the boldest step of all, which is best described in his own words:

'We decided to do the unthinkable: we made it known that we were about to close the whole system. The next day there was a turmoil of meetings … setting the date for closure of the system, like the sentence of death, concentrated the mind wonderfully.'[7]

This was the peak. Soon afterwards, after a period of tense discussions that involved the TUC, the disputes came to an end. Trains from Bedford to St Pancras (and Brighton) have been operated only by drivers ever since.

BR's fortunes during the rest of the 1980s were mixed, reflecting the wider economy of the nation, but the governments in power were not instinctively fond of the railway.

The diesel HSTs were now in service on a number of main lines and proved to be a tremendous success, transforming the fortunes of InterCity, one of the new business Sectors created in the 1980s as the eventual successors to the Regions, but the next-generation HST, the tilting Advanced Passenger Train, failed to stay the course.

After some trials in service between 1981 and 1984, the funding ran out and the project had to be abandoned. The core tilt technology was sold, and is now used in the 'Pendolinos' built by Alstom that run on the West Coast Main Line – the testing ground of the APTs.

The curious desire to convert railways into roads also raised its head more than once, and indeed a serious proposal to close London Marylebone and convert it into a coach station went far enough for BR to compile a detailed internal document, complete with a copious appendix of timetables.

This failed (and fortunately so, considering that Marylebone has since gained two more platforms but is still under pressure), but this did not prevent the advocates of rail-road conversion from raising their heads at times they considered to be appropriate, such as during rail strikes.

BR took the case that was being made seriously enough to produce a leaflet in 1982, entitled 'Why our trains should stay on the rails'.

In its introduction, Peter Parker commented:

'Turning the railways into roads is an old idea which still has nothing to say for itself … the railway would provide space for only one lane of road traffic in each direction, no hard shoulder, no capacity for safe overtaking, unacceptably low clearances through tunnels and under bridges…'

This did not entirely clear the air. Later in the decade, one typical advertisement demanded: 'What would you do to a department that only worked to 3% of its potential?', and continued,

'Published statistics claim that our railway system only works to 3% of its potential.

When it's not on strike, of course. And how would its full potential be realised? Simply by converting the under-utilised rail routes into a road network.'[8]

The call is still occasionally heard now, but the DfT has said that such conversions do not form part of official policy.

A serious accident at Clapham in 1988 proved to be caused by wrongly wired signals, with the result that the Southern Region changed the working practices of signal engineers.

The inquiry was chaired by Sir Anthony Hidden, and his report recommended the general introduction of Automatic Train Protection within five years, but the events of the 1990s prevented his recommendation – one of 93 – being carried out on more than a few lines. At least one major accident later on would have been prevented by it (see Chapter 24).

The Regions themselves were also running out of track by the end of the decade. A major BR initiative, Organising for Quality, transferred all functions to the rail businesses – InterCity, Network SouthEast, Provincial (later Regional Railways), Freight and Parcels.

As the decade came to an end, Chairman Sir Robert Reid (the first of that name) gave a presentation that included these words:

'In preparing for the 1990s what is British Rail preparing for? Is it just the ability to achieve a further set of objectives? I think not. British Rail in the year 2000 will bear little resemblance to BR now.'

In 1991 British Rail published a prospectus for the last ten years of the 20th century. It was entitled 'Future Rail: the next decade'.

Introduced by the second Chairman to bear the name Sir Robert Reid, it looked ahead to the opening of the Channel Tunnel (which was being built at the time) as well as Crossrail and a major upgrading of Thameslink. As this book is written in 2015, although the Channel Tunnel has been in business for more than two decades, the other two projects are still 'under construction'.

The Chairman wrote:

'The railways are at a watershed. We are faced with tremendous opportunities, but if we are to seize them, decisions on projects which will take a decade to complete need to be taken now. For many of them we need the approval of Parliament.'[9]

In fact, Parliament would soon be asked to approve something else – the break-up of British Rail.

Chapter 19

'More or less by stealth'

The Conservative Governments led by Margaret Thatcher from 1979 had been enthusiastic privatisers. Many state-owned industries were sold to the private sector in the 1980s, allegedly to encourage competition, raise money to reduce public debt, improve the quality of management, and encourage small-scale investment in major industries by millions of people.

The party's 1979 manifesto introduced the principle of privatisation in fairly broad terms:

'More nationalisation would further impoverish us and further undermine our freedom. We will offer to sell back to private ownership the recently nationalised aerospace and shipbuilding concerns, giving their employees the opportunity to purchase shares.'

By 1983, after several privatisations had been achieved, including nearly all the railway hotels, the next Conservative manifesto (which was followed by a second election victory) had become more frank, saying: 'We shall transfer more state-owned businesses to independent ownership.'

In public, the Conservatives had been careful not to alienate the employees of nationalised concerns. The 1983 manifesto went so far as to say: 'Most people who work in these industries work hard and have a sense of public service.'

Behind the scenes the verdict was less benevolent, because the party's position had been influenced by a strategy that originated with the Conservative Economic Reconstruction Group. This Group had been chaired by free market supporter Nicholas (later Lord) Ridley while the party was in opposition in the second half of the 1970s.

The Conservatives were smarting from their experiences earlier in the decade, when the Prime Minister Edward Heath had been forced into a corner by the unions. That conflict had led to shortages of coal and the imposition of a three-day week to save energy at the end of 1973. This was followed by a General Election in February 1974 in which Heath demanded 'Who governs Britain?', but the result was a hung Parliament. A second election in October sealed the Conservatives' fate for the time being, when Labour gained a small majority of three seats.

Ridley saw a primary case for curbing the power of the unions by breaking up 'vulnerable' state monopolies. His paper of July 1977 maintained that the measurement of unit costs was 'vital' and that 'in the nationalised industries the output is measurable and unit costs can be obtained', which might have been news

ABOVE: The remote goods depot at Longparish, near Andover in Hampshire, lingered until 1956, partly because the branch had been used for military traffic.

BELOW: Beeching's axe descended on the Guildford–Christ's Hospital branch in June 1965. A car crosses the line at Bramley & Wonersh in May 1966, while track lifting is in progress. In recent times, it has been suggested that this line should be reopened between Guildford and Cranleigh.

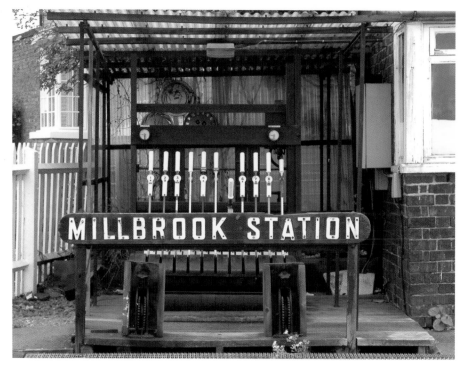

ABOVE: This lever frame lasted at Millbrook in Bedfordshire until the Bedford–Bletchley line was resignalled in the early years of this century.

BELOW: Some Victorian technology still survives, such as these single line token instruments at Battersby on the Whitby line.

ABOVE: The panel at Watford Junction, dating from the early 1960s, closed in 2014 when train regulation was temporarily transferred to Wembley. Later, the new Rail Operations Centre at Rugby will take over the southern section of the West Coast Main Line.

LEFT: Stafford No 4 box was only replaced in 2015, when the Stafford area became the first to be controlled from the new centre at Rugby.

ABOVE: First generation franchise: National Express operated Midland Mainline between April 1996 and November 2007.

BELOW: First generation franchise: First Great Eastern ceased to be a separate network when its routes became part of Greater Anglia in 2004. The winning bid for the new larger franchise came from National Express.

ABOVE: Second generation franchise: Transpennine Express, which began in April 2004, inherited the interurban routes of Arriva Trains Northern.

BELOW: Fifth generation franchise: Virgin Trains East Coast was launched in March 2015. East Coast had been operated by the Department for Transport's Directly Operated Railways for more than five years, having previously been run by GNER (twice) and then National Express.

TOP LEFT: Tom Winsor (now Sir Thomas) was Rail Regulator 1999-2004.

TOP RIGHT: Richard Bowker was Chairman and CEO of the Strategic Rail Authority 2001-2005.

ABOVE LEFT: Sir John Armitt was the last Chief Executive of Railtrack in 2001-2002, and continued as the CEO of Network Rail 2002-2007.

ABOVE RIGHT: Sir Richard Branson, whose Virgin Group has operated at least one franchise since 1997, mostly in partnership with Stagecoach.

BELOW: Two generations of tilting trains pose at the Crewe Heritage Centre in 2002. British Rail's ill-fated Advanced Passenger Train is on the left, while on the right is an Alstom Pendolino for Virgin Trains which uses a development of BR's original tilt technology.

ABOVE: Railtrack was repeatedly criticised for its stewardship of the network between 1994 and 2001. Certainly these platform lines at Derby looked a little worse for wear in 2002.

BELOW: There was no new electrification after privatisation until a short connection between Crewe and Stoke was energised in the autumn of 2003. This demonstration Pendolino was standing at Alsager.

ABOVE: HS2 continues to be a controversial project. The London tunnels for its high speed predecessor HS1 were bored in 2003-2004 and opened in 2007.

BELOW: More rolling stock is needed to deal with relentlessly rising passenger demand. This former London Underground District Line car has been converted to diesel power by Vivarail in Warwickshire.

to the British Railways Board, considering its fruitless struggles in 1971 and 1972 to discover if it possessed any profitable routes (see Chapter 17).

He had a poor opinion of nationalised industries in general, commenting that 'More and more the nationalised industries are run for the benefit of those who work in them. The pressures are for more jobs for the boys, and more money for each boy.'[1]

He went on to calculate how long the country could 'survive' strikes in various industries, concluding that the answer was 'zero' in the case of water, gas, electricity and the health service, but that the nation would be able to manage without railways for four weeks, coal for six, docks for eight and 'dustmen' for ten.

The survival period was said to be 'a long time' in the case of 'buses and tubes', posts and telephones, education, steel, air transport and the civil service, including the administration of tax. (Considering the effects on London of a single 24-hour Underground strike now, even when bus services are reinforced as much as possible, it might be thought that his assessment in the case of 'buses and tubes' erred on the optimistic side.)

He also considered whether workers in certain industries should be legally prevented from striking, as they are in the police, but concluded that withdrawing tax rebates and unemployment benefit from strikers would be 'far more likely to succeed'.

In addition, he ruled out placing a special 'strikebreaking' force on standby. (In the case of the railways at least, such a force would have been useless in safety-critical jobs such as those of drivers and signallers unless it had been extensively trained beforehand, but such preparations would have been difficult to arrange and, unless extremely covert, vigorously opposed by the unions – indeed, the training of outsiders to deputise for striking railway staff would have been seen as highly provocative and could easily have triggered industrial action in its own right.)

He advised the shadow cabinet: 'As a long term policy government should seek to manoeuvre the nation out of the position where it is vulnerable to monopoly unions in vital industries.'

Ridley also suggested a restructuring of the management of such nationalised industries as might remain, commenting that so far managers had been given a 'hopeless task'. Although they had a statutory obligation to break even or make a stated profit, in practice they had 'been constantly overlaid by requests from Ministers which vary from keeping rural telephone kiosks going to not putting up prices when they should. The objective is thus lost.'

The answer, as he saw it, was to separate Ministers and their officials from day-to-day administration, and to convert the existing top-level managerial groups into supervisory or 'holding boards', which would have the task of protecting the subsidiary managers further down from 'ministerial and bureaucratic pressures and interference'.

He was even willing to accept a token role for unions:

'If there was a statutory obligation (or it was thought prudent in relation to the circumstances) to have some worker or trade union directors on nationalised industry boards, they could be appointed to the holding board. Provided that they were in a distinct minority, they could do little harm.'

Ridley saw the challenges of privatisation in much the same light as one might regard a military campaign:

'The process of returning nationalised industries to the private sector is more difficult than ever. Not only are the industries firmly institutionalised as part of our way of economic life, but there is a very large union and political lobby wanting to keep them so. A frontal attack is not recommended…'

He continued that the policy should be to prepare the industries for a 'partial return to the private sector, more or less by stealth. First we should destroy the statutory monopolies; second we should break them up into smaller units; and third, we should apply a whole series of different techniques to try and edge them back into the private sector.'

He conceded that the ending of monopolies would need changes to the law, but added that 'this nasty little Bill is the only legislation called for in this paper'.

He went on to analyse the extent to which individual industries could be fragmented successfully, suggesting that the potential was greatest in such enterprises as coal, airports, car manufacturing and buses.

Surprisingly, considering the actual course of events in the 1990s, he believed that the chances of doing so were 'minimal' in the case of the railways.

It was evidently the tactics set out in the 'Ridley Report' that formed the basis of much of the hiving-off (as it became known) pursued by the Thatcher administrations during the 1980s. Thus the British Railways Board was instructed to dispose of its hotels and ships a full decade before the core industry was broken up.

Ridley was under no illusions about the potential unpopularity of his plan. In a 'confidential annex', he warned that 'There is no doubt that at some time the enemies of the next Tory Government will try and destroy this policy…'

He thought the opposition would be greatest in one of the 'vulnerable' industries such as coal, and suggested that one answer might be to 'provoke a battle in a non-vulnerable industry, where we can win. This is what happened when we won against the postal workers in 1971. We could win in industries like the railways…'

His notes of caution ('we must be prepared to deal with the problem of violent picketing') proved to be justified within a few years, when indeed there were pitched battles between police and striking coal miners at colliery gates.

Meanwhile, the foundations had also been well and truly laid for the eventual disaggregation of the railway industry, even if that would not be achieved until more than another decade had passed.

The earliest privatisations after 1979, which were intended to raise money for the Treasury as well as reduce the power of the unions, included British Aerospace, British Telecom and Jaguar. Other utilities followed later in the decade, together with British Airways, British Steel and Rolls Royce.

Margaret Thatcher lost the party leadership and therefore her position as Prime Minister in November 1990, but the principle of privatisation survived under her immediate successor John Major. His inherited position was confirmed in 1992 when the Conservatives won their fourth election in succession.

Mrs Thatcher had stopped short of privatising the core operations of British Rail, presumably because they were not profitable. In addition, as BR was considered to be a 'non-vulnerable' industry it was unlikely to have been a priority for the kind of political reasons set out by Ridley.

Of course, had BR been making net profits in the early 1980s it might have been moved much closer to the head of the privatisation queue, and the tracks and trains could then have accompanied the railway hotels and ships into private ownership.

The search for a 'profitable' railway had been under way for decades, but the problem had defeated the British Transport Commission, Beeching, the 1971 Special Studies Group and numerous Transport Ministers.

There had been a long-running debate about whether a profitable railway really existed at all – as we have seen, even pragmatic Stewart Joy had been forced to conclude that apparently commercial services might prove to be subsidised, in effect, by others which were acknowledged loss-makers, so that all the elements were leaning on each other.[2]

But was this really the position? This was the question that yet another committee of inquiry was set up to answer in May 1982.

It was chaired by Sir David Serpell, whose obituary in 2008 described him as a 'formidable Whitehall mandarin'[3]. He was already familiar with railway finances, having served as Deputy Secretary at the Ministry of Transport during the Beeching period and later returning to become Permanent Secretary of the Ministry and its successor, the Department of the Environment. In addition, he had been a part-time member of the British Railways Board since 1974, from which he resigned when his Committee was appointed.

His Committee on the Review of Railway Finances was convened by Transport Secretary David Howell (later Baron Howell of Guildford) who, like some of his predecessors as well as Mrs Thatcher, was alarmed at the size of railway costs. As we saw in the previous chapter, the industry had also just been damaged by a near-disastrous industrial dispute and tensions were still high. Partly because of the disruption caused by strikes, traffic figures had slumped to levels previously unseen in the 20th century.

The Committee's terms of reference evolved slightly while the inquiry was being set up, but the final version read:

'To examine the finances of the railway and associated operations, in the light of all relevant considerations, and to report on options for alternative policies, and their related objectives, designed to secure improved financial results in an efficiently run railway in Great Britain over the next 20 years.'

The Government may have regarded privatisation as an effective way of restoring the balance of industrial strength in its favour, but it could hardly sell an industry that needed hundreds of millions in Government grants each year (in 1983 the BRB received total grants of £958m, including £856m from central government). If, however, a profitable railway could be disinterred from the wreckage then here, we may surmise, was a chance to close another door on the unions.

The resulting Serpell Report is sometimes seen as an updated version of Beeching's 'Reshaping' recommendations almost 20 years earlier, but the two documents did not serve the same purpose.

Beeching had made a clear statement (rightly or wrongly) about the railway network – much of it was not worth having and should be closed.

Serpell gave no advice of this kind: his Committee's task was to set out costed options for the Government's consideration, not to choose a course of action. (Indeed, the report's introduction pointed out that '...our review has been concerned with the railway's finances, not transport policy'.)

The options were duly calculated and described in the form of maps, but the outcome was not promising. Just as Serpell's predecessors had discovered, measuring railway finances was about as easy as juggling with quicksilver.

Paragraph 12.16 of the report admitted morosely that 'forecasting the revenues and costs of a business as complex as the railway is difficult', which some of the details (such as they were) confirmed.

One example of this was provided by: 'Operating speeds almost certainly have an influence on maintenance costs, but there is no empirical data to estimate the size of the effect.' The same paragraph then referred rather vaguely to 'circumstantial evidence' that reducing the speeds of HSTs 'may cost some £3 million a year in extra brake maintenance'.[4]

In short, parts of the picture were so blurred that many of the Committee's calculations were inevitably tainted with uncertainty, and that uncertainty was increased to a critical level when one of its four members announced in the closing stages that he wished to disassociate himself from some of the main findings.

This was Alfred Goldstein, a highways engineer who was an ally of Margaret Thatcher's monetarist adviser Sir Alan Walters, and also Alfred Sherman, an advocate of converting railways into roads. He felt that his colleagues had concentrated too much on the short-term prospects for the railways, at the risk of neglecting the longer-term outlook.

In a 'minority report' that was printed as an annex, he explained:

'It is with regret that I have parted company from my colleagues. But the need for a long term review of and direction for the railway is so compelling that I can take no other course. In Committee we tried hard and for long, but could not, in the end, agree on important issues.'[5]

This lack of consensus recalled the differences of opinion that had afflicted the Stedeford Advisory Group more than 20 years earlier, but in that case the Government had been able to avoid any publicity.

On this occasion there was no choice. Her Majesty's Stationery Office was standing by to set out all the details, but when the Serpell Report was received by David Howell a few days before Christmas 1982 he did not hurry to share it with the nation.

If he and his colleagues had been hoping to be given the magic formula for a profitable and therefore saleable industry of any reasonable size, they were doomed to be disappointed.

The Committee had drawn up a number of options for the future network, which ranged from virtually the status quo to a vestigial system of just 2,623 route kilometres, down from a basic 'reference case' network of 16,206km.

It was thought that such a vestigial system would be profitable, but only because of the supporting revenue from freight. The Committee forecast that passenger services alone would still be in deficit by £32 million, but that freight income would provide a final annual profit of £34 million.

However, 'Option A' meant that trains would become no more than a memory in many parts of Britain, with nothing north of the Scottish central belt nor anywhere in Wales, apart from the main line from the Severn Tunnel to Cardiff.

There would be no railways south-west of Bristol, and no Midland Main Line. The East Coast Main Line would terminate at Newcastle, and Leeds would be at the end of a branch. All East Anglian lines would disappear, with the solitary exception of the main line to Norwich. Even south of London, just a handful of routes would have survived to such places as Brighton and Dover.

The publication of Serpell could not be delayed indefinitely, and media interest was whipped up by a series of leaks in early January (the Board was the chief suspect), with inevitably much of the attention being given to the draconian Option A.

Inevitably, the stories that resulted from these leaks were often incomplete or inaccurate. The edition of *New Scientist* for 13 January 1983 included a report that began: 'British Rail should save money by increasing the risk of railway accidents' and described Option A as a 'proposal'.

By the time Serpell was officially published on 20 January, the Board had been able to draft a response, in which it expressed its disappointment that the Committee had been divided over the important issues and had failed to encourage 'the need to maintain momentum'.

It soon became clear that Serpell was, to paraphrase at least one contemporary newspaper headline, already heading for the buffers. No one was pleased with the report, which did not recommend any particular network size but had certainly horrified many people with its map of Option A.

Even some of the conclusions appeared to be contradictory. The industry was left to make what sense it could of such statements as: 'We see many opportunities to improve the efficiency, and reduce the costs, of the railway while keeping it at broadly its present size', which was followed further down the same page by: 'It is clear to us that reductions in the size of the network will be required if the level of financial support for the railway is to be lowered substantially.'

Elsewhere, the tone of the report verged on the dogmatic, with such pronouncements as: 'There is no "right" to transport in the absence of payment for the resources consumed.'

This, as Michael Bonavia commented, was 'not a law of economics but a subjective, in fact some sort of moral, or ethical, judgment'.[6]

The clear recommendations the report did make concerned such relatively detailed aspects as improvements to maintenance (which was probably the inspiration for the *New Scientist* report of 13 January), fleet management, the future role of British Rail Engineering Limited, and marketing.

David Howell evidently found it hard to provide much of a welcome for Serpell. On 3 February 1983 he told the House of Commons:

'I certainly rule out extreme options. That includes the option that Mr Goldstein has since said was only included as an example and was not practicable. I refer to option A which is, nevertheless, an important illustration of a purely commercial railway. It shows just how far we are from having a railway system that can cover its costs. It is a valuable illustration, but not a practicable option.'[7]

In the event, Serpell was quickly forgotten. Unlike the first Beeching report, it was not followed by any major changes to the size of the network, but it had at least provided some grounds for believing that a profitable national railway, in cash terms, was now genuinely out of reach.

Ownership of the railways was still a potential discussion point but, although Mrs Thatcher's Governments continued their privatisation programme as the decade advanced, the core railway was largely left alone, although British Rail's shipping division Sealink had followed the last of the hotels into private ownership in 1984.

There were some attempts after the 1979 election to form partnerships with private enterprise: the British Railways Board explored the possibilities of selling the fleet of merry-go-round coal wagons, upgrading its freight ferry services from Harwich and building a new rail/air terminal at London Victoria. However, these and other projects of a similar kind mainly fell foul of the Treasury's aversion at that time to such partnerships. It insisted that such projects should be wholly self-standing, and that public money could play no part in private speculations.

The Board was not deterred. It went on to consider entrusting the electrification of the East Coast Main Line to a commercial company and allowing private enterprise to run Gatwick Express, but these proposals also foundered.

One of the more bizarre proposals in this period concerned the branch line from Slough to Windsor & Eton Central, when a company known as Rail Limited approached David Howell in late 1982 with an offer to lease and operate the route. This scheme was abandoned at the end of 1984 for 'financial and administrative' reasons.[8]

Apart from such abortive lurches in the direction of private enterprise, British Rail made significant progress in the decade following Serpell. As we have seen, the regional managements that had existed in one form or another since 1948 gave way to Sectors, ushering in the 'business-led railway'.

Passenger and freight traffic remained volatile but the general trend was one of recovery, so that the crisis year of 1982, when just 630 million passenger journeys were recorded, remained an all-time low.

As far as private enterprise was concerned, all the concrete proposals affecting the core railway until the second half of the 1980s had been project- or service-based. They were, in a sense, miniature 'hivings-off' that failed to survive close scrutiny or Treasury misgivings.

However, in 1987 the complete privatisation of British Rail began to be debated in earnest. It would take time, and there would be some rough riding along the way.

Part 3:

'The fragmented railway'

Chapter 20

'A competitive element'

The full privatisation of British Rail had been discussed by various commentators from time to time during the early 1980s, and the inspiration for such proposals was probably the flow of other privatisations under the Conservative administrations.

But most analysts who were in favour of renewed private sector involvement in railways had tended to stub their toes, metaphorically speaking, against the apparently intractable problem of the industry's losses, although some maintained that unnecessarily large costs were still contributing to the problem.

David Starkie, writing in 1984, drew attention to British Rail's long-criticised inefficiencies, saying: 'When inefficiency is substantial … the opportunity exists for a more efficient firm to set up in competition but producing at a lower cost.'[1]

His preferred solution was privately operated trains but infrastructure co-ordinated by the state – in other words, a partial privatisation that recalled the 'Landlord and Tenant' proposals suggested in vain by the LNER in 1946 (see Chapter 6).

The introduction to David Starkie's article began with the no-nonsense statement that 'British Rail will have to be denationalised sooner or later' (much more recently he has suggested seatless Third Class trains[2]).

His advocacy of privatisation in 1984 was expanded upon three years later by Kenneth Irvine, a former British Rail trainee manager who was to become one of the founders of Prism Rail, a company that secured several passenger franchises before it was taken over by National Express Group.

His views were published as a pamphlet by the Adam Smith Institute in 1987, on the eve of the General Election. He wrote:

'There would not need to be a radical upheaval to the management structure of the British Railways Board to introduce a competitive element in the use of railway track and stations. The principle can be extended to loss-making rural services by negative tendering.'[3]

This would be a first step. Eventually, Irvine saw a gradual evolution until private sector operators were buying paths from a private sector infrastructure owner.

His conclusion was hopeful – indeed optimistic: 'The above measures will hopefully lead to dramatic reductions in the PSO grant if not its phasing out, given the profitable rental and sale of property.'

Table 9: British Rail passenger totals, 1973-1992

Year end	Passenger totals (m)	Year end	Passenger totals (m)
1973	728	1983	695
1974	733	1984	701
1975	730	1985	686
1976	702	1986	738
1977	702	1987-88	798
1978	724	1988-89	822
1979	736	1989-90	812
1980	760	1990-91	810
1981	719	1991-92	792
1982	630	1992-93	770

Sources: 1973-1986 Department for Transport; 1987-1992 British Railways Board annual accounts

Irvine's plan – although still including some subsidy – was essentially adopted by the architects of the 1993 Transport Act. It was the same plan that went on to fail spectacularly with the placing of Railtrack in Railway Administration in 2001.

Irvine also believed that new technology could help to make multiple operators a reality: 'The argument that there can only be one train operator on the network has disappeared with the introduction of new signalling and train control.'

This remark was likely to strike anyone experienced in railway operation as odd. Mr Irvine did not provide any source for the 'argument' he cited, and chose to ignore the ample evidence of history. Railway companies had been running trains successfully on parts of each others' networks since the 1840s at least, initially in many cases without even the protection of semaphore signalling or the telegraph, which were both in their infancy at that time.

Even so, the present author has been unable to trace any railway accident in Britain caused specifically by the presence of more than one operator, although it is true that the introduction of standard bell codes used for communication between mechanical signal boxes was disgracefully slow, and one consequence was a triple collision that occurred at one end of Canonbury Tunnel in London in December 1881 because the signalmen in adjacent boxes were working for different companies whose codes were not the same.[4]

In our own time, the Rail Accident Investigation Branch reported as recently as 2013 that a non-standard (and unofficial) code had been in use near Stockton for many years.[5]

However, in these and similar cases it was a lack of consistency and not the presence of more than one operator as such that caused problems.

Mr Irvine went on to quote some instances of existing private sector participation on BR infrastructure, such as Foster Yeoman's stone trains and also, perhaps slightly less to the point, the Venice-Simplon Orient Express – which is no doubt admirable in its own way but hardly claims to be a transport service in the same sense as commuter trains from Orpington.

He was also pleased to note that 'a strong emphasis was given to the development of Company trains in the Beeching era since when there has been continuing investment in a substantial fleet of privately owned wagons'.

In fact, there was nothing particularly novel about 'private owner' wagons. In 1955, for example, well before Beeching and in the comparatively early days of nationalisation, there were 6,312 such wagons in use on British Railways[6], although it is true that the proportion of these in comparison with the BR fleet had become much higher by the 1980s. There were indeed more of them, but by then the total number of BR wagons had also fallen dramatically.

(Mr Irvine was not the only commentator who believed that the concept of the privately owned wagon was invented in the Beeching era. A House of Commons Library briefing note, intended to inform MPs, also claims: 'BR was encouraging the private ownership of wagons in the freight business as far back as the 1960s'.[7])

Mr Irvine's pamphlet apparently struck an approving chord in high places, and discussions about railway privatisation seem to have begun in earnest within Government in 1988.

The proposition gained the attention of Greg Bourne, who had come from BP and was now in charge of 'privatisation initiatives' in the Prime Minister's Policy Unit, but the issue came to the surface in an unusual way – in connection with a proposed closure.

There had been many railway closures since 1963 and, as Beeching had commented, the 'emotional upsurge' that a closure proposal caused usually died away once the deed had been done.

However, a prospective closure could be different, and there was at least one precedent. This had occurred in 1963, when Beeching's plan to withdraw the passenger service across the inner suburbs of north London from Richmond to Broad Street had aroused the articulate denizens of Hampstead and Highgate to such an extent that the service was reprieved in June 1965. (It has survived to become part of London Overground, although the eastern terminus is now Stratford.)

However, in 1988 the axe was poised over the scenic but increasingly decrepit 117km Settle & Carlisle line, which provides an alternative to the largely parallel West Coast Main Line.

It is one of the most impressive routes in the country, thrusting through the high Pennines across the 'roof of England', but the large number of structures along the way include the soaring Ribblehead viaduct.

It was the need for major and costly repairs to Ribblehead in particular that prompted a closure proposal from the Board in 1988, and Transport Minister David Mitchell revealed in May that the Government was minded to consent.

The vociferous protests that followed his announcement caused closure to be delayed so that ways of keeping the line open could be explored, and one alternative promoted by Greg Bourne was privatisation.

In the event the S&C was neither sold off separately nor closed (it has become increasingly necessary in modern times once again, particularly for freight), but the debate about this line was accompanied by reports that much wider railway privatisation was now on the agenda. It also became known that Bourne had been discussing various options with the British Railways Board.

In July it was announced that BR had made a record 'profit' of £291m in 1987-88, although this was only after grants of £871m had been taken into account. Even so, this improvement was calculated to attract renewed interest in returning the railways to private enterprise, although grants for some services, mainly those in the Provincial sector, would have had to continue if widespread closures were to be avoided.

It is not clear whether another contraction of the network was still contemplated at this stage, notwithstanding the Serpell debacle a few years earlier. Certainly Lord Faulkner of Worcester, recalling the 1980s, remembers that:

'When a senior official from the Department of Transport arrived as a new member on the British Railways Board, he announced that he was there at the Minister's behest to preside over the orderly rundown of the railways. That was the mood of the time.'[8]

In October 1988 the Transport Secretary, Paul Channon (later Lord Kelvedon), told the Conservative Party conference, with evident enthusiasm, that rail privatisation was now on the horizon:

'We all of us in this great conference hall know the advantages that spring from setting free the spirit – the entrepreneurial spirit – giving customers thereby a better service and increasing efficiency. I want to look at the whole of BR's future, to see whether privatisation is the way ahead.'

So the wheels were starting to turn, although slowly, and later in the same month Channon set out four possible options at a conference organised by the 'free market' Centre for Policy Studies on 28 October, entitled 'Reviving the Railways'. (It was also the day that InterCity had announced forthcoming increases in the price of long-distance season tickets of up to 21%, partly because some trains were becoming seriously overcrowded.)

Channon had begun by pointing out that rail privatisation, if it happened at all, was still distant. It is possible to detect a reduction of urgency in this speech when compared with his resounding sentiments in favour of the 'entrepreneurial spirit' at the party conference just a few weeks earlier:

'I want to emphasise at the start that Her Majesty's Government has not decided to privatise British Rail. There is no chance of doing so in the lifetime of this Parliament. What we have decided to do is to look at the long term options...'

Three of the options were already known – a revival of the regional companies, the creation of a track authority with separate operators, or the conversion of BR into a single plc (which the Board preferred). A fourth possibility, Channon now revealed, was the sale of each BR business (InterCity, Network SouthEast, Provincial, Freight, Parcels) as individual enterprises. However, he believed these options were not necessarily exclusive, continuing:

'There is no need to stick to a single option for the whole railway. It would be perfectly possible to combine aspects of more than one of the other options. For example a division into independent companies based partly on regions and partly on sectors might be possible...'

On the 'track authority' option, Channon made a perceptive comment:

'Competition between railway companies will be limited by the practicalities of rail operation and the main competition [for] many rail services would be from coach, car or air.'

Indeed, the conference as a whole did not warm to the prospect of a separate infrastructure owner selling paths to competing operators, tending to share Channon's view that such a monopoly could create pricing and quality problems, be remote from its customers and, most importantly perhaps, that investment 'would be hard to attract'. Sir Christopher Foster of Coopers & Lybrand was 'especially damning' about this model.

After the track authority option had been adopted in 1992 (it seems that the Treasury did not share the reservations voiced at this event, while Channon himself would leave government within a year), it became clear that it was not the practicalities of operation so much as their economics that would pose limits to competition, which is the main reason why franchised and open access passenger operators have proved to be such poor bedfellows (when the open access operators have been allowed in the bed at all).

A report of the proceedings was compiled by Conservative MP John Redwood, who commented in his introduction: 'The stance of British Rail is still essentially defensive. Many at the Conference felt that large market opportunities had been, and were still being missed.'[9]

He was also unimpressed with the Board's record of improving the railway network:

'They have failed to use their nationalised monopoly position to drive routes underground across London and to permit easy travel from the north and west of the country through to the South Coast and beyond to the European continent.'

The Board would have smiled wryly – perhaps – at such a comment. Its 'nationalised monopoly position' notwithstanding, BR had rarely if ever been granted access to the kind of capital funding that projects like this would have required, bearing in mind the competing demands for investment in rolling stock as well as the continuing need to make up the arrears of maintenance in buildings and infrastructure that had resulted from the war and its aftermath.

There had been plans for a new Underground line – 'Route C' – across central London since 1948 at least, but London Transport (another nationalised monopoly) had only been granted the funds to build the main Walthamstow-Victoria section by a reluctant Government in 1962.

As for the BR Board itself, it had been refused funds for several major projects in the 1980s alone. One of these would indeed have provided cross-London tunnels of the type suggested by Redwood, connecting lines coming into Paddington and/or the Euston-St Pancras-King's Cross group with the Southern Region from Victoria or Waterloo[10], while others that also fell by the wayside included an extension of electrification to much of the network[11] and the completion of the project for the tilting Advanced Passenger Train.

The same conference also considered the financial prospects for a privatised railway. Transport analyst Richard Hannah believed that the City would make funds available 'providing first that a system of grants was formalised so that shareholders would know what support railways were going to obtain from the Government'.

That, of course, was the crux. Whatever privatisation might achieve, no one expected that the result would be a truly commercial railway.

We can only speculate whether it was Channon's apparent dislike for the track authority option that helped to encourage Mrs Thatcher to detach him from Transport, but she appointed Cecil Parkinson to replace him in the Cabinet reshuffle of 24 July 1989, and Channon did not serve in government again. (The generally accepted reason for Channon's dismissal is an indiscretion in connection with the investigation of the terrorist bombing that had caused the air crash at Lockerbie.)

Meanwhile, the BR Board had started to discuss the implications of privatisation with merchant bankers Lazard Brothers and management consultants Coopers & Lybrand (now PwC).

When the 1989 Conservative Party conference was held in October it had became the responsibility of Paul Channon's successor Cecil Parkinson to bring the party – and the nation – up to date about rail privatisation. Channon had already insisted that it was a long-term project, which Parkinson confirmed:

'As Paul Channon said last year, privatisation may be the best way forward. He set work in hand to find out whether and how best it could be done. And that work is making good progress, but those decisions are for the future.'[12]

It was hardly a ringing endorsement, but then privatising the railways had rarely charmed Margaret Thatcher, who was still Prime Minister at the time. She was known to dislike the industry and the people who ran it and, according to one colleague, she 'thought the railways were so bloody awful she wouldn't wish them on the private sector'[13], while Parkinson had allegedly resisted her wish to leave railway privatisation out of his speech altogether, pointing out that such an omission would have appeared to signal a policy u-turn.[14]

It was not the end of the matter. Parkinson remained relatively bullish about reforming the railways, and on 16 October, during an interview for the BBC programme *Panorama*, he set out his personal stall rather more plainly:

'The more essential the industry, the more essential it is that it doesn't stay in the public sector... I don't think public sector industries are, in the end, run for the benefit of the customer.'

Gourvish has speculated[15] that Parkinson's favourite was the track authority option, to judge by remarks made by his wife in March 1989, but when Parkinson gave his interview in October of the same year, he was non-committal:

'I suppose if you did break [British Rail] up into separate companies you'd get competition by emulation ... smaller units, more accountable. For instance, InterCity has responded very well to becoming a separate business within British Rail.'

In the same programme, it was claimed editorially that the current favourite was the sale of each BR sector as a vertically integrated unit, a stance confirmed by economist and transport consultant David Starkie (who had predicted in 1984 that privatisation would be inevitable 'sooner or later'). At this remove it is impossible to know if he or *Panorama* might have been right at the time.

Even so, the Government's transport emphasis remained on roads rather than railways. On 14 November 1989 Cecil Parkinson spoke of forthcoming transport investment, which he said would total more than £13bn over the following three years. Roads were to get £7.7bn, British Rail £3.7bn and London Transport £1.7bn. In the following March Margaret Thatcher promised 'we're not going to do away with the great car economy' during an environmental awards ceremony.

By this time she had other problems, which may be one reason for the lack of progress with railway privatisation during her last year as leader. The heady days following the 1987 election had gone, and this time there was no 'Falklands factor' available to rescue her. She faced her first leadership challenge in December 1989 (from backbencher Sir Anthony Meyer) and would be out of 10 Downing Street less than a year after that.

Her successor was John Major, who inherited the office of Prime Minister on 28 November 1990. One of his first actions was a Cabinet reshuffle that included the appointment of Malcolm Rifkind as Transport Secretary.

Rifkind revealed at least some of the Government's evolving railway policy on 28 May 1991, when he addressed a transport conference:

'I must declare myself, enthusiastically and unequivocally, as desiring to see far more traffic, both passengers and freight, travelling by the railways. This would help to relieve both road congestion and take advantage of the capacity which exists on the railways.'[16]

As a start, he added, there would be new 'green grants' to encourage companies to use railfreight services. However, he maintained that what the railways really needed was a competitive element, and that meant an end to British Rail's monopoly:

'We intend to allow anyone who wishes to provide rail services for freight or for passengers, and who can meet the necessary standards for safety and competence, to be able to do so. They will no longer require British Rail's permission or be obliged to use their staff or rolling stock. Monopolies are no more acceptable on the railways than elsewhere.'

The end of a nationalised British Rail as such lay further ahead, he explained, but eventually it would be sold to the private sector as well.

This was the clearest indicator of the Government's intentions so far, and went much further than Cecil Parkinson had done – but there had also been a recent change of Prime Minister.

Had Mrs Thatcher maintained the confidence of her party in 1990 and remained in office the timetable for railway privatisation would probably have been different, and it might not have happened at all before Labour won power in 1997.

John Major waited until March 1992 before calling the next General Election, which he was to fight as leader of the Conservatives for the first time, and this time the party's manifesto confirmed which way the privatisation wind was blowing:

'We believe that the best way to produce profound and lasting improvements on the railways is to end BR's state monopoly. We want to restore the pride and local commitment that died with nationalisation. We want to give the private sector the opportunity to operate existing rail services and introduce new ones, for both passengers and freight. A significant number of companies have already said that they want to introduce new railway services as soon as the monopoly is ended. We will give them that chance. Our plans for the railways are designed to bring better services for all passengers as rapidly as possible. We believe that franchising provides the best way of achieving that. Long term, as performance improves and services become more commercially attractive as a result of bringing in private sector disciplines, it will make sense to consider whether some services can be sold outright.'

The election on 11 April resulted in a workable Conservative majority of 21, and the new Government soon moved ahead with its railway industry reforms.

Serpell had tried to demonstrate that a commercial passenger railway was not possible. It remained to be seen if private sector disciplines could make any difference.

Chapter 21

'Radical changes'

The decision to privatise the railways had taken a long time, but the actual task needed to be completed as quickly as possible after 1992. There was no assurance that the Conservatives would retain power in the following General Election – indeed, as time went on there was increasing reason to believe that they would not – while an incoming Labour Government might well leap on a railway privatisation 'in progress' and attempt to halt it in its tracks, so to speak.

As the proposals became clearer, more critics emerged from the undergrowth – some of them in surprising corners of the forest.

Richard (Lord) Marsh had served as a Labour Minister of Transport in 1968 and 1969, and left Parliament to chair the British Railways Board in 1971, a post he held for five years.

He announced in 1978 that he had become a supporter of Margaret Thatcher and intended to vote Conservative at the next General Election. After she had become Prime Minister in 1979 he was rewarded for his support in 1981 with a life peerage and the title of Baron Marsh of Mannington, sitting in the House of Lords as a Crossbench peer.

This mixed political heritage tended to make him unpredictable, but he was in no doubt about the broad merits of privatisation when he was interviewed in July 1991:

'In general, I am totally in favour of privatising anything which it is sensible to privatise – all the evidence shows that there are major problems with industries which are state-owned. In relation to the railway, I think that's a very different problem, and I cannot myself see a sensible argument for privatising it or a sensible way of doing it.'

Marsh also warned that the problem of investment would not go away:

'The capital requirements for modernising the railway are vast. If you take an example, Mrs Thatcher has recently said that the Channel Tunnel railway, the cost of that, should be met by private companies. That I think is a perfectly sensible way of approaching it. It can only be done because the Channel Tunnel railway will be basically a businessman's railway, paid [for] by companies. That is not true of British Rail. You will, whatever you do, come back to a situation where the public and the politicians will rightly demand that this major chunk of the nation's transport system conforms to some sort of central policy, whatever that policy may be. I cannot see the purpose of the exercise, other than possibly taking the issue of privatisation to nearly the same level of dogma that we got with the arguments for nationalisation.'[1]

At the same time Kenneth Irvine also reappeared on behalf of the Adam Smith Institute, where support for railway privatisation had not wavered. He believed that the problem of capital could be met by private investors:

'I think we've already seen – was it with the Channel Tunnel? – that the City is willing to undertake long-term horizons and take long-term investments, rather than take the short-term easy option, because they see it as being important to the long-term economic future of this country.'[1]

Marsh's successor at the Board, Sir Peter Parker, was relatively philosophical about the prospect of privatisation, saying: 'I suspect that a patchy political compromise will be the outcome.'[2]

As we now know, later events were to prove Sir Peter right. The current BR Chairman, Sir Bob Reid, could hardly launch an all-out war on the Board's owner, but he also sounded his own note of caution:

'Every time you say let's break it up, let's privatise it, you have to be clear what the objective is. If the objective is, well, let's have fun and see what we can do, that's one objective, it wouldn't be mine. Mine would be, let's find a better way of looking after the customer and running a highly competitive railway.'[3]

Meanwhile, arguments about 'dogma' were to be pursued relentlessly by both sides in the debate, with each accusing the other of following a path of blind ideology rather than considering economic and social factors.

We know that one of the main reasons, if not the initial inspiration, for privatisations since 1979 had been the Conservatives' desire to reduce the power of the unions (see Chapter 20), and the future shape of industrial relations was still a sensitive aspect of the proposals to reform the railways.

Jimmy Knapp, the General Secretary of the National Union of Railwaymen, was asked whether a break-up of British Rail would prevent national strikes in future. He answered:

'You could ballot all the companies at the same time and pull them all out at the same time, so the whole thing's a nonsense. If that's the only yardstick they're going to use to determine the standard of service that the British public deserve, then I think they'll get the thumbs down for that as well.'[3]

It is worth recording, perhaps, that there has never been coordinated industrial action in the privatisation era involving all the employees of National Rail operators simultaneously, although a lengthy pay dispute came close to causing a nationwide walkout of many Network Rail staff in the spring of 2015, which could have been almost as disruptive.

The first detailed vision of rail privatisation eventually evolved by John Major's Government (and, of course, the Treasury) was set out in a White Paper published in July 1992, entitled *New Opportunities for the Railways*.

The proposals included what could only be interpreted as distinctly lukewarm praise of existing BR management:

'Regular users know that the performance of the railways is not good enough. BR's staff and management work hard to improve services. But they are limited by the structure of the industry in the public sector. The industry is more insulated from the demands of the market than its private sector airline, coach and road haulage competitors. It therefore has fewer incentives to improve its performance and less freedom to respond to what the customer wants. Radical changes are needed.'[4]

This White Paper pointed out that investment in the railways had 'greatly increased', and was now 'more than 50% higher in real terms than in 1980'. This was true, but these calculations had started from a low base.

The railways had been expected to tighten their belt after the 1979 election, and a paper for the Cabinet from the Chief Secretary to the Treasury dated 9 July that year had set out rail investment cuts totalling £104m between 1980 and 1984.

This paper had noted blandly: 'Reductions ... have been made because officials do not consider that adequate financial progress has been made to justify investment at the level proposed.' This was in spite of the fact that the Board had, as the paper went on to admit, 'emphasised the serious consequences for the renewal of existing assets of maintaining the present investment ceiling'.[5]

In other words, although railway investment was now increasing (the White Paper quoted £1,005m for 1991) it had been critically low for many years, with major proposals such as widespread extensions of electrification and cross-London tunnels (see Chapter 21) being dismissed out of hand.

The White Paper explained that privatising British Rail as a single entity or as 'geographical units' was not practicable, because in both cases the resulting businesses would need continuing financial support. Neither could the Sectors be sold as individual enterprises, because again some of them would not be commercial.

The answer, it said, was an end to vertical integration and the creation of a new track authority, which the White Paper dubbed Railtrack.

Railtrack was intended to be self-standing from the beginning, apart from the possibility of capital grants for schemes which 'although not earning an adequate financial return, provide a satisfactory cost-benefit return when wider benefits are taken into account'.

Apart from this, revenue grants would be 'targeted directly to the provision of services' – in other words, they would be payable to at least some of the new operators, although the Government 'would hope to receive payments from franchisees for the right to operate profitable InterCity services…'. The outright sale of InterCity routes was considered, but the White Paper conceded that 'it is not clear that the business as a whole could improve its performance sufficiently to allow sale in this Parliament'.

Indeed so. When the franchised operators took over only one small component of InterCity (Gatwick Express) turned out not to require subsidy, in the early years at least. This outcome was so at odds with British Rail's claim that this Sector had become profitable in the 1980s that one can only wonder whether InterCity had, in fact, been paying its full share of system overheads or, alternatively, whether the passenger franchise model was really as cost-effective as its promoters were claiming.

The requirements that new passenger operators would need to meet (the description 'franchise' was a little strange, but it has more or less stuck until the present day) would become much greater if they had been obliged to find the capital to pay for their rolling stock, and although the White Paper said there would be 'no standard duration' for contracts, franchise lengths seemed certain to be shorter than the life of most rolling stock (which can easily be 30 years or more). Therefore, the White Paper said, operators would be able to lease their rolling stock from private sector leasing companies.

The interesting point here was what would happen to BR's passenger fleet, which included some recently built rolling stock as well as a large number of comparative veterans. There was no real answer provided at this stage, except a very general statement that existing rolling stock would be available for operators to rent. Unless BR was to continue its existence as a single monolith rolling stock leasing company (which would have surely raised questions about whether imposing such a monopoly supplier on the passenger operators was fair), this implied that BR's trains would also need to be sold outright to the private sector, but to banks and finance houses rather than operators, which is in fact what happened.

Railtrack itself was to begin life as a BR department, but once train operations had been privatised it would become independent as well. (This plan changed later: in the event Railtrack was launched on 1 April 1994 as a separate organisation, although still in the public sector.)

The eventual flotation of Railtrack was also indicated with the words: 'In the longer term, the Government would like to see the private sector owning as much as possible of the railway. Powers will therefore be taken to allow the future privatisation of all BR track and operations.'

Railfreight and Parcels would be sold outright. For them, it would be sink or swim.

The fate of stations was a little vague, although the White Paper conceded that 'in some cases it may be appropriate for franchisees to take responsibility for stations for the period of their franchise', which is what happened to nearly all of them. However, it continued: 'The Government is prepared to consider other disposal arrangements...'

This open-ended proposition proved to be the entrance to one of railway privatisation's truly blind alleys – at least at the time of writing. Railtrack would be given theoretically temporary custody of the largest stations – those that were believed to have the brightest commercial prospects through such revenue sources as rents from station traders – but a later plan to create 'Independent Station Operators' by selling off these sites never came to fruition.

Other key players in this brave new world were to be a Regulator and a Franchising Authority. Bearing in mind what has happened since then, particularly after the ending of the Strategic Rail Authority (which was not part of the original vision) in 2006 and the resulting domination of railway matters by the Department for Transport, we may note the hopeful aspiration in the White Paper that there would 'less scope and justification for Government involvement in managerial issues'.

One flag of hope was raised as far as future open access operators were concerned:

'The Government wishes to encourage the greatest possible development of commercial rail services. It will therefore establish a framework and procedures through which companies wishing to provide new railway services, who can meet the necessary operational and safety standards, will have a right of access to the railway network.'

As we shall see later on, the phrase 'right of access' would not, in practice, mean quite what it said.

Before major legislation could be enacted, a 'paving' Bill was needed first, which would authorise the British Railways Board to prepare for privatisation by transferring its functions to other bodies when required to do so.[6]

This Bill's rather leisurely progress (it was introduced on 7 May 1992 but did not become law until 19 January 1993) meant that the following main Railways Bill was also delayed, being introduced in the Commons on 21 January.

The Second Reading took place in the Commons during the afternoon and evening of 2 February.

It was a long debate: the resulting Hansard report runs to more than 52,000 words. Transport Secretary John MacGregor, presenting the motion, told the House:

'Those who work in BR and the system have been constrained by the nationalised industry form of organisation, which has now been found wanting for all the other industries that we have privatised. The railways and their customers will benefit as much as other industries from a change in the culture and the system under which they have to operate. We therefore aim to create a new regime for the railways. Our objective is to improve services for passengers and freight customers, while maintaining high safety standards and other necessary safeguards, including a commitment to the provision of subsidy to maintain loss-making but socially necessary passenger services.'

Although the Bill had yet to become law, Mr MacGregor revealed that the British Railways Board was already being instructed to start creating train operating units (as they would become known), which would form the basis of future franchises:

'I wish to announce the first groups of services which I am asking British Rail to reorganise and prepare for transfer to private sector operators under our franchising proposals ... My right hon. Friends the Secretaries of State for Scotland and for Wales have been consulted throughout. The groups of services will be: the InterCity east coast main line; the InterCity Great Western main line to south Wales and the south-west; ScotRail; the London, Tilbury and Southend line; the south-west division of Network SouthEast; the Victoria-Gatwick express; and the Isle of Wight line.'

The imminence of this debate had been met by Labour's publication of its own 'Ten point plan' for the railways that morning, in which it called for the creation of a new railways commission. Mr MacGregor was scathing:

'Only two points said anything new... The two points were a new independent railways commission with wide-ranging powers to oversee British Rail – who is talking about bureaucracy? – and powers for British Rail, still wholly in the public sector, to borrow from private funds free of all Treasury constraints, just as the French railways do. What is the consequence in France? It is a total debt of £14bn, compared to British Rail's £2bn; an annual interest payment of £1.3bn... No wonder the Opposition do not like to hear this. That annual interest payment of £1.3bn – a colossal burden on French taxpayers and rail users – compares with British Rail's £80m. The result is that 20% of SNCF's annual costs are debt interest payments, compared with British Rail's 1.5%. If that is Labour Members' prescription for British taxpayers and rail users, I tell them to beware – it would be a total disaster.'

In spite of Mr MacGregor's condemnation of a railway funded on the never-never, Railtrack would be able to borrow on the open market. Although the resulting debts were officially those of a public limited company and therefore not backed by the Treasury, this situation turned out to be more or less illusory when Stephen Byers placed the company in Railway Administration in 2001.

(The collapse of Railtrack would recall the situation that had arisen in 1962, when it had become clear that the reconstituted British Railways Board would not be able to service the debt that had been the result of issuing more than £1.4bn-worth of British Transport Stock since 1948, most of which paid a guaranteed 3%. On that occasion the Treasury had been obliged to come to the rescue too.)

The access charges to be paid by train operating companies for use of the network would be determined by the Rail Regulator (it was provisionally announced during this debate that the first person in this post would be John Swift QC), but although the broad intention was that Railtrack's revenues would be sufficient to allow it to function profitably, Mr MacGregor also confirmed that some operators would be supported:

'Railtrack will operate on commercial lines, making an appropriate rate of return, which the Government will fix nearer the time that Railtrack goes live. But franchisees will have to pay only the track charges that they can afford. The proposals for charges for freight operators are specifically designed to maintain flexibility to protect marginal operators while charging more to those who can afford it.'[7]

The reference to 'charges that they can afford' was a little misleading, at least in the light of later events, because it almost seemed to suggest that franchised operators would be means-tested. In fact, track access charges would be calculated on a more or less standard scale (they did vary according to the type of rolling stock used), but part of this liability would be met by agreed subsidies where non-commercial passenger services were involved. These subsidies would come from the Franchising Director and be made to the operators, who would then pay Railtrack in full.

Such an arrangement was the birth of a railway 'money-go-round' that would become more complex as privatisation matured and Railtrack gave way to Network Rail, as we shall see.

John Prescott, speaking for the Opposition, was deeply critical:

'Never has a Bill changed so many times. Never has a Bill been so universally condemned. Never has a Bill lost its essential justification – that private competition and privatisation would provide the means by which to change the service. All that the Secretary of State seemed to claim was that there will be a change in the culture. That was his essential point. He is to replace public management with private management, and there will be fundamental changes. Of course there will – one of them will be the pay increases for the bosses at the top who will be running the system.'[8]

There proved to be more doubters as the Bill progressed through both Houses of Parliament. In April 1993, the Commons Transport Committee gave its own, if rather cautious, approval:

'In no country with a rail system of comparable size and density of use is there an example, either in operation or even under consideration, of a complete scheme such as that contained in the Railways Bill? This does not of itself mean that it cannot succeed. To take that argument to its logical conclusion would mean that no innovation ever took place. What it does mean, however, is that because of the lack of previous experience to draw upon, the risk that something could go badly wrong is that much higher. To put it another way, the system of railway operation proposed by the Government probably can work, but, in the words of one witness, it may need to be made to work.'9

Speaking in the Lords on 1 July, Lord Carmichael described the new structure as:

'A unique venture, separating the trains from the tracks on which they run and requiring that both the providers of the infrastructure and the operators of the train services … operate commercially. Nowhere else in the world, nor in the entire history of the railways of this country, have these things been done.'10

The noble Lords were also concerned that some bidders might succeed in obtaining a franchise but later on cease trading without notice, leaving some lines without a service. On 5 July Lord Tordoff explained that he was particularly doubtful about the prospect of bus companies winning rail franchises:

'The truth is that a number of people who are likely to bid for the franchises may be of no great substance. I have heard reference to certain bus companies wishing to take up franchises. If he were to consider their balance sheets, I hope that the franchising director would feel that they were not necessarily people worthy to obtain a franchise. However, it is possible that people will slip through the net. Assuming that they do, the chances are that there will be bankruptcies.'11

(It might be worth recording here that the only 'bus company' to withdraw from a franchise because of financial difficulties has been National Express, which did not become insolvent as a Group but did decide that its InterCity East Coast franchise could not continue after 2009.)

The Railways Act received Royal Assent on 5 November 1993. Section 25 ruled out certain types of organisations as bidders for passenger franchises, such as Ministers of the Crown, central government departments and local authorities.

As the result of a Lords' amendment on 5 July it did not specifically exclude British Rail from bidding, although it did give the Franchising Director authority to do so (after consultation) if, for example, it was felt that such an exclusion would promote competition or encourage new entrants to the passenger railway industry.

This was a very broad brush power, and the Franchising Director would go on to wield this particular brush with such vigour that in practice BR was never permitted to compete. The pros and cons of allowing the public sector to bid for franchises are still the subject of a lively debate today.

The pace of reform now increased. British Rail continued its preparations for the forthcoming break-up (BR Chairman Sir Bob Reid II had described the effort required as 'formidable'[12]), while Railtrack had already come into notional existence as a BR division in April 1993, in preparation for its full launch a year later.

One unlooked-for side effect was that the preparations for privatisation were now tending to preoccupy white-collar managers. Train drivers, station staff and depot fitters continued to sign on as usual, but staff in managerial grades spent considerable amounts of time attending briefings and considering their future. Many of those who helped to run the infrastructure were planning to move to Railtrack, but as most of its trackside functions were to be delegated to private contractors its workforce would be relatively small – in the region of 12,000 – compared with the modern Network Rail total of some 35,000.

Those who intended to stay on the 'operational' side were hoping for a transfer to one of the new franchises, but as none of the passenger contracts had yet been offered – much less awarded – their future was far from clear.

Others, again, began to investigate what they might receive if they chose to take early retirement. As a result, in many cases the industry was to lose the benefit of their experience at a time of critical transition, when it could have been particularly valuable.

In all, the level of managerial distraction seems to have been considerable. One insider commented to the author during this time: 'This railway is being run at the moment by Supervisor grades and below.'

Meanwhile, Government mounted a campaign to inform the industry and the wider public what it intended to do with the railways.

The Department of Transport published a detailed explanation in March 1994, entitled 'Britain's Railways: A New Era'. The forthcoming structure was seen to consist of essentially three types of organisation, making it a relatively complicated privatisation.

Those in the first category would be wholly in the private sector, such as freight operators, infrastructure maintenance contractors and rolling stock leasing companies. Later on, open access passenger operators would also be in this class.

Passenger franchises (25 in all) would form a second category. Although owned by the private sector, these operators would hold contracts with Government to run specified passenger services, taking much of the commercial risk in order to do so. But these contracts would not be indefinite – in the event, most would be awarded for terms between seven and 15 years.

The last category had only one member – Railtrack – which was to inherit the track maintenance and train regulating functions of British Rail together with 16,528 route kilometres of railway, 2,482 stations and a myriad of equipment and structures that included around 90,000 bridges and almost 1,000 tunnels. This new organisation would remain in the public sector for the time being, but the Government was determined to sell it as soon as reasonably practicable and certainly before the next General Election, which could not be later than 1997.

It was a short and demanding timetable, planned and executed in haste – and destined to be repented at leisure.

Chapter 22

'The Government's resolve'

The start of the privatisation of the core railway is an elusive date to pin down. It could be argued to have been the publication of the White Paper in 1992, the passing of the Railways Act in late 1993 or the start of the first passenger franchises in February 1996.

Until this last date, apart from the complete 'hivings-off' of such activities as hotels, ships, Travellers' Fare station catering and British Rail Engineering, private sector participation in the railway had been confined to a few routes and services, such as the Foster Yeoman stone trains from Somerset.

A new enterprise called Charterail was formed in 1990 to lease 'piggy-back' wagons from Tiphook and diesel locomotives from BR, using them to provide a road-rail service between Pedigree Petfoods in Melton Mowbray and London, Manchester and Glasgow. This venture, in which BR had a 22% stake, had gained ministerial support and was launched by Transport Minister Roger Freeman in July 1990.

Its operations were then expanded with a further service connecting Cricklewood Yard in north London with Warrington and Scotland in June 1992, supported by 13 companies, including Safeway and Heinz.

Transport ministers, busily developing their vision of a privatised railway and about to publish their White Paper, were enthusiastic about such a partnership.

At the launch of the Cricklewood service, Transport Secretary John MacGregor said:

'The equivalent of 10,000 lorry movements a year will be removed from motorways and trunk roads between London and Glasgow. But that is only a start. Charterail plans to extend its service to Aberdeen in the autumn, and then much further afield, and of course into Europe. These plans will be instrumental in removing even more lorries from the roads. This is obviously very good news.'[1]

However, difficulties with the locomotives and allegations that BR was charging too much for the use of its locomotives and crews were followed by financial problems. Charterail ceased trading at the end of August 1992, still owing the BRB £1m. It was not a promising demonstration of the potential for private enterprise investment in the railway, and it was also a damaging straw in the wind for railfreight in general, whoever the operator might be.

Rail Freight Group director Julia Clarke was quoted as saying, 'The confidence in railfreight is already so fragile … I don't know how people can go back to the likes of Safeway and Heinz and say, "Why don't you use rail?"', while Charterail Managing

Director Robin Gisby warned that its closure could 'only be unhelpful to developing the railfreight business in the UK'.[1]

Ministers refused to be publicly discouraged. Transport Minister Roger Freeman said on 28 August that the 'unfortunate history of Charterail ... in no way shakes the Government's resolve to press ahead with British Rail privatisation'.[2]

In spite of this official determination, the Charterail episode left some awkward questions unanswered. How could private sector rail operators shield themselves against protectionist tariffs? Who would control track charges?

The problem was summed up in these terms on 10 September by *Commercial Motor* (whose road haulier readers had no reason to welcome an expansion of railfreight):

'Some of the factors which contributed to Charterail's problems remain and do not bode well for the development of railfreight... Despite repeated calls from organisations such as the Rail Freight Group and Transport Development Group for money to alleviate the high cost of the track, the Government looks unlikely to move. This means that despite the benefits of privatising BR's railfreight businesses and liberalising operations ... rail looks set to remain more expensive than road.'

In October, Roger Freeman told the House of Commons:

'I regret the demise of Charterail, but that had more to do with the recession and the company's optimistic plans than the charging regime, which is currently not in place but is operated ad hoc by British Rail. I do not believe that we can fault British Rail for Charterail's demise.'[3]

In spite of the Charterail debacle, a further step in the direction of liberalisation had been taken by Stagecoach (still, at this stage, only a bus operator) when it proposed entering the passenger rail business by providing overnight 'seated' services between London King's Cross and Aberdeen to exploit BR's withdrawal from this market. (Anglo-Scottish sleeper services still ran from King's Cross at this time, although they have long since been transferred to Euston.)

The service was launched on the night of 11 May 1992. It consisted of six vehicles branded Stagecoach, attached to BR's intercity trains. This experiment lasted for just five months, once again putting the economics of private sector train services into doubt.

By the spring of 1994, with the Railways Act safely on the statute book, the Government was continuing to ignore these ominous signs. Railtrack was detached from BR and became a separate organisation – although still in the public sector – on the ominous date of 1 April. The three BR passenger businesses ceased to exist at the same time, and their routes were divided between 25 new 'train operating units' – five of which became 'shadow franchises' in April alongside Gatwick Express, which had already become the first 'shadow' in October 1993. The territories of the new units, which became known within the industry as TOUs, were based on existing 'profit centres' within the previous passenger businesses.

A campaign to inform staff about the purpose of Railtrack had already been started. One widely distributed folder, entitled 'Railtrack: an introduction to the new structure', included a message from Railtrack Chairman Robert Horton:

'An efficient and economically sustainable transport network is vital to Britain's well-being and to our quality of life. We must make the best possible use of the rail network and every opportunity to improve its efficiency must be grasped. In the years to come Railtrack will be the hub of that network and the importance of thorough preparation now is enormous.'

Railtrack was to be divided into ten zones, ranging from the single zone covering the whole of Scotland to smaller areas such as South (Kent and Sussex), South West (essentially the western half of BR's former Southern Region) and Great Western, which included the lower half of Wales as well as the West Country and the South West peninsula.

The months that led up to April 1994 were evidently hectic ones for the new organisation. The Director of Railtrack Great Western, Martin Reynolds, told his staff: 'We are working, rather out of sight just yet but nonetheless extremely hard, all too aware that 1 April 1994 is approaching fast, and then we *must* be ready to take over.'[4]

While the employees of the embryonic Railtrack were preparing to occupy their new zones, British Railways Board administrators were also busily converting the first of the new train operating units into shadow franchises, as well as preparing for the outright sale of other activities such as freight, parcels and the infrastructure maintenance units as well as a rather amorphous grouping that had been given the collective title of 'central services'. These included BR Telecommunications, the train catering division OBS Services, BR Projects, BR Occupational Health, and Quality and Safety Services.

Rolling stock was transferred to three new BR companies known as ROSCos, which were expected to become rolling stock leasing companies in the private sector by the end of 1995, while three new freight companies – Loadhaul, Mainline Freight and Transrail Freight – took over Trainload Freight's existing contracts on 1 April 1994.

In May Red Star Parcels was offered for a second time (an initial attempt in 1993 had failed, so some restructuring was carried out). Freightliner was put on the market at the same time, but this would also prove to need some restructuring before it could eventually be sold.

The assets of the Charter Train Unit were also sold in May, while Railfreight Distribution began operating through the new Channel Tunnel in June.

This period was accompanied by many compromises so far as publicity intended for passengers was concerned. The old British Rail businesses were fading away, but their immediate successors – the TOUs – were only interim organisations themselves, and there was little point in devising elaborate new logos or corporate identities that were unlikely to be to the taste of the incoming franchisees. In spite of this one or two novelties did emerge briefly, such as a 'sunburst' design for InterCity East Coast, the shape of which vaguely recalled the long-gone symbol of the LNER.

This transformation was not the same as the previous changeover at nationalisation on 1 January 1948, when the companies had given way to the new Railway Executive at midnight precisely. This time the transition was gradual, and each newly liberalised train operating unit took its own decisions, relatively untouched by the headquarters organisation. The double-arrow logo disappeared from timetable booklets, but elements of the old sector branding tended to survive for a while.

Sometimes full privatisation seemed to have taken place already. The introduction to the Chiltern Lines Summer 1994 timetable booklet (the franchise would not begin until July 1996) read:

'As a new passenger train business we inherit a line in which passengers and staff alike can feel justifiably proud … our goal is to improve all aspects of the service we offer our customers … this is only the start of our programme to reshape our services to be more closely attuned to the travel needs of the communities and individuals we exist to serve.'

The unwary passenger (or customer) might have been excused for assuming from this that a new franchise had already started. However, the warier reader (with good eyesight) might have also noted the very small print on the back cover that admitted that the timetable was published by 'Chiltern Lines T.O.U.' – even though no explanation was offered for this mysterious abbreviation.

British Rail was still publishing a hefty national timetable book, but the organisation's title appeared on the cover for the last time on the Winter 1993 issue; from May 1994 it became the 'Great Britain Passenger Timetable', although here the double-arrow was allowed to continue.

(Responsibility for the full timetable itself was inherited by Railtrack, then Network Rail, but the officially printed version succumbed to a combination of lack of demand, increasing operational complexity and internet competition in 2007.)

One minor question arose over the future of the 'InterCity' logo, which had been derived from a typeface known as 'Novarese' since the 1980s. This logo, which was thought to have a better reputation than the core 'British Rail', might have survived as a subsidiary brand for the new intercity franchisees. In preparation for this it was registered as a trademark, but the precaution proved to be unnecessary; in practice the logo soon disappeared from trains and publicity once private enterprise had taken control.

The transfer of British Rail's train operating units to the private sector was the task of OPRAF – the new Office of Passenger Rail Franchising – and by the second half of 1995 it was preparing to let the first of 25 contracts.

This process was to continue until all BR passenger services had been taken over by private sector companies. But who would these companies be? Fortunately for the promoters of rail privatisation, the break-up of the National Bus Company almost a decade earlier proved to be a useful if unlikely factor, because privatising the bus industry had encouraged the formation of several large passenger road transport groups that were comparatively well placed to move into rail.

The reforms of the bus industry, whose keystone was the 1986 Buses Act, had essentially followed the Conservative strategy set out by Nicholas Ridley in the late 1970s. He had suggested that one preparatory step towards the privatisation of an industry could be to break up large organisations into smaller ones – essentially, bite-sized chunks that would be easier for future owners to swallow. This did not apply in every case, such as the sale of British Airways, but the bus industry was a natural candidate.

Accordingly, the regional operators owned by the National Bus Company had been divided into smaller units before being offered to the market. The result, at first, had been the emergence of several local NBC operators in regions where just one or two companies had existed before.

These local companies were then sold – in other words, genuinely privatised – unaffected by the constraints of franchise contracts or an Office of Bus Regulation (which did not exist). Neither was there any equivalent of a track authority.

Many of the original bus operators had been bought out between the wars, and the result was that by 1939 most of them had come to be owned partly by the large BET or Tilling combines and partly by the main-line railways. Although railway interests were no longer involved in the 1980s, it was probably inevitable that history would repeat itself and that the new generation of smaller bus companies would start to merge once again, particularly because the more successful members of the industry began a process of deliberate acquisitions – again following the precedents of BET and Tilling.

By the mid-1990s this process had produced some major operators – Stagecoach, based in Perth; Cowie (soon to become Arriva), which had originated in the North East as a car-leasing company; FirstBus, another Scottish enterprise that was the result of a merger in 1995, and National Express, the privatised descendant of the National Bus Company's long-distance coach division.

Another group of potential rail bidders was newly created for the purpose. These included Prism Rail (privatisation supporter Kenneth Irvine was one of its founders) and others that were often set up to bid for one particular franchise.

Companies of this type would include M40 Trains (a successful bid by BR managers at Chiltern, supported by 3i and John Laing), Great North Eastern Railway (a subsidiary of Sea Containers, which won InterCity East Coast), and another management buyout known as Enterprise Rail, of which more in a moment.

The first franchises were awarded in late 1995, with the pioneering signatures being placed by Stagecoach Holdings on the South West Trains franchise on 19 December. The pens were needed again the following day, when the Great Western franchise was signed by Great Western Holdings – a management and employee buyout supported by 3i and FirstBus.

The third franchise to be signed was LTS – London, Tilbury & Southend – which had frequently been put forward in the past as a natural candidate for early privatisation because of the self-contained nature of its route. The successful bid had been made by existing BR managers, who had obtained the backing of 3i and Gresham Trust and were trading as Enterprise Rail.

The formal signing of the first three franchises, which were all due to take over on 4 February 1996, was duly celebrated. On 20 December 1995 the Transport Secretary Sir George Young told the House of Commons:

'All three franchises are committing themselves to significant improvements in services and have imaginative plans for developing their businesses. I look forward to the first franchised services operating in the new year and to passengers experiencing for themselves the benefits which privatisation will bring to the railway.'[5]

In spite of this, a spoke was about to be placed in the Government's wheel.

The London Travelcard had been introduced in stages during the second half of the 1980s (originally it was known as the Capitalcard), and it was valid on nearly all London Transport and British Rail services in Greater London.

Travelcards could be bought at stations managed by either undertaking, but the precise share of the resulting revenue depended on where the ticket had been bought.

British Rail auditors visited LTS early in 1996, shortly before the scheduled handover from BR to Enterprise Rail. They were curious about sales of season tickets, because the number issued at Fenchurch Street had gone up sharply for no obvious reason, while those at Upminster had fallen.

Their inquiries soon uncovered that many of the tickets being sold at Upminster – managed by London Transport and served by the Underground as well as LTS – had been printed at Fenchurch Street, which was managed by LTS and where there is no Underground connection. The net effect of this adjustment was to reduce London Transport's share, and it was later suggested (although never confirmed officially) that as much as £7,000 a week could have been diverted to LTS in this way.

We do not know what would have happened had the discovery been kept behind closed doors, but the auditors' findings were soon leaked to the *Evening Standard*. This meant that the Government had to be seen to take action, especially as it was about to confirm a major contract with the apparently guilty party.

It was pointed out that this alleged fraud had been carried out by British Rail staff and not private enterprise (the franchise had not yet started), but even so the consequences were dramatic.

The Commercial Director of LTS (who had been a member of the buyout) resigned almost immediately, although there was nothing to suggest that he had been personally involved.

A tense period followed, at the end of which Sir George Young halted the privatisation of LTS – reportedly just nine hours before the scheduled handover.[6]

Other managers (again they were not necessarily directly accused, but nonetheless there was talk of 'lax financial management') were either transferred to other parts of BR or suspended.

The scandal was a potentially major blow to the Government's plans for rail privatisation. It also raised doubts about the fairness of allowing BR managers to bid at all, considering their superior knowledge of the finances of a train operating unit.

Sir George Young rallied, as ministers must, and on 5 February he told the House of Commons:

'The board immediately instituted an investigation, which is still continuing. The Rail Regulator is also carrying out an investigation under his powers under section 55 of the Railways Act 1993. In the circumstances, the franchising director decided that the transfer of LTS to Enterprise Rail should be postponed pending the outcome of the investigations. For the time being, LTS Rail will therefore continue to provide services as a subsidiary of the British Rail Board. The House will understand that, as there remains a possibility of legal action, it would be inappropriate to comment on the specific allegations…'[7]

As this amounted to little more than a 'holding answer', it predictably failed to damp down the flames of political controversy. Labour MP Clare Short, representing Birmingham Ladywood, was quick to pour more fuel on the fire:

'May I ask the Secretary of State to understand how serious this matter is, and that deliberate fraud in the public services – franchised or not – is a terribly serious matter for the country? Will he give us an undertaking that the offer to the LTS management team to allow it to run that service will be withdrawn, because it has shown itself to be a corrupt management team – [Hon Members: "Withdraw."] – if the allegations are true. Will he agree to reopen the tendering process and now allow British Rail to bid for this and other franchises? Can the Secretary of State tell us whether a criminal investigation is taking place, and, if not, why not? Will he confirm that the fraud was discovered because the British Rail auditors held an inquiry and that, a few days later, they would not have had the authority to do so? In the future, how will he ensure that such fraud does not take place in companies that have been franchised?'[8]

Sir George, in turn, was quick to divert the responsibility for making uncomfortable decisions in another direction:

'Depending on the outcome of the investigations, it may not be necessary to re-tender, but it is too early to say. In relation to the police, it makes sense for British Rail to complete its internal investigations. However, British Rail has assured me that it will not hesitate to call in the British Transport Police if that seems appropriate in the light of the investigations. As for British Rail making a bid, again that is a matter primarily for the franchising director.'[9]

After further consideration the award to Enterprise was cancelled, although no one seems to have been prosecuted – possibly because there was no evident motive of personal gain. Fresh bids were invited (although still not from the British Railways Board), and this time the winner was Prism, which therefore gained LTS as its first franchise.

We may surmise that those responsible for the 'irregularities' at Fenchurch Street and Upminster had not been intending to boost BR's revenue as such, but rather to establish a new pattern and thus unobtrusively lay the foundations for a process that would have benefited Enterprise in the longer term. Since Travelcard revenue is pooled, it is impossible to say how much Enterprise would really have gained – various sources have since presented varying estimates – but nevertheless the franchising process had to be restarted.

The Government had been justifying its privatisation programme by praising the opportunities presented by the private sector – its superior management, its greater focus on its customers and its willingness to invest and innovate.

The LTS episode served to demonstrate that unleashed private enterprise could have a less attractive side as well.

Chapter 23

'An imprudent hurry'

As a possible portent of things to come, South West Trains gained the unforseen privilege of running the inaugural franchised train service because of railway engineering work in South Wales. The result was that the first franchised train, an eight-car electric multiple unit, left Twickenham at 05.10 on 4 February 1996, bound for London Waterloo.

South West Trains and Great Western had both taken control of their networks at 02.00 as scheduled, although there must have been a thoughtful silence that morning at the LTS London terminus of Fenchurch Street, where British Rail would stay in charge for a little longer.

The first privatised passenger train run by a franchisee should have been the unadvertised 01.50 Great Western service from Fishguard Harbour, which, had it departed on time, would have moved seamlessly into the new era somewhere near the site of the former Jordanston Halt.

The Independent, however, reported with ill-disguised glee that the 'train' was actually a late-running rail replacement road service, and that the hour of handover had struck just as the incoming bus was approaching its terminus at the harbour to pick up a small group of ferry passengers and journalists.[1]

The unpunctual 01.50 was not unlike the rail privatisation programme itself (originally, it had been hoped that the first franchises would have been awarded in 1994), and time was not on the Government's side.

After 4 February another 23 passenger franchises remained to be awarded, and privatisation would only be completed when Railtrack moved into the private sector as well.

But since publishing its White Paper in July 1992, the Government had been forced to modify its plans. Some of these modifications were legal (the Railways Bill was repeatedly amended during its passage) while others were the results of some prudent rethinking.

The White Paper had made much of the 'right of access' that could be exploited in future by would-be operators, but further consideration had led to the conclusion that too much competition would endanger the business of the franchised companies and therefore their financial relationship with the state.

Many franchises – such as those in the retailing sector – generally rest on a commitment from the franchisor to spread out its outlets, so that each has a reasonable geographical area in which to trade. This means, for example, that someone who invests in a high street franchise to sell ABC fried chicken can be assured that another branch of ABC will not be opened next door, or across the road.

In railway terms, this implies that a linear monopoly is all but essential along the franchisee's routes, otherwise 'open access' operators (that is to say, operators who do not possess a franchise) may start price wars, as well as occupying train paths that the franchisee needs.

The realisation that unhampered open access would make a nonsense of the passenger franchise system came quite quickly. To quote a later commentary, 'The requirement for competition was essentially a non-starter and open access was quietly dropped by the Regulator in 1993.'[2]

Thus one of the main arguments in favour of privatising the railways had been lost before a single franchised operator had moved so much as a wheel.

In fact, the commentary quoted above exaggerates slightly. Open access was not entirely 'dropped' (it could not be abandoned or even restricted to freight without an amendment to the 1993 Railways Act, and such a change would also have been at odds with European rail policy), but it had certainly ceased to be a core component of privatisation before the Act was even passed, and instead would be subject to 'moderation of competition'.

As a result, the 1992 White Paper notwithstanding, open access operators were not welcome to sprint down the main lines in pursuit of franchised services, at least not if their perceived purpose was primarily 'abstraction of revenue'. Policy u-turns of this kind only confirmed that some of the hasty privatisation proposals set out in 1992 were quite unworkable in practice.

It was also not the first time that the pot of gold labelled 'competitive profits' at the end of the railway rainbow had dazzled the Treasury – such yearnings had previously been set out in the White Paper preceding the 1953 Railways Act, which had included the more or less fatuous suggestion that a 'healthy rivalry' could be developed between the BR Regions (see Chapter 9).

In ordinary business life, 'abstraction of revenue' is normal, legal and to be expected. A new supermarket opens and others in the town lose some of their customers to it; this is essentially 'abstraction of revenue', but it is one of the pieces on the board in the game of private enterprise.

The railway franchises, however, would now be protected from unrestrained competition, at least at first. In July 1993, during the passage of the Railways Bill, the Earl of Caithness told his fellow Lords:

'While we have accepted that some moderation of competition will be necessary to get franchising under way, our aim ultimately is to create a competitive market for railway services, with operators competing for custom and bidding for train paths. Only through this process will the railway be turned around so that the focus is on providing the services rail customers really want.'[3]

As far as open access is concerned the situation has not changed significantly since, although franchising has now been 'under way' for two decades.

In spite of moderation of competition, the open access issue did not lie down or go away. Indeed, in the early years of the following century, the ambitions of one such operator would lead to a legal battle in the High Court (see Chapter 28).

Meanwhile, the priority for OPRAF in 1996 was to let more passenger franchises as quickly as possible.

The awkward member of the squad, LTS, was re-awarded (to Prism Rail) on 9 May and started on 26 May. By then Connex South Central, Gatwick Express, GNER and Midland Mainline had also begun (all on 28 April).

There was then a perceptible pause; the next franchise, Chiltern Railways, did not begin until 21 July, and another gap followed until Cardiff Railway, Connex South Eastern, Island Line, South Wales & West and Thames Trains all started on 13 October.

The rest would wait until 1997: Anglia Railways, CrossCountry, Great Eastern and West Anglia Great Northern all began on 5 January, to be followed by Merseyrail Electrics on the 19th of the same month. This left a rump of seven. Central Trains, North Western, Regional Railways North East, Silverlink and Thameslink started on 2 March, with West Coast Trains following a week later.

ScotRail came at the tail of the queue on 31 March – having been delayed, it was said, by detailed negotiations with Strathclyde Passenger Transport Executive.

In all, 25 passenger franchises had been launched over a period of just under 14 months, and with the start of ScotRail the British Railways Board ceased to be an operator of passenger services.

Contract lengths varied considerably. The longest, with 15 years and three months, was Virgin's CrossCountry franchise, while at the other end of the scale the little vertically integrated Island Line would be run (and maintained) by Stagecoach for an initial period of just five years. The most common length was seven years, or slightly more, while both Great Western and Midland Mainline were to run for ten. Apart from CrossCountry, the other 15-year contracts went to Connex South Eastern, Gatwick Express, Prisms' LTS and West Coast Trains – which had also been won by Virgin.

The longer franchises all included commitments to introduce new rolling stock, while only Gatwick Express would pay premiums from the start of its contract, although several others were expected to move into profit later on.

Meanwhile, privatisation of the railway infrastructure had also been achieved over the same period. Railtrack, originally to be a division of the British Railways Board, had started life as a separate organisation on 1 April 1994, but on 24 November of that year the Transport Secretary, Dr Brian Mawhinney, told the Commons that the company was to be floated 'within the lifetime of this Parliament'. He continued:

'The Government believe that privatisation offers the best future for Railtrack, for passengers and freight and for train operators. It will allow greater use of private sector skills in managing the network, improving Railtrack stations, delivering efficient track maintenance and encouraging investment in the upgrading of railway lines.'[4]

Labour members greeted this proposition with hostility and doubt. Michael Meacher, representing Oldham West, responded:

'Is not it clear that this privatisation is now being hurriedly brought forward because there is little or no investor interest in the franchises, for the very good reasons that the train operators' profitability will always depend on political decisions about the level of subsidy and that their major fixed costs – rail access charges – will remain outside their control?'[5]

Just under a year later, in October 1995, the next Transport Secretary, Sir George Young, confirmed to the Conservative Party conference that Railtrack would be offered to the market in the spring of 1996.

What was the Government selling? Figures published by Railtrack stated that in September 1995 the company's net book value was £4,349m, and its net assets after indebtedness were worth £1,601m.

However, it is not the capital position of a company alone that attracts investors – it is also its revenue prospects. Here, Michael Meacher had made a pertinent point. Although some of Railtrack's customers would be genuinely private sector companies, most of its revenue would come from the track access charges paid by franchised passenger operators. In 1994-95, passenger track access charges accounted for 86% of Railtrack's turnover.

The revenue of franchised operators, in turn, would depend crucially on how much financial support the passenger railway was granted. In short, although the money was filtered via the operators, a privatised Railtrack would be the ultimate recipient of Government subsidy.

It could be argued that increasing numbers of franchised operators would operate in the black in due course, because their subsidies were due to fall during the years ahead until they became premiums.

This, however, ignored all the lessons of history, which taught that passenger railways rarely make a profit – in any part of the world – unless there is some unusual external factor.

To bring the story almost up to date for a moment, recent figures from the Department for Transport show that the English franchised train operators paid a total of £1.68bn to the DfT in 2012-13, which appears to be a gain for the taxpayer until the effect of revenue support (paid by the DfT to eight of the 15 operators) and the Direct Grant received by Network Rail (which has the effect of reducing track access charges) is taken into account. The final figure is an annual subsidy of £2.23bn for the passenger rail industry in England, or an average of 4.2p for every passenger kilometre travelled.

It was also in late 1995 that Railtrack published its first Network Management Statement, which set out plans to invest 'in excess of one billion pounds' annually over the following decade. More than half of this expenditure would be on renewals, rather than 'day-to-day' maintenance.

But this plan was at odds with figures that had been produced by CDG – a BR civil engineering consultancy. CDG was commissioned by Railtrack in March 1995 to assess the costs of returning the railway infrastructure to a 'stable state', and it calculated that strengthening tunnels, bridges and sea defences alone would cost £11bn over the next decade. This total was not to Railtrack's taste, and a second study carried out by another consultancy produced a more acceptable estimate of £1.39bn, which went on to be quoted in the prospectus for flotation.

The Times quoted a Railtrack spokesman as saying:

'The BR report was not felt to be a realistic estimate and was on the old public sector principle of asking the Treasury for far more than you are actually going to get. You have to remember that BR's annual spend on this kind of work was only about £150m. When [the CDG report] was presented to us it turned out to be based on very little actual evidence.'[6]

Whether £150m had been sufficient is another matter, but the fact that a reduction on BR's infrastructure spending was now being accepted, apparently to serve the purposes of the prospectus as much as anything else, can only raise doubts in retrospect about the adequacy of Railtrack's longer-term budget for maintaining its system.

The Network Management Statement also explained an elaborate plan to modernise the West Coast Main Line. Features of the scheme included Automatic Train Protection and in-cab signalling, on new 225km/h tilting trains. It was an ambitious and technologically courageous proposal. Within six years its failure would help to bring Railtrack down.

In the meantime, however, the prospectus was published. It included a determined attempt by Labour to head off the whole idea, which had originally been presented by Clare Short in the form of a speech. This had to be brought to the attention of potential investors to comply with Stock Exchange rules, and it included a warning about what would happen after a Labour Government came to power:

'Matters of public policy are properly the concern of an elected government, and the relationship between the Secretary of State and the Regulator will be adjusted to reflect that fact. Once that has happened, the new Labour government will have at its disposal substantial instruments for achieving its policy objectives for Railtrack. These include the direction of Railtrack's investment spending, controls on its access charges, restrictions on disposals of its valuable land assets and the clawback of substantially all of its property disposal income. The powers will also be used to make

Railtrack far more responsive to its dependent users including in matters of safety. They will be used to review – and if necessary alter – the economic arrangements which impose financial penalties on Railtrack for delays and cancellations, and in other areas. These are things which are at the heart of Railtrack's business. They may change substantially.'

This might have deterred some investors, but there is no evidence that it did so.

On 28 April, just three weeks or so before the launch, *The Observer* told its readers: 'Once it is in the private sector, watch out for Railtrack's property development plans.' The article predicted that 'retail outlets and office blocks could proliferate at 14 major stations…'

Meanwhile, the Government had no scruples about using taxpayers' funds to sweeten the offer. The prospectus included an undertaking that some £69m in dividends would be paid in the first year, by using the profits that had been made when the company was still in public ownership. The document added: 'This and the other incentives make the first year yield on the partly paid shares close to 20%.'

Certainly the shares found ready takers when they were offered. On 20 May *The Times* reported:

'Investors who applied for more than 300 shares in Railtrack will see their allocations scaled down by up to 75 per cent, the Government said yesterday. Last night City dealers were forecasting an instant 20p profit for investors on each partly paid 190p share when trading starts this morning … private investors have applied for almost twice as many shares as are being sold to them. The demand has delighted ministers and City advisers to the sale, which has been dogged by political controversy and public suspicion.'

So, accompanied by mixed cries of delight and suspicion, the privatisation of the railway industry moved towards its conclusion.

Apart from the unfortunate false start at LTS, there were relatively few problems at first, although the pioneering franchise SWT – South West Trains – did blot its copybook about a year after it had taken control by reducing the number of its drivers to an incautiously low level as part of a 'Driver Restructuring Initiative'.

Having offered redundancy packages, SWT then discovered that it now had too few drivers who were 'route-cleared' for some lines. Cancellations started to occur in February 1997 and continued into March, and OPRAF decided during that month that SWT was risking a breach of its franchise agreement. Accordingly, a draft enforcement order was prepared and SWT was told to display a copy at all its stations. Unless SWT ran 98.5% of its scheduled services in April, the enforcement order would become substantive and be accompanied by a £1m fine. Further failures could be followed by termination of the franchise.

SWT avoided this fate by taking urgent action, and the number of cancellations fell dramatically as a result.

It was, however, a critical time for Stagecoach and its future prospects in rail. The Group's chief executive at the time, Brian Souter (now Sir Brian), told a railway industry conference many years later that the episode had 'scared us skinny'[7]. The problems had arisen because inexperienced rail franchise owner Stagecoach had been attempting to run SWT like a bus company, where the rules and restrictions (particularly in relation to drivers and the routes they are allowed to work) are rather different.

By the spring of 1997, on the eve of the next General Election, privatisation of the national railway network had reached its peak. Within a few years, the high tide of private ownership would start to ebb. Some passenger operators would be returned rather erratically to the public sector from time to time, while the collapse of Railtrack would not prevent a near-disastrous attempt to involve the private sector in London Underground in the first few years of the new century, which later had to be reversed.

But, as Stephen Glaister later described the early years of railway privatisation: 'Although dauntingly complex, imperfectly articulated and implemented in an imprudent hurry it worked reasonably well for a period of some years.'[8]

However, fresh trials for the newly restructured industry lay just around the corner, because some of the principles that underlaid the privatisation matrix would soon be called into question.

Chapter 24

'Collective nervous breakdown'

Since the early days of railways, the large number of individual companies had posed a potential threat to safety – not because there was more than one operator, but because the various companies developed different and sometimes inconsistent ways of working.

These variations became critical where one company's territory met another, or where running powers were exercised over the lines of 'foreign' companies.

One of the tasks of the Railway Clearing House had been to encourage uniformity and standardisation, together with its primary function of keeping the industry's accounts. One accident involving a triple collision caused by the differing bell codes used by signalmen in adjacent boxes has already been mentioned (see Chapter 20), while it was not until the 1890s that the Board of Trade managed to persuade the companies to arrange the layouts of semaphore signal arms at junctions and other potentially confusing places in a consistent way.[1]

The merging of more than 120 companies into just four in 1923 should have made standardisation easier to arrange, but even after that date the Great Western Railway's semaphore signals continued to drop by 45 degrees to indicate permission to proceed, while the signal arms of the other three companies rose by the same angle.

This particular difference – known as lower and upper quadrant – has persisted into modern times, because the Western Region of British Railways continued to insist on lower-quadrant signals, in accordance with time-honoured practice. It even went so far in some cases as to replace upper-quadrant signals with its own versions when the WR took over the management of a route from another Region.

This variation seems likely to survive until semaphores themselves disappear, and does not in practice cause any great harm. Both indications – whether upper or lower – are quite clear and cannot be mistaken for anything else, while 'stop' is universally indicated by a level arm that is neither up nor down.

Apart from semaphore signals, many of the other differences between the former companies were slowly ironed out during the decades of nationalisation, and in any case by no means all these differences had safety implications.

But the fragmentation that resulted from privatisation brought about a new and potentially serious threat to safety, which does not seem to have been anticipated.

The break up of the 'vertically integrated' railway into infrastructure and train operators, together with the employment of hundreds of outside contractors, would soon become a fruitful source of misunderstandings and breakdowns in communication, partly because of the large number of individual parties that were once again involved.

There was also another factor, which was new. This was the commercial relationship between the infrastructure owner – Railtrack – and the train operating companies.

The train operators paid track access charges. If infrastructure failures such as a signalling fault caused delays, Railtrack was now liable to pay compensation to the operators affected. (They, in turn, were supposed to pass on at least some of this to their passengers on the delayed trains.)

This structure worked both ways. If a train failed, blocking a line, the operator was liable and Railtrack would now be entitled to compensation – unless it could be established that the problem on the train had been caused by an infrastructure fault.

This system, known as 'delay attribution', soon involved hundreds of people around the industry, whose sole job was to analyse the causes of each incident and negotiate on behalf of their employers.

The need to avoid delays was impressed on all concerned, because time now literally cost money (quite apart from the fact that statistics of 'performance' could be used to penalise defaulters, as South West Trains was one of the first to discover in 1997. Such statistics, later dubbed the Public Performance Measure, or PPM, also became an increasingly political hot potato as the years went by).

Inevitably, awareness of the penalties associated with the delay attribution system had an effect on the way that the railway was controlled.

The traditional method of regulation had been to give higher classes of train priority over lower ones. (These classes are not to be confused with accommodation for passengers but indicate the type of train, for the information of the staff.)

Letter codes were used until 1962, but from then on all passenger trains were in Class 1 (broadly, the expresses) or Class 2 (the rest). Freight trains started at Class 3 (perishable) and went down to Class 9. (Some of these classes were changed again in 2013, so that the freight categories are now based on the maximum speed rather than the type of cargo.)[2]

In January 1995, with the new 'commercial railway' bedding in, the traditional rule that higher classes of train should be given priority was revised, although not without some controversy.

The result was a change to the track access conditions, approved by the Rail Regulator and known as Condition H11. This said, in brief, that the objective of train regulation was 'to be the striking of a fair and reasonable balance between minimising overall delay … maintaining connections, avoiding undue discrimination, protecting the commercial interests of Railtrack and each affected train operator, and the interests of safety and security.'

Tom Winsor, who would become Rail Regulator himself, was acting as the legal adviser to the Regulator John Swift at that time. Later he was to say: 'I believe that that consideration [of commercial interests] is potentially dangerous to the interests of safety and security. It was put in … against my advice.'

By the time he said this, his words had a new significance that might not have been so readily understood before 19 September 1997. For the reason why, we must visit Swansea on that date, where a Great Western High Speed Train was about to depart for London Paddington.

The passengers on board might not have been willing to stay in their seats had they known that of the two train protection systems installed in the leading cab, one (British Rail's Automatic Warning System, or AWS) was faulty, while the other (the newer and more comprehensive Automatic Train Protection, or ATP) was turned off because the driver was not fully trained to use it.

(ATP takes control if a driver attempts to pass a red signal. AWS sounds warnings but only intervenes if a driver fails to acknowledge an adverse signal. Both systems have been essentially superseded for the time being by TPWS – the newer Train Protection and Warning System – which, like ATP, monitors train speeds and applies the brakes if necessary. TPWS, in turn, will eventually give way to the European Train Control System – ETCS – which includes train control and also features in-cab signalling.)

Without AWS or ATP, control of the train from Swansea to Paddington was wholly in the driver's hands – if he made an error, nothing could intervene to save his train.

Passengers at some intermediate stations later reported that the driver had his feet on the control desk in the cab, but apart from this all seems to have gone well until Reading had been passed (he had been accompanied by a Railtrack employee checking signal positions between Swindon and Reading, but from there he was on his own).

Past Slough, and therefore well into the London suburbs, the driver encountered a signal showing two yellows, then another showing a single yellow, but in defiance of the Rule Book he did not reduce speed. For reasons that have never been made clear, he did not realise that he was in trouble until Southall, where he saw a red signal about 1,200m ahead.

He then made a full brake application from 200km/h and retreated into the body of the leading power car, because he could now see that the signal was protecting a freight train crossing the main line.

Seven people were killed and more than 100 hurt in the collision that followed. The driver faced a manslaughter charge, which was later dropped, but the operator Great Western Trains was fined £1.5m under health and safety law.

A key question raised in the eventual inquiry under the chairmanship of Professor John Uff (which was delayed for some two years by the protracted criminal proceedings) was whether a Class 6 freight train should have been allowed to cross the main line in the path of a Class 1 express.

Before Condition H11 had been introduced, long-standing railway practice would have given the Class 1 HST 'right of way', and the freight train would have been held clear of the main line until it had passed.

Was privatisation to blame? The priorities for train regulation had tended to change from the 1970s onwards because automatic route setting systems were becoming more common, while freight trains now had better brakes. The automatic systems were designed to reduce 'overall delay' but also to 'weight' the decisions in favour of higher classes of train, so the old principles were not abandoned completely.

It was not until Condition H11 had arrived in the privatisation era that 'commercial interests' also became a factor, and listed, possibly significantly, ahead of 'safety and security'.

By the time the Southall inquiry was held in late 1999, Tom Winsor, part of whose evidence has already been quoted, had become the Regulator. He said:

'Signallers are obliged … to comply with safety obligations first. Therefore they have an essential and overriding objective of running a safe railway. Insofar as … the commercial interests of the companies conflict with safety, then, in my opinion the safety considerations should always be paramount. If there are arrangements in the industry which prejudice those, then they are arrangements that I would like to change.'[3]

If time was now so valuable (rather than merely important), then had the new delay attribution rules influenced Great Western's decision to allow the train to stay in service, or the way it was regulated?

It would appear not. The reasons that emerged at the inquiry were a complex dog's dinner of ambiguous notes and unorthodox lines of communication, laced with a generous helping of misunderstandings – for example, a member of staff in a control room received a call before the accident that could have changed the course of events, but failed to take appropriate action because she had only been in the job for a few weeks and did not fully understand the railway terminology.

When Great Western Trains was later prosecuted and fined, Mr Justice Scott Baker criticised the lack of a working train protection system, but said: 'It has not been suggested that the accident in this case was the result of a deliberate risk taken in pursuit of profit.'

But even if privatisation was not directly to blame, the fragmentation that had accompanied it was still a factor, to judge by this recommendation in the official inquiry report:

'10. Railtrack must ensure that Rules and Group Standards applicable to operators, including drivers, are clear and unambiguous. In particular, Railtrack should urgently complete the review of operating Rules to ensure they are workable in the privatised, fragmented industry.'[4]

And what of Condition H11? The inquiry had established that the signaller who had given priority to the freight train was not to blame. Professor Uff commented:

'I do not believe that, in the circumstances, the decision made by Signaller Forde had any safety implications, given that the crossing had to be achieved at some point in the face of regular HST and other passenger services on both main lines. Nor did it involve any consideration of the overall commercial effect. In my view, the regulating policy as applied by Signaller Forde cannot be said to have caused or contributed to the accident.'

But he also recommended:

'38. There should be a review of Condition H11 of the Access Conditions which should make clear that no regulating decision is to be made on the basis of protecting commercial interests. Safety and security must be paramount considerations.'

So privatisation came out of the dock after Southall not quite without a stain on its character, but not really the guilty party, either. As with many previous accidents, including some during the nationalisation era, Southall proved to have been caused by a fatal combination of errors and lack of communication rather than an overriding commercial interest.

But the picture was darkening, even so. The Southall inquiry was still under way when another accident occurred on the same main line.

This time two passenger trains were involved, in a near head-on collision. Many more people were killed than at Southall, and although again privatisation was not the primary cause, various parts of the privatised railway industry – particularly Railtrack – would stand indicted of poor management practices.

For the first time, the nation became aware that signals had numbers, and that the number of the beast was SN109.

The crash – on 5 October 1999 at Ladbroke Grove Junction – occurred because a newly qualified Thames Trains driver had failed to obey the red aspect being displayed by SN109, and collided with an approaching up Great Western HST.

The inquiry, chaired by Lord Cullen, discovered that there were contributory factors, including the fact that SN109 had a poor history, having been the site of eight incidents of a signal being passed at danger (known as SPADs) in the previous six years.

A signal sighting committee was supposed to deal with such problems, but it had not met since Railtrack had taken over from British Rail in April 1994. Although auditors from Railtrack Assurance and Safety had warned of this in March 1999, still nothing had been done by September. Lord Cullen said this amounted to 'a serious and persistent failure … due to a combination of incompetent management and inadequate procedures'. In addition, there had been a 'lamentable failure on the part of Railtrack' to respond to the recommendations of inquiries into two previous serious incidents on the Paddington approaches.

The track layout was also highlighted because it lacked 'flank protection', essentially a crossover that could have guided a train overrunning SN109 safely on to another track.

Meanwhile, Thames Trains had not been training its drivers consistently or well. The report said:

'Driver standards managers conducted their classes as each of them thought best. Training material was not validated. There were gaps in the training. I conclude that the safety culture in regard to training was slack and less than adequate; and that there were significant failures in communication…'[5]

Signallers at Slough IECC – the signalling centre – were also criticised, having reacted only slowly to the fact that the Thames Trains service was overrunning SN109. Lord Cullen concluded:

'The evidence of the signaller and other members of the staff at the IECC indicated that there was a serious under-rating of the risks involved in SPADs, a failure to realise the importance of immediate and direct communication with the driver where that was possible, and a dangerously complacent attitude to SPADs as being simply a matter of driver error. The root cause of these deficiencies – which should have been picked up by senior management – lay in the running of the IECC.'

The public consequences of Ladbroke Grove, in which 31 people were killed, were more widespread than Southall had been. At Southall, the failure of an operator to ensure that a train protection system was working had been compounded – indeed, fatally reinforced – by driver error. In the case of Ladbroke Grove, several departments of the industry were found to have been wanting over a long period of time.

Cullen's remorseless beam had even highlighted Her Majesty's Railway Inspectorate, which had now found a home within the Health & Safety Executive:

'An internal inquiry within the HSE after … Ladbroke Grove questioned whether the approval process for the first phase of the resignalling had been operated with sufficient urgency, but it was asserted on behalf of HMRI that they had been overwhelmed with work. In such circumstances they should, in my view, have pressed for increased resources. As regards the activities of HMRI in general, it was candidly accepted by the Director-General … that they could have done more. I make my observations on the reasons which were given for this deficiency, which were a lack of resources, a lack of vigour in pursuing issues, and the placing of too much trust in duty holders.'

The Southall accident inquiry started to hear evidence in September, having been delayed for two years by outstanding criminal proceedings. This inquiry was still in progress when the Ladbroke Grove collision occurred on 5 October, resulting in a new and understandable wave of public concern about railway safety.

The view taken by the *Evening Standard* was typical:

'Successive governments for many years have shirked investment in our public transport infrastructure, and this generation of British travellers is paying a wretched, and now also tragic, price.'[6]

As Railtrack would concede in May 2000: 'Confidence in the rail industry was shaken and every aspect of safety was called into question.'

At the same time, the company announced a major programme of improvements, covering all the sensitive areas:

'Railtrack is committed to ensuring that lessons learned are rapidly translated into action. Work has already started to accelerate the installation of the £330m Train Protection Warning System to fit it throughout Railtrack infrastructure by the end of 2002. A National Safety Task Force has been established to facilitate and co-ordinate safety matters across the industry. A Confidential Safety Reporting System is being rolled out nationally, best practice is being disseminated throughout the industry on prevention and mitigation of SPADs. Actions have been taken at the 224 signals most often passed at danger and all complex layouts have been risk assessed.'[7]

As a shopping list this read well, although by now Railtrack was in deep water so far as its modernisation of the West Coast Main Line was concerned (of which more in Chapter 26).

The Ladbroke Grove report had yet to be published when the Government, still very concerned about railway safety, decided to remove one of Railtrack's responsibilities. Accordingly, on 22 February 2000 it announced: 'Prescott takes safety regulation away from Railtrack':

'The responsibility for deciding whether train companies are safe to operate is to be stripped from Railtrack and given to the Health and Safety Executive, following Deputy Prime Minister John Prescott's decision to accept the recommendations of a high-powered rail safety review. Mr Prescott told the House of Commons today that the review had confirmed fears of a potential conflict of interest within Railtrack's Safety and Standards Directorate.'[8]

Apart from a fundamental change to safety assessment, another long-term result of this decision was the creation of the modern Rail Safety & Standards Board, which is funded by the industry but functions on its own account.

This was a major reform, which removed one of the flaws in the original vision for privatisation.

October 2000 marked the publication of the first 'periodic review' by the Rail Regulator, which set out Railtrack's budget for the next five years. Tom Winsor had been in post for 15 months, and at first sight his assessment of the success of railway privatisation was bleak:

'The railway industry, and Railtrack with it, was privatised in a hurry, with inadequate attention paid to the fitness for purpose of the regulatory and contractual matrix which is essential for the proper functioning of a separated industry which must continue to operate in so many respects in a co-operative and integrated fashion. Railtrack was privatised in 1996 with a weak financial structure which gave it little or no incentive to invest. That was a poor birthright for an industry which needed to promise and deliver so much, so soon.'[9]

However, Mr Winsor could also see many gleams of hope:

'The railway is not in decline. It is growing at a pace and to an extent neither seen nor foreseen in modern times. It is a time of considerable opportunity.'

The essential point, as he saw it, was to make sure that Railtrack was in a position to invest in this growing industry, and that was why he was introducing a new framework:

'It creates a virtuous circle of effective incentive-based regulation, strong and empowered management, clear contracts and sound accountability.'

Railtrack had to carry out its side of the bargain as well. There would be new restraints on asset disposal and a firm requirement to compile a reliable register of all its assets. He concluded:

'The shortcomings of the current regime are swept away, replaced by a sound framework for investment and the finance to carry out a rail renaissance whose momentum must increase strongly and quickly. Thus endowed, Railtrack has no more excuses.'

Some of the key figures included increases in annual revenue, including grants but not track access charges, from £826m in 2001-02 to £1,004m in 2005-06. Railtrack's total revenue for the next five years, including track access income, was set at £13.4bn (Network Rail's revenue for 2014-19 is £38.4bn at 2014 values).

Winsor's statement was dated 19 October 2000, which was in some ways unfortunate, because just two days earlier an intercity train operated by GNER had been passing through Hatfield at high speed when a rail disintegrated beneath it, into what was later reported to be 300 pieces. Four people died in the catastrophic derailment that followed. The following day, Railtrack Chief Executive Gerald Corbett offered to resign (although in the event he did not depart straight away).

The Hatfield accident was followed by a time of unprecedented crisis. The cause was found to be 'rolling contact fatigue', a progressive deterioration of the railhead, and no one – including Railtrack – could say whether the rest of the network was safe.

Wholesale emergency speed restrictions were immediately imposed on many lines, causing much more disruption than any single accident could.

It emerged later that the rail had been known to be in need of renewal – indeed, its replacement had been lying alongside the track since April – but the necessary engineering possession had not been arranged because, yet again, there had been protracted and repeated breakdowns of communication between Railtrack and its contractor Balfour Beatty.

The fragmentation imposed by privatisation, and particularly the arms-length character of Railtrack's dealings with its principal contractors, could no longer be ignored.

Sir Alastair Morton, who had been chairing the newly constituted Shadow Strategic Rail Authority since it had been set up the previous year and had been critical of both Railtrack and the Rail Regulator, famously dubbed the post-Hatfield period a 'collective nervous breakdown'.

But the origins of this breakdown could arguably be traced back to Southall – and certainly Ladbroke Grove, where Lord Cullen's uncompromising criticisms of the industry could not be dismissed.

Drivers and signallers were not being trained properly, many Railtrack managers appeared to be spending far too much of their time explaining why things had not been done (such as the convening of signal sighting committees), and even the long-revered Railway Inspectorate had been caught out.

Hatfield undoubtedly marked a new level of crisis. But the worst was yet to come.

(**Note:** In April 2004 Thames Trains was fined £2m after it had admitted two health and safety offences in connection with the Ladbroke Grove collision. The judge said he accepted it was 'not a case of putting profits before safety' but that Thames, which should have been aware of the risk, had made 'serious omissions' in its training courses for drivers. In March 2007 Network Rail was fined £4m in connection with the crash, as the legal successor to Railtrack. Following the Hatfield derailment, Balfour Beatty pleaded guilty to health and safety offences in July 2005. It was originally fined £10m, but this was reduced on appeal to £7.5m. Railtrack's successor Network Rail denied health and safety charges, but was found guilty and fined £3.5m.)

Chapter 25

'The fragmented railway'

The years on each side of the turn of the last century were notable for several developing strands, all of which would prove to have significant consequences for the railway and its relationships with Government and the nation.

The aftermath of Hatfield was one potent and malign influence. As the derailment had come so soon after the Ladbroke Grove collision, public confidence in the railway fell, and this situation was almost certainly worsened by the disruption associated with the emergency speed restrictions that followed the accident. One result was that the growth in passenger numbers, seen every year since 1995, virtually levelled off for a while.

Labour had been in power since 1997, but in spite of its warnings before the election – such as the remarks by Clare Short that had figured in the Railtrack prospectus – the Government led by Tony Blair had not made any changes to the structure of the privatised railway during its first two years in office, leaving both the Office of Passenger Rail Franchising and the Rail Regulator to get on with their jobs in accordance with the 1993 Act.

However, the new Government had revealed some of its thinking in a White Paper, *A New deal for Transport: Better for everyone*, published in July 1998. It included an introduction by John Prescott, whose cabinet responsibilities included transport, and explained that behind the scenes, the wheels had been turning:

'We have not put everything on hold until this White Paper. We are already working to extend the range of transport choices across the country and are investing more in public transport to improve its quantity and quality. We have secured new and imaginative ways of funding to modernise our transport system. We are giving high priority to maintaining and managing the nation's transport infrastructure.'

By 1999 some changes were on the way. The first practical development was the creation of the Strategic Rail Authority, which was to replace OPRAF but still work alongside a separate Rail Regulator, whose role was broadly preserved.

Railtrack, meanwhile, was in trouble over its blue-chip project to modernise the West Coast Main Line. A new intercity franchise had been launched on the route by Virgin in 1997, based on a business plan that included 225km/h tilting trains. The trains (although late) would start to arrive in 2002, but would the West Coast line be ready for them?

New trains were now on order for the third rail network south of London but they would prove to be hungrier for power than the slam-door stock they were to replace, and the inadequately predicted but essential upgrading of the traction current supply equipment would go on to cost at least £800m (on 11 April 2004 Strategic Rail Authority Chairman Richard Bowker told an industry conference that 'The new trains programme on the Southern Region is a fine example of chaos in retreat').

By the time 2004 arrived, both Railtrack and the Rail Regulator had faced some fundamental changes, which culminated in a full-scale Rail Review.

To return to the start of this period, the embryonic Strategic Rail Authority had come into existence in July 1999. As it could not take executive action until the law had been changed, the new organisation existed initially in shadow form as the 'sSRA' (or Shadow Strategic Rail Authority), while under the umbrella it provided both OPRAF and the British Railways Board continued to exercise their statutory powers. (In spite of the extensive changes brought about by privatisation, the BRB had continued to exist because of various statutory and contractual obligations, such as those relating to international services.)

Sir Alastair Morton was appointed to chair the sSRA and the BRB. In his introduction to the first sSRA annual report, he implied that railway renationalisation was no longer on the agenda (if, indeed, it had ever truly been there):

'We shall emphasise service, to be delivered by private sector operators and suppliers, to provide what the consumers and the areas served show they want, through consultation and through the farebox. The SRA will not be an operations driven, command-and-control authority managing the rail system.'[1]

The cynical reader could have been excused for wondering whether this outpouring of jargon had been caused by the likelihood that the SRA would really do very little, apart from taking over the franchise responsibilities of OPRAF and, apparently, providing an industry talking shop. (Within a couple of years, the SRA would stand accused of having 'no strategy and not a great deal of authority'.[2])

The changes needed to give the SRA legal standing were contained in a Transport Bill, which received its Second Reading on 20 December 1999. This was a portmanteau measure, which not only affected the structure of the railways but also included changes to aviation law as well as new provisions concerning buses, local transport plans, road charging and workplace parking levies.

The main responsibilities of the Strategic Rail Authority were to 'promote the use' and 'secure the development' of the railway and, tellingly, 'to contribute to the development of an integrated system of transport of passengers and goods'.[3]

These provisions, which had originally been published a few months earlier as a separate but now-abandoned Railways Bill, included powers to transfer the British Railways Board's rights, liabilities and remaining property (which included disused railways) to the Secretary of State, and for the eventual dissolution of the Board itself, while the post of franchising director was to be abolished, with all its responsibilities and functions transferred to the SRA.

The use of the word 'integrated' signalled the formal return of an old friend that had not been seen nationally since Labour's last major transport measure but one, the ill-fated Transport Act of 1947. This Act, it will be recalled, included various statutory shackles that had so hampered the British Transport Commission that it was unable to make the kind of progress that had been hoped, although the BTC had admittedly made the situation even worse by then wasting many of the opportunities it was offered by the Government-funded 1955 Modernisation Plan.

Would this sad saga be replayed by the SRA some half a century later?

There were some important differences between the two bodies. The BTC had been required to 'provide, or secure or promote the provision' of a 'properly integrated system of public inland transport'[4], while the SRA's duty was merely to 'contribute to the development' of an integrated transport system (a duty that was now also shared by the Rail Regulator).[5]

Making a 'contribution' to integrated transport was a considerably less demanding requirement than being responsible for providing it. Indeed, the SRA lacked the power to operate any transport service at all, except as 'operator of last resort' should a passenger rail franchise fail.

There was one common factor between the two Acts: neither attempted to define what 'integrated' meant so far as transport services were concerned, although Prescott's 1998 White Paper had devoted a chapter to integrated transport that showed such commendable examples as bicycles being loaded on to trains.

The task of integration had previously defeated the British Transport Commission, and the SRA and the Rail Regulator now faced a much tougher job if they were to make any real contribution.

The most important alternative public transport mode to rail is the bus, but since 1986 all bus services outside London had been deregulated, so that bus operators were bound by little more than a commitment to run the services they advertised and to notify the regional Traffic Commissioners of any significant changes to their timetables, giving at least 42 days' notice.

However, they were permitted to vary the times of departures by up to five minutes in either direction without giving any notice at all, even to their passengers, while fares were (and are) entirely a matter for them. (The notice period for bus timetable changes was extended to 56 days in 2004, and the five-minute timetable easement has been abolished.)

The task of integrating two forms of transport, one of which was regulated by statute and also generally bound by standard twice-yearly timetables, with another whose timetables could be changed every few weeks, was all but impossible unless the connecting bus services were so frequent that their timetables became irrelevant.

Nonetheless there were some genuinely useful initiatives, such as a rail-road link from Redruth station to Helston. This was branded the 'Helston Branch Line' and had started running in 1999. But the DfT-funded Cornwall Centre for Excellence summed up some of the difficulties that had been encountered:

'The need to comply with the rail industry's regulations did hamper progress. Other contractual problems arose due to the nature of the project as it involved rail and road integration.'[6]

The special link to Helston launched with such high hopes in 1999 has long since become just another FirstGroup bus route. One despondent correspondent on the 'Trip Advisor' website commented in 2014: 'The timetable is certainly changing… These changes are being made at very short notice and it will probably be several months before the rail websites catch up.'

Although some progress has been made in recent years with the aid of the industry initiative PlusBus to display maps of local bus routes at stations, the task of keeping these maps up to date proved almost impossible thanks to the unpredictable changes in the bus industry, with the result that the maps have been simplified considerably to avoid showing too much fragile detail.

So in 2000, as in 1947, the law-makers had set their sights too high. In any case, the SRA – which had no control or influence over buses – would prove to have much larger (and less fragrant) fish to fry.

By the time the Transport Bill received its Second Reading, John Prescott had just outlined his new and evolving ten-year plan for transport.

In a speech to the Institute of Public Policy Research earlier in December he had promised a 'comprehensive programme' to be published by the summer of 2000. However, he said the private sector would continue to be involved:

'The key to better transport is to engage the best of the public sector and the private sector to invest in a better future. That means higher investment and it means effective investment, with work done to cost and on time… It can't all be done through taxpayers' money… Nor can it be left to mindless privatisation. Public Private Partnership, PPP, is our key to open up future investment, and it works.'[7]

But not all the MPs in the Chamber for the Second Reading of the Transport Bill were convinced that the SRA was necessary. This debate was also notable for its sharp exchanges between Prescott and free market advocate John Redwood, representing Wokingham for the Conservatives:

(Prescott) 'We are carrying out our policies to reduce congestion, create a better public transport system and improve the environment, all of which objectives are opposed by the right hon. Gentleman. For far too long, politicians have dodged the hard decisions and sacrificed long-term gain for short-term popularity. I have no intention of doing that.'[8]

(Redwood) 'To come to a judgment about the Bill, we need to know the answer to many important questions… When will there be a tube public-private partnership? How much more delay will there be? How much cash does the Secretary of State have for the tube over the next two years? We were told last Wednesday that he had zero in the budget for next year and zero in the budget for the year after. Is it still zero? Nothing will come of nothing – he has been filleted by the Treasury… We think that the authority is a cop-out by the Secretary of State and the new Minister for Transport. They should make many of those decisions and regulators exist to deal with the regulatory issues. The authority is a great red herring.'[9]

Opinions were therefore sharply divided, but Gwyneth Dunwoody, Labour's member for Crewe & Nantwich and a redoubtable member of the Transport Select Committee, which she chaired for many years, came to John Prescott's rescue:

'The railway system is in the most frightful muddle; that is the truth of the matter. Recent terrifying accidents were only a demonstration of that lack of clarity and lack of coherence. The Strategic Rail Authority is not only necessary; it is essential. Without an attempt to put together this kaleidoscope of broken pieces, the railway industry in the next century will be totally unable to serve the needs of the United Kingdom.'[10]

The Transport Act received Royal Assent on 30 November 2000. It was a complicated measure, with 280 sections and 31 schedules, but it gave the Strategic Rail Authority statutory teeth and, hopefully, the means to rejoin the pieces of Mrs Dunwoody's kaleidoscope; it also paved the way for the eventual abolition of what was left of British Rail.

By now, however, other parts of the railway cauldron were coming to the boil. One increasingly distressed piece of flotsam in the swirling currents was Railtrack, which was under increasing pressure from the Regulator over network performance.

In August 1999 the new Rail Regulator Tom Winsor (who had taken over from John Swift in July) had threatened to serve an enforcement order, which produced this response from Railtrack:

'A 12.5% improvement requested by the Regulator against the background of further industry growth, coming on top of three years' improvement of over 40%, is a huge hurdle. We have made a 10% improvement in performance in the first quarter on passenger delays against the same period last year, but much will depend on how well autumn and winter go.'[11]

A week later the shadow Strategic Rail Authority also weighed in, when its Chairman Sir Alastair Morton said:

'I expect Railtrack to provide continuous improvement in a network offering better performance, more capacity, faster trains and better provision for freight. The industry needs more investment focused at meeting these requirements.'[12]

By early October Sir Alastair had sharpened his sword a little more. In a major speech to City investors, which by coincidence was delivered just hours before the Ladbroke Grove collision, he made it clear that Railtrack's priorities had to change:

'It is a fallacy to assert, as some do, that Railtrack's primary duty is to its shareholders. They bought the right to profit from a monopoly by proving highly efficient in delivering the conditions under which that monopoly is licensed to operate. The most significant condition is No 7. Railtrack must meet the "reasonable requirements" of users (TOCs) and funders (the SRA). I do not believe Gerald Corbett seeks to avoid this duty, though some of his team are not yet comfortable with the thought of meeting the "requirements" of others. Gerald's current task is twofold – to obtain an incentivised return on investment and to deliver a greater volume of investment than Railtrack has yet seemed capable of. I wish him well: a crippled Railtrack is no use to any of us. I believe the company is more likely to cripple itself by poor delivery than be crippled by its terms of reference.'[13]

It is possible, with the benefit of the hindsight that is one of the historian's most useful tools, to see a pattern emerging in the last few months of 1999, when the plight of Railtrack was deepening. The company was labouring under the shadow of two major accidents, questions continued to be asked about the practicality of the ambitious West Coast Modernisation Scheme, while industry criticism of its general management of the network was becoming more vocal.

The creation of the sSRA had provided a new source of discontent (OPRAF was much less likely to have commented on Railtrack's affairs), which reinforced the Regulator's strictures.

Tom Winsor's next target was the progress – or lack of it – in modernising the West Coast Main Line. On 5 November 1999 he warned that enforcement action was now being taken, and that the company could be fined unless it could demonstrate real progress:

'By failing to complete adequate strategic reviews, despite undertaking to do so by March this year, Railtrack is likely to breach its network licence. It is likely to commit a further breach if it cannot demonstrate how it will provide the additional capacity on the WCML it has committed to provide by 2005.'

One major problem with which Railtrack was grappling was the type of signalling to be used on the West Coast route. Ambitious plans for an unproven 'moving block' system had faltered, and the Regulator was now getting impatient:

'I am not satisfied with … progress … nor am I persuaded that Railtrack can produce credible plans before it has taken key decisions on the signalling system to be employed on the WCML upgrade.'[14]

sSRA Chief Executive Mike Grant said he was disappointed that regulatory action was necessary, but that he 'fully supported' the action that the Regulator was taking.[15]

Railtrack responded on the same day, saying that it had agreed the details of Passenger Upgrade 2 ('PUG 2') with Virgin Trains in 1997, which involved moving block signalling and a 225km/h line speed. But second thoughts, proverbially often better, had evidently prevailed, particularly after similar technology had been adopted prematurely on the London Underground Jubilee Line extension. Before that line had opened signalling contractor Westinghouse had been forced to admit that moving block would take much longer to introduce than had been first thought, and Railtrack did not want to fall into the same trap:

'The moving block approach, never before implemented on the scale of the West Coast Main Line, would involve fitting 1,800 trains with high technology equipment which then communicates, via transponders in the track, with control centres. Line side signalling is not required. As with the Jubilee, a "big bang" implementation is required. The lineside signalling is removed, and all 1,800 trains switch over to moving block. This is very high risk.'[16]

Although this was a sensible attitude it was, in retrospect, unfortunate that this 'very high risk' had not been taken into account at the time PUG 2 had been signed.

By now, Railtrack's sorrows were not single spies but in battalions. A report commissioned by Winsor's predecessor from consultants Booz Allen & Hamilton and completed earlier in 1999 had shed doubt on the company's stewardship of the network:

'Railtrack appears to have focused its investment efforts on assets likely to generate performance improvements in the short run, such as renewal of rail, rather than investments in long term drivers of performance and quality, such as for example ballast renewal. Although performance outputs have been maintained, there has been some (temporary) decline in asset quality and an increased risk of deteriorating long term asset condition.'[17]

Such conclusions had caused concern in the Regulator's office, and on 25 November Winsor published new proposals. These included an amendment to Railtrack's network licence to bring it into line with the company's status in the private sector, as well as the compilation of a new asset database and a system to monitor the condition of those assets. The problem, as Winsor saw it, was that far from improving the network, Railtrack had actually failed to maintain its inheritance:

'Although Railtrack asserts that it has spent considerable sums on the network, the report states that it is likely that there has been a decline in the underlying quality of the network assets as a whole. The implication of this is that, in some respects, the national railway network may be in a poorer condition in 1999 than it was when it was in the hands of the nationalised state corporation, the British Railways Board.'[18]

Railtrack's response was a combination of dissent and humble pie. The company said that it totally accepted 'the need to improve its asset management and responsiveness to customers and it has already put in place a whole series of measures to address these issues', but lest the Regulator might think he was getting it all his own way, it went on to point out that 'we take issue with what we see as a partial and unbalanced perspective of our record as steward of the network. A balanced perspective should also acknowledge the successes.'

It also highlighted some related factors, particularly 'the challenges of the fragmented newly privatised railway with many more relationships to manage, the sudden growth in demand for passenger and freight, and higher customer expectations'.[19]

The 'challenges of the fragmented railway' were now indeed becoming clearer. The Rail Regulator, although still occasionally conciliatory, was hardening his attitude perceptibly as 1999 drew to a close, while Railtrack evidently felt that it was being treated harshly.

The following year would see publication of the delayed Southall accident report, although the report into the Ladbroke Grove collision – with all its damning conclusions – would not appear until 2001.

Meanwhile, sparring between the Regulator and Railtrack would also continue. On 20 March 2000 Winsor rejected Railtrack's proposals for improved performance, setting out plans to fine the company £2m for each percentage point in any shortfall, which could double to £4m if needed 'to provide sufficient incentive'.

Railtrack's gloves came off in turn later in the same month, when it refused to accept a 'modified enforcement order' in connection with the troubled West Coast Main Line project.

John Prescott published his ten-year 'transport plan' in mid-2000, which contained proposals for major investment in both heavy and light rail, but the year would soon take a downward turn again. The widespread disruption that had followed the Hatfield derailment on 17 October lasted well into 2001, and this triggered the start of a fresh conflict between Railtrack and the train operators.

John Robinson became the Chairman of Railtrack in July 2001, replacing Sir Philip Beck, but by then the company was almost on its last lap. Before 2001 came to an end, the Railtrack dream would be all but over.

Chapter 26

'A much patchier condition'

The Strategic Rail Authority had yet to gain its statutory powers when the still-new passenger franchises began to come under fresh scrutiny in the second half of 1999. Connex had already been launched on what would prove to be a downward path to oblivion in the British rail franchise world, when it had been refused a longer South Central franchise the year before. This, if granted, would have confirmed an option in the original contract to extend it from seven to 15 years. Then in August 1999 the franchising director invited ideas from operators for a replacement South Central franchise, together with new contracts for Chiltern and GNER.

This was followed in November by an invitation to start negotiations, when the Franchising Director Mike Grant said:

'My aim is to secure long term franchises that provide high levels of performance for passengers. I want to see proposals that will provide additional capacity coming on-stream as early as possible, and in exchange for this I am prepared to consider franchise terms which would last between 10 and 20 years. I shall also be looking forward to receiving proposals from other interested parties.'[1]

Against apparent expectations, passenger figures had been rising steadily since the first franchise round had been completed in 1997. The total for 1996-97 of 801m had already risen to 848m in 1997-98 and would reach 892m a year after that. This trend suggested that the franchises agreed only a few years earlier would rapidly become unfit for purpose. Their leased rolling stock had been inherited from British Rail (apart from one small batch of new diesel units for Chiltern, no new post-privatisation trains would come into service until 1999, although several major fleets were on their way), while Railtrack, as we have seen, was struggling to keep the existing infrastructure in some kind of order. There would be, for example, no new electrification schemes until a short section was completed between Crewe, Alsager and Kidsgrove Junction in 2003 to form a much-needed West Coast Main Line diversionary route.

Even if Railtrack was lagging (not least because it was becoming increasingly mired in the complexities of West Coast Main Line modernisation), the operators needed to be encouraged to adjust to the rapidly growing demand as much as the constraints of the network would allow, and the only practical source of such encouragement was the Franchising Director, Mike Grant.

He, in turn, was limited by the terms of the existing contracts that had been let so hurriedly; the obvious answer was to replace them sooner rather than later. Some were probably best left to run to their full term, and this was particularly true of the long 15-year franchises, which all included large new fleets.

Although both the Virgin contracts fell into this category, the fact that neither of them survived – at least not in accordance with their originally agreed terms – was due more than anything else to infrastructure failings dominated (inevitably) by the basket case that was the West Coast Main Line.

In December Mike Grant widened the possibilities. Up to another four franchises would also now be considered for early replacement, he explained (although this time the candidates were not named), and he went on to emphasise that the franchise boundaries were up for renegotiation as well.

The interested parties were given until 1 February 2000 to respond and, considering that some recent franchises have taken the DfT more than a year to award, in hindsight the rate of progress seems remarkable.

Some of the unpredictabilities of dealing with the private sector emerged in the same month, when MTL Holdings was bought by the bus group Arriva. This acquisition allowed Arriva into rail for the first time, because MTL brought the Merseyrail Electrics and Northern Spirit franchises with it.

Grant was cautious: Arriva was given just 12 months on the understanding that the longer-term future of both franchises was in the melting pot. (It is fair to add that Arriva, now part of Deutsche Bahn, has maintained a presence in the British rail franchise sector ever since.)

By March the franchising wheels at the shadow Strategic Rail Authority were revolving faster, and it was revealed that Central Trains and South West Trains were the latest candidates for a rethink. (South West Trains would be retained by its incumbent Stagecoach Group, while the Central Trains contract, owned by National Express Group, was extended twice but did not survive unscathed. Its routes in mid-Wales were transferred to the new 'shadow' contract Wales & Borders in December 2001, while the rest of Central Trains was finally abolished in 2007 when its English routes were mostly divided between the new London Midland and East Midlands Trains franchises, except for a couple of the longer-distance services that were included in the re-tendered CrossCountry.)

True to his warning that the original franchise boundaries were not necessarily carved in stone, Grant also unveiled a plan for a new TransPennine franchise. This would take over the faster inter-urban services run by Northern Spirit.

The shortlisted contenders for the first three restructured franchises were announced on 14 March. East Coast would be a choice between the present operator GNER and a consortium of Virgin and Stagecoach. Although GNER would win on this occasion, it was not to be the last time that the other two would bid for East Coast. (They finally succeeded in taking over the franchise in early 2015.)

Chiltern was to be fought for by its existing operator M40 Trains and Go-Ahead (again, the incumbent won), while the two shortlisted for South Central were Connex and Govia. This time, the result would be different. Not only did Govia win, but it did so ahead of time by taking over the last two years of the original South Central contract in August 2001. Connex was not pleased. When the franchising director's decision was announced in October 2000, it said:

'We believe that our proposals were robust, more than met the core franchise requirements set out by the SRA and provided unprecedented passenger benefits across all aspects of rail travel at the lowest cost to the UK taxpayer. Our bid had a high level of financial commitment and risk guaranteed by our parent company, Vivendi Environment.'[2]

Although the early takeover was achieved by negotiation rather than confiscation, Connex also commented dryly: 'We wish our competitor luck with the South Central franchise and are curious to learn full details of their franchise commitments and the level of real financial risk that they are taking.'

Apart from the stillborn Enterprise Rail, Connex was probably the first operator to feel stung by the workings of the British rail franchise system. It would not be the last.

The reverberations of the post-Hatfield speed restrictions had continued to vibrate during the autumn of 2000, eventually provoking the Association of Train Operating Companies to lodge a formal complaint with the ORR just before Christmas. This alleged that Network Rail's failure to restore its infrastructure following the derailment amounted to 'multiple breaches' of its licence, and that the network had been 'in chaos' ever since. ATOC also dismissed a national recovery plan that had been published earlier in December as 'not fit for purpose'[3].

In fact, Tom Winsor had already virtually defended Railtrack's actions after Hatfield, saying in a radio interview that 'it's not a question of them being fined or being penalised, they have the obligation to run a safe railway, and that's what they must do.'[4]

However, ATOC could not be dismissed so readily, and Winsor accordingly warned Railtrack on 2 January that it must now prepare operator-specific recovery plans by the 18th of that month and provide supporting information about the wider recovery plan by 16 February.

The weaknesses of the fragmented railway under pressure were now more evident than ever before, as tempers shortened and each party jostled for position in the post-Hatfield maelstrom.

Winsor was told on 15 January that Railtrack had accepted his final conclusions about its budget for the next five years. He welcomed this as a 'positive step', but also acknowledged that the consequences of Hatfield would leave the company in a 'materially worse financial position'. One remedy he suggested was to bring forward (but not increase) some of the grants that the SRA was due to pay in the forthcoming Control Period, but he also opened the door to the possibility of an 'interim review' – in other words, a reassessment of Railtrack's financial position before the next five years had elapsed.[5]

In spite of this brief gleam of hope, the pressure on Railtrack increased again when it became known in mid-February that the company's estimate of the budget for upgrading the East Coast Main Line was seriously inadequate. Deputy Prime Minister John Prescott expressed his 'grave concern', while Mike Grant, now Chief Executive of the SRA, warned that the Authority's refranchising programme would be affected:

'We are examining with Railtrack the details of these cost increases which could range between 20% and, if specific provisions for contingencies are included, nearly 100%. We have been asked by the Deputy Prime Minister to advise him urgently of the reasons behind this rapid increase in costs. Obviously, this new information must now generate a pause in the refranchising process for the East Coast Main Line while we review the contents and causes of this increase.'[6]

This particular impasse ended on 2 March, when a general increase of less than 20% was agreed by the SRA and some of the more ambitious (and costly) improvements envisaged by Railtrack were set aside on the grounds that they would offer only 'marginal' improvements in journey times.[7] We also get a glimpse of the financial approach at Railtrack in this period, when the SRA commented that the abandoned elements had added 'fees and contingencies upon contingencies' to the total cost – effectively doubling it.'

By this time rumours were spreading that Railtrack might no longer be viable, and one fertile source of these speculations (if that is all they were) was apparently the Strategic Rail Authority.

For example, a few days after the disarray of the East Coast budget had been revealed, *The Guardian* reported on 19 February that the company was 'facing bankruptcy'. The story relied on 'senior sources' at the SRA, while the Authority's Chairman Sir Alastair Morton was alleged to have ordered a halt to any further funding for rail maintenance because of what the SRA saw as 'managerial incompetence' at Railtrack. Railtrack responded by saying that its financial position had not changed since its last Stock Market statement a month earlier, although at that time it had called for grants worth around £1bn, which were due in 2006, to be provided earlier in the new Control Period.

At the end of February the wider industry had been depressed once again by another serious accident. Early on the morning of the 28th a Land Rover towing a trailer loaded with a car crashed through the fence protecting a railway embankment alongside a road bridge at Great Heck, near Selby in North Yorkshire. The Land Rover came to rest on the up East Coast Main Line, where it was almost immediately struck at speed by a GNER train from Newcastle.

The leading bogie was derailed, but the moving train stayed upright and in line. However, before it could be brought to a stand it was deflected by points and struck an oncoming Freightliner coal train weighing more than 1,700 tonnes, with the appalling results that can only be expected from a collision involving a joint closing speed of almost 230km/h.

The passenger train became entirely derailed and most of its coaches overturned. Ten people were killed, including both drivers and two other members of railway staff.

The driver of the Land Rover pleaded tiredness, but was found guilty on ten counts of causing death by dangerous driving and jailed for five years.

The accident led to a debate about the adequacy of crash barriers and fencing at railway bridges, but the responsibility rested with the Department of the Environment, Transport and the Regions rather than Railtrack and, in any case, a claim from the car driver's insurers that the strength of the fencing had been insufficient was later dismissed in court.

This was one accident where neither Railtrack nor any train operator could be accused of negligence, and the coldest of cold comfort could, perhaps, be drawn from that.

Meanwhile, the post-Hatfield recovery was still dragging on, and on 20 March the Rail Regulator took enforcement action.

Tom Winsor conceded that Railtrack had made some progress since January, but he also warned that 'after Easter 16 passenger and two freight TOCs will still face emergency timetables or running normal timetables with significant delays'.

Railtrack had set itself a revised target of 21 May for nearly all routes to be returned to normal, and Winsor said the purpose of his order was to 'concentrate minds'. He continued:

'The industry cannot allow further drift of deadlines for the restoration of a reliable network if it is to deliver the growth and new services envisaged in the government's ten year plan. The current problems on the network highlight longer term stewardship issues. The Regulator has therefore required Railtrack to produce a network quality assessment by the middle of April.'[8]

The SRA had ceased to be a 'shadow' following the passing of the Transport Act and moved nearer to the centre of the stage in March, pronouncing that 'Railtrack cannot do it all'. This was one key phrase in a new 'Strategic Agenda'[9], in which the SRA set out its plans to improve the railway network over the coming decade (it also included an over-optimistic prediction that 'by Autumn 2001 the post-Hatfield National Rail Recovery Plan will be history'). This document followed the publication of the Government's ten-year transport plan in July of the previous year, which had allocated £60bn to railways.

This was followed in April by a further SRA announcement that the East Coast Main Line upgrade was now to be undertaken by a public-private joint venture including the SRA, Railtrack, the future franchise operator, a project management company and external investors.[10]

The proposed upgrade included numerous track improvements, such as new freight loops, a flyover just north of Hitchin station to carry Cambridge-bound trains over the main line, an enlarged station at Peterborough and an additional platform at London King's Cross – all of which now exist, although it was well into the Network Rail era before they were completed. (The additional platform at King's Cross was only opened in 2010, while the Hitchin flyover was not available to traffic until 2013.)

Meanwhile, Tom Winsor had agreed in March that Railtrack might approach the Strategic Rail Authority directly for more funds. It was agreed on 1 April that £1.5bn from Control Period 3, which was to start in 2006, could be brought forward to CP2.[11] At the same time a proposed funding structure (called the 'RenewCo') was sketched out. This would have created 'revolving credit' worth up to another £1.4bn, secured on future grants payable to Railtrack.

Having secured its £1.5bn from the SRA, Railtrack announced on 2 April that:

'The acceleration of this income … will provide a stable financial basis for the Company and will ensure that a credit rating within the A category is maintained. The satisfactory resolution of this issue means that Railtrack need not now approach the Regulator for an interim review…'

At the same time, Railtrack warned that it was expecting to report a 'substantial loss' for 2001-02, and the outlook remained 'extremely challenging'. One consequence was that the interim review had only been postponed, and Railtrack now expected to ask for it in the summer of 2002. The main reason, perhaps inevitably, was Hatfield.

Detailed proposals for significantly longer franchises were also now appearing, and one of these was to be East Coast. In early May the SRA said it was still dealing with several outstanding issues, such as 'technical feasibility and value for money, financial risk and the extent to which proposals are deliverable'. Even so, the two contenders – GNER and Virgin Stagecoach – were being offered a 20-year contract that, to quote the SRA, was 'as significant to Britain's rail system as the West Coast Main Line franchise, held by Virgin Trains.'[12]

What the industry needed, apart from an accelerated refranchising programme, was a calmer period in which to recover from Hatfield, then start moving forward again. This was confirmed by the Transport Secretary, Stephen Byers, on 18 June:

'We've now got the framework in place – with the Transport Act and the funding set out in our Ten Year Plan – to improve the quality of the rail network. So I am not going to embark on big structural changes. What the industry needs now is a period of stability and certainty so it can concentrate on the vital job of delivering safe, reliable services for passengers and freight.'[13]

It would have been a nice idea, but even as the Transport Secretary was expressing his pious wish for stability the winds of change were already rising. Just over a week later, in an otherwise broadly sanguine speech, Sir Alastair Morton described Railtrack as 'the cracked principal structure supporting our industry'[14].

By the autumn these winds would become a hurricane, demolishing a key part of the privatised industry's painfully constructed but far from invulnerable structure, and imposing 'big structural changes' once more.

The original vision for railway privatisation, which in 2001 was less than a decade old, had included a private sector infrastructure authority called Railtrack that would be nourished by a series of profitable, competitive intercity and freight operators. Socially necessary passenger routes would receive appropriate subsidy from public funds, so that their operators would also be able to pay fully 'commercial' track access charges. This flow of revenue should in turn have allowed Railtrack to raise funds for investment on the open market as well as pay dividends.

Unfortunately, this rosy vision was never to be more than an unrealisable aspiration, inspired and encouraged by advocates of the free market and a hawkish, profit-seeking Treasury.

Railtrack inherited a network in 1994 that had suffered from many years of under-investment caused by Government restrictions on British Rail spending. It did not know the true state of affairs about the condition of its network (in 2001 the compilation of a reliable asset database still lay in the future), but it was expected to deal with sharply rising demand that had not been predicted in the early 1990s, while network capacity had been systematically reduced for many years.

As PricewaterhouseCoopers observed in August 2001:

'In the Government's second term there needs to be an increase in momentum in investment in our railways to accommodate rising numbers of passengers and improve service performance.'[15]

Railtrack therefore faced a series of problems, at the core of which lay a decaying, inadequate network that had suddenly and inexplicably become popular once again. (Railtrack Chief Executive Steve Marshall was quoted by the *Daily Telegraph* on 25 July 2001 as saying that 'the network was in a much patchier condition than we previously understood'.)

Another factor, which certainly prejudiced safety, was the general fragmentation of the railway industry and particularly the multitude of external contractors that Railtrack employed. The consequent breakdowns in communication cost lives on several occasions.

The final straw on Railtrack's back was the West Coast modernisation scheme. This had run out of control – both financially and technically – bringing Railtrack into conflict with the Regulator and also Virgin Trains, which had based its original Intercity West Coast bid on the prospect of gaining a 225km/h railway, complete with capacity enhancing moving block signalling.

By 2001 these unattractive chickens were coming home to roost with a vengeance.

This became clear when the new Railtrack Chairman, John Robinson, had a meeting with Transport Secretary Stephen Byers on 27 June, where he spelled out a situation that was threatening to become a full-blown crisis.

Among the problems the company faced was its comparative isolation within the industry – Railtrack was quite definitely not the most popular child in the class. Robinson said that the way the company had been privatised was flawed, and that the financial situation was worse than he had been expecting.

The minutes of this meeting ('restricted') show that he warned Byers that Railtrack would need to raise more cash by the autumn, but 'this would be an impossible challenge if others in the industry continued to undermine the company through the media'. In particular, relations with the Regulator were 'very poor'.[16]

Worse still, Winsor's assumptions for the next Control Period were 'unworkable', although his willingness to take the longer-term financial implications of Hatfield into account was 'really an opportunity to reassess the assumptions underpinning rail funding more generally'.

We cannot know Byers' private reaction to this clutching at straws, but he did tell Robinson that 'for better or worse the current situation was likely to be in place for some time', and also repeated his already publicly expressed view that he had 'no plans for major structural reforms'.

The proper function of the Strategic Rail Authority was also brought into question at this meeting, with Robinson saying that Railtrack had 'often walked away from its own strategic responsibilities, expecting the SRA to play this role'. (Was this a reference to the SRA's new East Coast joint venture?) 'He wanted to take lead responsibility for this in future, to get across the message that the Railtrack Chairman had the main responsibility for delivery.'

Byers welcomed this idea, but the fact that the relative duties and responsibilities of Railtrack and the SRA needed to be discussed in this way – and in such circumstances – was really an overdue condemnation of the vague way that the Transport Act of 2000 had been drafted.

The minutes of what must have been a tense discussion ran to just ten paragraphs, but its neat sentences probably summed up the harshest internal verdict on railway privatisation that had been produced so far.

Again using hindsight, it is surprising that neither Byers nor his officials seemed to recognise the storm clouds that were gathering, in spite of Robinson's frankness. Indeed, the last paragraph records that Byers still believed 'the industry could be turned round'.

This appears to be a definite case of mind over matter, considering that he had just been informed that a major – in fact, structurally essential – part of the industry was cordially disliked, fighting for position and running out of cash.

Nonetheless the Chairman was evidently told, in effect, to go back to his office and carry on the good work, while he was left to get such comfort as he could from a valedictory assurance that he had an 'open line' to the Secretary of State.

A further meeting was held with Robinson, Byers and his officials on 25 July, and now the news was much worse.

Robinson told them that he believed 'it would take another year to return to pre-Hatfield performance levels and probably three years to get performance to a level the company could be proud of. Turning things round was not a question of more investment, but rather running the company properly.'[17]

Even so, the financial situation had proved to be even more serious than Robinson had previously thought. Railtrack's relationships with other parts of the industry were still poor, although in the case of the Regulator he was 'trying to build a better working relationship' in spite of the fact that the current regulatory framework was placing 'great burdens' on Railtrack while the Regulator was simultaneously demanding that Robinson should 'put away the begging bowl'[18].

Meanwhile, outspoken SRA Chairman Sir Alastair Morton had been pursuing what seems to have amounted almost to a vendetta. Recent comments he had made about Railtrack's ability to raise money in the markets had been 'unhelpful', Robinson believed. (Byers attempted to pour some belated oil on troubled waters at this revelation, and said he would 'be stressing to the Rail Delivery Group the need for all players in the industry to show discipline in their public comments'.)

Robinson also revealed his full hand during this discussion. His preferred option was to restructure the company under the banner 'Project Rainbow', but this part of the conversation was considered to be so sensitive that it was minuted only in outline, at Robinson's request. (The official notes say merely that Robinson 'was working on a number of proposals relating to the company's short term and longer term finances which it would be helpful to discuss with Government.')

Robinson appears to have been reasonably confident about the outcome, and in 2005 he would say in evidence that he had believed a rescue plan would be supported by both the Government and the SRA.[19]

This view is consistent with the fact that he told Byers that Railtrack was now seeking either a 'soft letter of comfort' from the Government to reassure the company's bankers, or else extra public funds.

His justification for this request was simple. If neither proved to be available, 'it was clear that on 8 November, when Railtrack was due to give its interim results, it would be unable to make a going concern statement'.

The crisis at Railtrack was no longer just a threat. It had arrived.

Chapter 27

'Dogged ignorance and hostile agendas'

All the evidence suggests that Robinson's proposals for Project Rainbow had not convinced nor even attracted the Government. The Treasury, in particular, would have been deeply opposed to the notion of pouring an unquantifiable amount of public money into a nominally private enterprise that had been giving signals of distress for years and was now sinking with all hands.

Therefore, any idea of bailing out Railtrack gave way to an acceptance in Government circles that the end was at hand – and, as we shall see, tentative plans to replace the company may have existed at least as far back as June 2001.

Accordingly, Byers began consultations with financial and banking advisors to see what the best – or the least painful – solution might be.

These consultations appear to have been limited in their scope. Although Byers had discussed Railtrack's critical situation with Robinson he did not go on to take advice from Tom Winsor, who had a statutory duty to regulate Railtrack's financial affairs but only discovered that Railtrack's game was up when he was unexpectedly summoned on 4 October to a meeting with Byers the following day.

Unusually, Byers' private secretary 'would not or could not' tell Winsor what the meeting was about, so 'I took with me briefing on a variety of subjects, including network and train operator performance, the West Coast route modernisation and the Enterprise Bill. None of this was needed. It was immediately apparent why.'[1]

What is clear now is that Byers had decided to end the Railtrack era without reference to the Regulator because he did not want Winsor to provide more funding for the company, possibly via an emergency interim review.

Such a review could have increased the level of track access charges, but in the end these would have been paid by the Government after the franchise contracts had been amended to take account of them.

It also may have been an early indicator that Winsor himself was no longer commanding full confidence in Whitehall and Westminster, and indeed he would be detached from his role within the governance of the railway industry within three years.

Winsor noted that the mood of the meeting was 'stiff and formal', and that Byers was 'cold', while his Permanent Secretary David Rowlands 'looked distinctly uncomfortable'.

What they had to tell the Regulator was probably without precedent in British Government circles.

Robinson had suggested that Railtrack should be refinanced, but that had been considered and rejected; the company was insolvent, particularly because of the spiralling costs of West Coast Main Line modernisation – the Government considered that the project was now out of control – and also because of the continuing aftermath of Hatfield, the impact of which was 'severe'.

Robinson's proposals had also included a suspension of the 'regulatory regime' for the next three to four years – an idea that plainly shocked Winsor, who later noted that in such a case Railtrack would be able to spend taxpayers' money without 'any accountability whatever':

'It would be free on any grounds to deny access to its network to train operators, to charge them unreasonably high amounts for its use, extract abusive terms for the acceptance of new rolling stock and organise maintenance and renewal works … to its own advantage and the detriment of users. There would be no available appeals against abuse of its monopoly…'

He also implied in the same note that he had been unimpressed with Railtrack for some time, which went some way to account for Robinson's earlier complaint that relations with the Regulator had been 'very poor'. Indeed, Winsor's private assessment of a Railtrack freed from its statutory restraints proved to be withering:

'Enforcement of its obligations under its network licence would be lost, including … essential stewardship of the network, and the controls on abuse of its dominant position under the Competition Act 1998 would be disapplied. In my time as Rail Regulator and before, it has been hard enough to regulate this sort of behaviour on the part of Railtrack, although we have been doing so in the face of great resistance. The weakness of the first generation of access contracts between Railtrack and the train operators – particularly in terms of remedies against breach – has meant that the Rail Regulator is about the only effective protection the operators have… Removing the company's regulatory accountability would open the floodgates to an abuse of power by a Railtrack which consistently shows its inclination to such abuse…'

Winsor had not been told that Railtrack was insolvent and felt that he had been deliberately left in the dark. ('Why, if things are so bad, has the company not informed the Regulator? I said it would have been incumbent upon the company to approach the Regulator if its finances were so precarious. Neither Mr Byers nor Mr Rowlands gave me any answer…')

Winsor could still have authorised an interim review (indeed, he offered to help Railtrack during that last weekend, without success), but this was not a risk that the Government was prepared to allow:

'I said that John Robinson's reaction … is likely to be an immediate application to me for an early interim review… Mr Byers said they had thought of that, and that if such an application were made he had the authority of the Prime Minister and the Chancellor immediately to introduce emergency legislation to entitle the Secretary of State to give instructions to the Regulator.'

Winsor, for once, appears to have been back-footed by this:

'After pausing to consider whether I had really heard what I had just heard, I asked whether that would be to overrule me on an interim review or in relation to all my functions. Mr Byers said it would cover everything, but its first use would be in relation to an interim review which the Government did not wish to proceed.'

At this Winsor evidently hardened, telling his audience that such action would throw the Government's policy of encouraging private sector participation in national industries into doubt: ('It would have very serious adverse implications for the constitutional position of independent regulators in other industries ... [including] the position of the PPP arbiter in the London Underground PPP...')

He even suggested that Virgin's agreements to lease two large fleets of 'Pendolinos' and 'Voyagers' could go into default, with a consequent loss of premiums to the Treasury in years to come, but Byers refused to be cowed. He insisted that if an interim review were to be attempted, the Government would restrict the powers of the Rail Regulator.

It must have been a testing conversation, but Winsor had manifestly failed to convince his audience. As we have said, the revelations plainly shocked him, especially as he had been set aside, then warned, essentially, to keep his fingers out of it.

Tom Winsor is a careful and methodical lawyer, so we gain some idea of his state of mind when in his subsequent notes of the meeting, dated 6 October, he recorded that he had been requested on 'Friday 4 October' to attend the next day, which would therefore have been Saturday. Not so: in 2001 the 4th of October was a Thursday. It was a trivial but very uncharacteristic slip.

Not all the King's horses and all the King's men, and certainly not the Rail Regulator, could save Railtrack now.

Railtrack Chairman John Robinson succeeded Winsor in Stephen Byers' office at 16.45, after the markets had closed, where he was told that there was to be no more Government money for his company.

Robinson had no alternative but to declare Railtrack insolvent, now that public funding worth £1.5bn a year had been withdrawn. He said later: 'The whole relationship we have with our banks is based on the Government supporting us.'[2]

In this he confirmed the ambiguous status of Railtrack as a private sector company, which in its concept had tended to recall the famous comment of Samuel Johnson about a dog walking on its hind legs: 'It is not done well; but you are surprised to find it done at all.'

In this case, the dog was back on all four legs. An order placing Railtrack plc in Railway Administration was granted by Mr Justice Lightman during an emergency hearing in the High Court at 17.00 on Sunday 7 October, on the petition of the Transport Secretary, Stephen Byers.

Was the ending of Railtrack inevitable? Certainly, the texts of internal emails that emerged later suggested that Byers had been considering winding up the company as early as June, although he was later criticised for giving a misleading answer on this point to the Commons Transport Committee.

Sir John Major, whose Government was responsible for creating and privatising the track authority, is in no doubt: he maintains that 'Stephen Byers killed Railtrack'[3].

Railtrack shareholders brought a civil High Court action against Byers in 2005, claiming compensation on the grounds that he had committed a misfeasance in public office, but they lost their case. He has remained unrepentant about the way he dealt with the company, saying, 'I have never regretted my decision to refuse Railtrack further taxpayers' money and then to apply for it to be put into administration. It was quite simply the right thing to do.'[4]

Meanwhile, Tom Winsor (now Sir Thomas Winsor) has described the end of Railtrack as 'an extraordinary episode'. He says, 'During my term of office, there was a significant degree of political interference with Railtrack, almost all of it unwarranted.'[5]

He also believes it would been neither easy nor simple to overrule the jurisdiction of the Rail Regulator – certainly not as simple as Stephen Byers had seemed to imply on 5 October 2001:

'I had no expectation that the Minister would ever take the steps that were taken in relation to me. If it was expected that I should be intimidated, I was not: it was very clear to me that if my independence, my jurisdiction or my job was to be taken away or changed then it could and should only be done with the authority of Parliament, and my message to the Secretary of State at the time, although not in these words, was, "If you intend to make that change, then go and get the authority of Parliament, and until then I am sitting tight"… It was very clear that if private investment in the railway was to continue then independent economic regulation needed to be protected, and the government drew back from that.'[6]

Friday 5 October 2001 was not only the day that Stephen Byers told Railtrack that the money well had run dry – it was also the second anniversary of the collision at Ladbroke Grove, which had been followed by Lord Cullen's report and its serious criticisms of various parties in the railway industry (see Chapter 24).

Now, however, the Transport Secretary had some better news. All trains using Paddington would be equipped with protection systems that went beyond the limited functions of BR's AWS.[7]

ATP, or Automatic Train Protection, would continue to be used on the fleets of

Great Western and Heathrow Express (and also Chiltern), while TPWS – the new Train Protection and Warning System – was being fitted to the trains of other operators using the terminus, which at that time included a couple of services run by Virgin CrossCountry.

The slow progress in installing modern train protection systems may have been another consequence of privatisation. Although ATP had been a major recommendation in the inquiry report that followed the accident near Clapham Junction in December 1988, national installation was then rejected on the grounds of cost.

Ironically, ATP had been fitted to the Great Western HST that collided with a freight train at Southall in 1997, but it was not in use because the driver was not sufficiently trained. On the other hand, either ATP or TPWS should have prevented the next major accident at Ladbroke Grove, although it would have had no effect at Hatfield, where crumbling infrastructure was the cause.

Railtrack's safety record, like its financial performance, had not been good, but there was still anger and disappointment after Byers decided to stop supporting the company.

On 8 October, the day following the granting of Railway Administration, the effects of his decision started to be felt. The shares of Railtrack plc were suspended, while John Robinson issued a statement:

'Until last Friday evening we believed that the Government was giving serious consideration to the Board's proposal. It has now been made clear to us that the Government has decided not to provide further financial support to Railtrack in its current form. The Directors are extremely mindful of their duty … but under current circumstances, and recognising the duty of the administrator also to act in the interest of both the shareholders and the creditors, we have concluded that we should co-operate with the administrator in ensuring a smooth transition.'[8]

His calm and constructive tone was not matched by that of chief executive Steve Marshall, who was plainly very angry indeed with the Rail Regulator as well as the Government:

'Government's treatment of my company, and its shareholders, has been shoddy and unacceptable. Commitments, whether financial or otherwise, are made to be kept not broken. Mr Byers will learn that 40-year-old rails are broadly neutral on the public:private partnership debate. Either way, they need hard cash to replace them and soon. The needs of the rail network are huge and will not go away. It is a pity I have never had the opportunity to put this to him personally. I will leave the industry with regret. Many are surprised to hear that it is full of bright and able people whose energies and initiative are constricted by intrusive and largely uncontrolled over-regulation. They deserve better and I hope they get it.'[9]

Railtrack's replacement was to be a 'not for dividend' company, limited by guarantee, with 'members' rather than shareholders, to be known as Network Rail.

The new company took over completely a year later. While Railtrack was still in charge, although in Railway Administration, another serious accident occurred on 10 May 2002 – again, this was directly linked to badly maintained infrastructure and a broken chain of communication between Railtrack and the responsible contractor. It also occurred on the same main line.

As at Hatfield, a train travelling north at speed became derailed, this time on the approach to Potters Bar station. The train was a four-car West Anglia Great Northern unit bound for King's Lynn, and although the front three vehicles stayed in line and were brought safely to a stand beyond the station, the fourth became derailed. After careering across a bridge and dislodging debris that fell into the road below, it came to rest on its side on one of the station platforms, wedged under a canopy.

Six people who had been travelling in this vehicle died, while an unlucky elderly pedestrian who had been walking under the bridge also lost her life after she was hit by some of the debris from above.

The inquiry revealed that a pair of facing points on the approach to the station had moved under the last coach, derailing it. The cause, again as at Hatfield, was poor maintenance. In this case, bolts on the stretcher bars that secure the rails were found to be loose or missing. Several previous warnings about 'rough riding' on that section had apparently been disregarded.

It was the last in the series of major accidents in the Railtrack era, and as before it triggered a storm about railway safety. Former BR safety manager Peter Rayner commented:

'All this is down to the continuing malaise that we have experienced since 1994. People should not put this down to Railtrack or the fact that Railtrack is now in administration. It's more about the problems that have been encountered over the last four or five years.'[10]

Some commentators saw Potters Bar as the latest symptom of Peter Rayner's 'malaise':

'The privatisation of British Rail can now, more than ever, be seen as one of the most reckless acts of ideological vandalism ever perpetrated by a British government. The quixotic belief that a profit-maximising company could ever remedy decades of underinvestment while moving towards minimal government subsidy – the twin propositions at the heart of privatisation – was risible. Yet New Labour must shoulder a share of the blame too. It spent almost five years complaining without taking substantive action. Meanwhile, it swallowed the half-baked free-market "wisdom" that private ownership would guarantee not only efficiency, but safety too.

Determined not to take Railtrack back into public ownership, it devised a time-consuming alternative: putting Railtrack into administration and reconstituting it as a public interest company. Although a vastly superior structure to that devised by the Tories, the Government has lost yet more time.'[11]

This newspaper leader did not use the word 'fragmentation', but it was at the heart of the problem. At Potters Bar – as at Southall, Ladbroke Grove and Hatfield – communications had failed, either within the core industry (so that someone in a control room did not understand the significance of 'AWS isolated', for example) or between that core and the seemingly limitless number of contractors who were a key element of railway privatisation.

Supply chain companies are, of course, essential – and have always been there. In the 19th century many components were made by outside firms rather than the companies themselves, such as signals and lever frames, rails, building materials, engineering components and sometimes complete items of rolling stock, including locomotives. The ticketing system on which railways around the world relied for many decades was devised by a former railwayman from the north of England who developed a very substantial business indeed. British Railways also bought widely, and it experimented with diesel locomotives from a number of third party engineering firms during the Modernisation Plan period.

Contractors to maintain the railway itself were also employed by some companies in the old days. But by 2001 privatisation had 'disaggregated' a formerly unified industry to an unparalleled degree. In some cases the effects were simply inconvenient and annoying, such as when the employees of one train operator could give no information to passengers about another operator's services, but the lack of data and understanding could also pose a risk to safety – in a few cases spectacularly so.

Labour had attempted to close this gap by creating a new railway authority, but all too often the SRA proved to be just one more link in a rather loose chain. It had been created to promote and integrate the railway with other forms of transport and also to manage the awarding and performance of passenger franchises, but its other tasks included funding Railtrack (then Network Rail) and also making the best use of the network. The first draft 'route utilisation strategy' (or RUS), covering the Midland Main Line and the East Midlands, was published by the SRA in June 2003, with the definitive version following in March 2004.

In this first RUS, Sir Alastair Morton's successor as Chairman and Chief Executive Richard Bowker said:

'This Strategy is designed to provide a coherent planning framework for one of the country's busiest lines. It is designed in particular to foster a significant improvement in performance without any dependence on infrastructure changes.'[12]

The early RUSs were therefore concerned with how to make the best use of the existing network, rather than to sketch out bold plans for major investment. Later versions (now published by Network Rail and known since 2012 as studies in the Long Term Planning Process) often go further, and are willing to examine proposals for investment where there is a promising business case.[13]

But the first few years of the SRA were not happy ones, partly because of the sticky relationship between its first Chairman Sir Alastair Morton and Railtrack. It was also a time of franchise changes that have already been mentioned, but the industry was confronted with some rethinks on policy after Morton gave way to Bowker, which could be bewildering.

One example was that only one 20-year franchise was awarded (to Chiltern Railways) before contract lengths shortened again. Another brief aspiration was to concentrate the services at each London terminus so that only one franchised operator was involved.

This was already true at London Waterloo, where only South West Trains was present, and was achieved at London Liverpool Street from April 2004 when the 'Greater Anglia' franchise, which combined Anglia Railways and First Great Eastern, was awarded to National Express.

(After FirstGroup had failed to be shortlisted for Greater Anglia, it bought GB Railways, the owner of Anglia Railways, which had stayed in the running. The stratagem failed – possibly the SRA did not care for it – and the result was that First lost Great Eastern but was left with GB Railways' subsidiary GB Railfreight, which it sold on to Eurotunnel in 2010.)

Paddington followed suit when 'Greater Western' took over in 2006, absorbing the previously separate suburban operator in the process.

Other stations did not fit this ideal. It would have been hard to achieve at Victoria, for example, which still follows a long-established tradition by catering for Southeastern and Southern ('South Central') services, while it would have been even harder at London Bridge with its three suburban operators – currently known (in early 2016) as Southeastern, Southern and Thameslink.

Euston was apparently a near miss, where there was talk for a while of amalgamating the Intercity West Coast franchise run by Virgin with the suburban services, which in the event survived to be run until 2007 by National Express, branded Silverlink, and since then by Govia's London Midland.

Meanwhile, the troubled West Coast route modernisation plan was running out of steam by 2001 as costs mounted relentlessly, even though the will-o'-the-wisp of moving block signalling had faded away, having been formally abandoned at the end of 1999. An original budget of less than £2bn would grow to a predicted £14bn or more, and there was even talk of that figure doubling again.

Virgin West Coast had committed itself in the 1997-98 (PUG 2) agreement with Railtrack to lease a fleet of tilting 225km/h trains as part of a business plan that assumed a properly upgraded route with the capacity for up to four intercity trains an hour between London and Birmingham and three between London and Manchester. This had been intended to last until 2012 when the West Coast franchise was due to expire, but be followed by open access rights on the London-Manchester route, with lower frequencies, until 2027.[14]

In November 2000 Virgin Trains Chief Executive Chris Green was still looking forward to launching the complete service in 2005, and welcoming the first tilting trains three years before that.[15] The first 'Pendolinos' did start running in 2002, but the 225km/h railway was as far away as ever (and at the time of writing it still is).

Because the route would not be upgraded by 2002, Railtrack was clearly in breach of its revised agreement with Virgin, and Virgin accordingly claimed the lion's share of a £305m compensation pot that Railtrack and Network Rail paid to operators on the West Coast route.

The West Coast franchise was also no longer financially workable, and it was suspended in July 2002 to be replaced by an 'interim agreement' with the SRA under which Virgin received a fixed 2% share of revenue as a management fee. Virgin's CrossCountry franchise was also suspended (in return for 1% of the revenue), because it too was affected by the West Coast problem.[16]

A bid to relaunch CrossCountry in 2003 ('Operation Princess') had to be considerably modified in the light of experience, after the complexities of sharing so many routes with other operators proved to be too difficult.

The SRA also clipped the CrossCountry network during the management contract period, so that although many of the new 'Voyager' diesels had visited such places as Portsmouth to be ceremonially named for the locality (in this case *Solent Voyager*), after the SRA had modified the network Portsmouth proved to be one of several places that were no longer on the CrossCountry map.

The West Coast franchise was restored on new terms in 2006, but these meant that premiums of some £1.2bn, payable in the later years of the original contract, had become subsidies of about the same amount. The costs of the West Coast failure were not therefore confined to Railtrack and Network Rail alone. Meanwhile Virgin and the SRA failed to agree over CrossCountry. It was therefore relet and taken over by Arriva in November 2007.

What had gone wrong on the West Coast Main Line? A National Audit Office report concluded that there had been 'a lack of clear governance arrangements and direction for the programme'.[17]

Railtrack had wasted several hundred million pounds developing then abandoning plans for moving block signalling and a new control centre, and the project was further endangered by the placing of the company in Railway Administration in October 2001.

The project was then 'de-scoped' (in other words, reduced) in a joint effort by the SRA and Network Rail in 2003, and the threatened costs of more than £14bn came down to around £9bn.

Although Virgin was eventually able to launch much-improved West Coast services in 2008, they do not run at 225km/h and there are three rather than four trains an hour between London and Birmingham, while large sections of the route have needed further upgrades since then, such as the multiple blockades that affected Watford Junction periodically in 2014 and early 2015. In other words, West Coast Main Line modernisation (now an 'upgrade') is still going on, long after its original parent Railtrack disappeared.

The Rail Regulator had the task of deciding the financial arrangements for Railtrack and its successor Network Rail, but Tom Winsor's approach to this task brought him into collision with the Government in late 2003, when he announced an additional £7.4bn in funding for Network Rail, taking its income for the five years 2004-09 to £22.2bn.

This was followed by criticism from politicians who felt that Treasury approval should be needed for such spending. The matter came to a head in early 2004 when the Government announced a review of the railway industry's structure. This was followed in April by a report from the Transport Select Committee that accused Winsor of being 'high handed' and of failing in his 'core function of effectively regulating the stewardship of the national rail network'.[18]

It commented that 'the Regulator, Network Rail and the SRA clearly differ about who exactly runs the railway infrastructure', and continued:

'Our inquiry exposed an astonishing and fundamental disagreement between the Government and the Regulator about the extent of the latter's powers. According to the Minister, the Government had a choice about whether to accept the Regulator's access charges settlement; but the Regulator considered that the Government had no option but to accept his decision. This is a prime example of the confusion which lies at the heart of the present structure of the railway...'

The Committee was particularly unhappy about the Regulator's award of an extra £7.4bn to Network Rail. He replied that the report 'contains many significant errors of elementary fact on which its fundamentally flawed conclusions are then based. I reject entirely the unfounded allegations in relation to my office, and am disappointed the report fails to acknowledge the very real achievement of regulation and the railways in the last few years'.

The Committee wanted to go further by abolishing both the Strategic Rail Authority and Network Rail and replacing them with a public sector Rail Agency, while it urged that there should not be one all-powerful Rail Regulator – instead, it wanted industry regulation to be carried out by a Board.

It was also outraged that £58m had been used to support the Connex Southeastern franchise for a year before the contract had been terminated by the SRA in 2003 (this marked the final departure of Connex, following its early handover of South Central to Govia), and concluded: 'The SRA's management of this franchise has been woefully poor'.

The Committee's report included a pertinent summary of what had really changed in the area of railway costs and control since the 1993 White Paper:

'Mr Winsor's defence of regulation fails to address the shift of emphasis away from the original vision of a privatised railway in which private sector franchisees would have significant freedom to extend and enhance their service, and to take commercial risks, to the present, highly subsidised and much more strictly delineated franchises.'

And that, more or less, was that. Some of the Committee's recommendations were adopted: the SRA was soon abolished under the terms of the 2005 Railway Safety Act, although Network Rail remained and there was to be no Railway Agency. Neither would franchises be freed from being 'strictly delineated'. But the end was in sight for the single Rail Regulator, and his office became the Office of Rail Regulation (it is now the Office of Rail and Road).

Just before Tom Winsor left, he wrote a long letter to his colleagues and successors on the curiously appropriate date of 4 July 2004. This was indeed the start of his personal independence as he left the ORR and returned to private legal practice, but then he had always insisted on the independence of the Rail Regulator, as his letter pointed out:

'It should not be underestimated just how effective the constant repetition of unjustified criticism and imaginary facts can be in shaping political and public opinion. In 1999, I gave hardly a thought to the issue of independence. It was a given, and not seriously in doubt, or so I thought. But when it came under pressure first, fire later – from the Department, the Treasury and, most of all, the SRA – the corrosive potential was serious and had to be resisted. If we had simply stayed quiet, it would not have washed over us, it would have washed us away. We began the defence with attempts at private persuasion, but the assailants were determined and it became necessary to make the case publicly. And at the time of greatest peril – when Stephen Byers threatened to legislate – our policy and our approach paid off…'[19]

Winsor had met many people in his five years as Rail Regulator, and had plainly been unimpressed with some of them:

'I caution you against the dogged ignorance and hostile agendas of supposed expert commentators in otherwise reputable consultancies, policy institutes and elsewhere. Some of these have used the cloak of the respectability of their organisations to steal past the defences of government and the serious press, and to get themselves listened to and believed by people who ought to know better. When that happens, it becomes necessary to explain, explain, explain, to counter the wild ideas which Ministers and others will hear based on misconceptions or worse. The struggle is constant...'

With Winsor's departure from the ORR, a railway era would come to an end. The responsibilities of the SRA would pass to the Department for Transport. Network Rail survived the Government's Rail Review, but some franchised operators would fall by the wayside. They might not have had the freedom that was once envisaged for them, but commercial risk was still as real as ever.

Chapter 28

'A wholly artificial construct'

Railway passenger franchisees are Government contractors, so competing 'open access' services (however laudable in free market theory) have proved to be unwelcome when they would have been rivals to services still attached to the state, even if they were no longer owned by it.

Protection of franchisees was achieved by the hasty invention of 'moderation of competition' – which gave the lie to one of the core planks of railway privatisation as it had been presented to the nation in 1992.

The implications of a truly free market were ominous, although these implications had been conveniently overlooked by the authors of the White Paper. If that document had been interpreted literally, any company qualifying on the grounds of competence and safety could have expected 'right of access' to the network.

Rarely has a potential legal right been extinguished so quickly. Indeed, the Office of Rail Regulator was considering the implications as early as 1994 – before any franchise had even been offered, much less awarded.

An ORR consultation document was published in July of that year. In it, the Regulator described the open access problem as a 'paradox', and was frank about the hurdles that a privatised industry faced:

'British Rail uses profit from some services to reduce the subsidy requirement on those which are maintained for social rather than commercial reasons. Within a franchise, the franchisee may operate both "commercial" and "social" services. Such operators are vulnerable to raiding by competitors if the latter are able to serve the profitable flows while avoiding the poorer markets the incumbent has to serve. In these circumstances, the incumbent suffers a loss of profit with which to cross-subsidise poorer performers and the requirement for subsidy from the taxpayer will go up or the pressure to reduce or withdraw services will increase.'[1]

To those who paid attention to transport history, this should have been a familiar problem. Rogue operators who existed only to 'skim the cream' from profitable routes rather than to provide a comprehensive service had threatened the bus industry in the 1920s. This was solved by various Acts of Parliament that eventually created London Transport as a unified transport authority in the capital and enforced the licensing of bus routes by regional Traffic Commissioners elsewhere.

However, many of the advocates of privatising the railways had either been unaware of the lessons of history or had chosen to ignore them, apparently on the specious and wholly unjustified assumption that somehow it would be different this time.

However, less than a year after the Railways Act had been passed it was already becoming obvious that a true 'right of access' could cause a free-for-all, followed by commercial and even operational chaos.

Accordingly, the ORR adopted a cautiously staged approach. The first stage was an explicit restriction of open access operation in the shorter term, while the franchises settled down. But the Regulator John Swift was vague about what might happen after that:

'I believe that a period of exclusivity, followed by a further period of restricted competition, is necessary for the development of a more competitive environment in the longer term. The initial period will provide a stable environment in which the market can prepare for increased competition and in which I will be able to gather more information to assist me in developing a policy appropriate for the longer term.'[2]

At least this demonstrated that the 1992 White Paper had been little more than a hopeful essay rather than a calculated set of proposals, while even the Rail Regulator seemed to have been seduced on occasion by the air of nebulous optimism that so often marked the early rail privatisation years:

'Franchising should … create some new competitive opportunities. Firstly, there will be a competitive bidding process for the award of franchises. Secondly, where the services of franchises overlap, or where they provide alternative routes to the same destination, competition may be expected to arise between them to serve the market they cover.'[3]

This was an echo of the forlorn wish for a 'healthy rivalry' between the Regions of British Railways, which had been predicted in the White Paper preceding the 1953 Transport Act (see Chapter 9), but in the event few franchises have ever competed with each other, apart from a few exceptional corridors such as London-Birmingham (where there are three main operators and also two distinct routes), London-Peterborough and London-Gatwick Airport. In the other cases where two or more franchises share a section of line there are rarely many 'operator specific' fares (apart from highly discounted Advance bookings), which makes competition all but meaningless.

Instead, operators sharing a section of route usually share the revenue according to industry standard formulae, although the operator that actually sells the ticket receives a small slice as commission before the rest is divided up.

In addition, although the Regulator could not have been expected to anticipate it in 1994, within a few years of his consultation on competition some of the original franchises were being combined or amended so that some larger territories were then mainly served by only one operator. The first of these was Wales & Borders in 2001, followed by Greater Anglia in 2004, then Greater Western two years later. This kind of 'remapping' of franchise boundaries removed even the limited opportunities for competition that might have previously existed between First Great Eastern and Anglia Railways, or between Great Western Trains and Wessex Trains. Neither was it evident where competition could possibly exist on most routes in Scotland.

In general, the real possibilities of rail-on-rail competition were offered by open access operators, as the 1992 White Paper had pointed out. But prudent second thoughts had soon prevailed, because a profusion of such operators was likely to 'abstract' revenue from the franchises and cost taxpayers more, as the Regulator warned in 1994.

The last of the original franchises had taken over from British Rail at the end of March 1997, but apart from the separate Heathrow Express, which did not compete with any franchise and began in 1998, Hull Trains did not begin running its open access services on the East Coast Main Line until September 2000. The majority owner of Hull Trains was GB Railways, the group that had also won the Anglia Railways franchise, but 20% was owned by Renaissance Trains, a group of former BR managers who had formed a company to promote open access services. (This operator became First Hull Trains after GB Railways was bought by FirstGroup in 2003, but two Renaissance shareholders still have the minority share.)

The franchised East Coast intercity operator GNER was running one train a day between London and Hull, and Hull Trains effectively quadrupled the service when it provided three more trains each way. (The service has grown since then, and First Hull Trains started to serve Beverley as well in February 2015.) Open access competition will also be seen on the West Coast Main Line before the end of the decade, when Alliance Holdings will start to run off-peak services between London and Blackpool.

Generally speaking, however, open access operators that want to provide passenger services have rarely been able to surmount the barrier presented by moderation of competition, although the MoC rules were eased slightly by the ORR in 2004.

However, if the purpose of an open access application is thought to be primarily abstractive then the application is still refused. To have any chance of success, a prospective operator must be offering through services on a route that is at best barely included in the franchised system (such as London-Hull) and preferably not catered for at all (such as London-Sunderland or Paddington-Heathrow Airport).

The 'abstraction' argument was the downfall of the first proposal in 2003 from Grand Central for services between Newcastle and Preston. This, it was feared, was likely to damage the forthcoming TransPennine Express franchise, so Grand Central was told to go away. It was more successful with London-Sunderland, then a second route between London and Bradford, but even so open access passenger services have continued to be rare beasts.

Grand Central did not achieve even its Sunderland route easily or quickly. The application was rigorously opposed by the franchised operator GNER, which was particularly concerned that Grand Central also proposed to call at York.

This is an important station on the East Coast route, and particularly attractive to railway operators because there is no airport nearby to compete for passengers (unlike Leeds, Newcastle or Edinburgh).

In March 2006 the ORR announced that it would grant access rights to Grand Central for its London-Sunderland route, including the York calls, and also allow Hull Trains to run an additional daily service between London and Hull, calling (like other HT services) at Doncaster.

GNER had won a new ten-year franchise in 2005 from the SRA that involved premiums worth £1.3bn but the storm clouds were soon gathering, mainly because of a growing financial crisis at GNER's parent Sea Containers.

By 2006 the future of GNER itself was in doubt, but the Department for Transport, which had now taken over from the SRA as the administrator of rail franchises, refused to renegotiate the terms of the contract, apparently on the grounds that it would set an undesirable precedent.

The ORR's award to Grand Central of its route to Sunderland via York was too much for GNER, which had lodged objections after the Grand Central application had been published. A full regulatory hearing was held by the ORR in March, which resulted in confirmation of the earlier decision, and GNER responded by saying it would seek judicial review. Interestingly, it seems to have been supported in this by the DfT, which was said to be dubious about the legality of how the ORR charged for open access.

One point that franchised operators often highlighted was that they paid more in track access charges to Network Rail than open access rivals. This was because both were liable to the 'variable' component of the charge, which depends on the number of trains, type of rolling stock and operating times (peak paths are more expensive), but up to the time of writing only franchises pay the 'fixed' component.

GNER's case was that as Grand Central was running on the same route and serving some of the same stations (the London-York sector was the sensitive one), it should pay the same track access charges.

Mr Justice Sullivan ruled on 27 July that the ORR's interpretation of both UK and European law was correct, and that granting a licence to Grand Central did not amount to discrimination.

By now, Network Rail was receiving some of its income by direct grant from the DfT, and the judge ruled that the amount that was left to be recovered from operators was 'entirely a product of horse-trading between the DfT, Network Rail and the ORR'.

He went on to point out that while franchise operators paid more, they also enjoyed the protection of a contract that included compensation in certain circumstances:

'In their negotiations with the DfT franchise bidders are able to, and do, obtain protection by way of indemnity ... against any increase in charges resulting from access charges reviews. They may also negotiate "cap and collar" risk sharing agreements with the DfT which give them (and the DfT) a measure of protection if revenues fall (or rise) below (or above) certain specified levels. Since none of these protections against the imposition, or subsequent alteration, of a charge that is a wholly artificial construct, are available to open access operators it would be contrary to non-discriminatory principles ... if the fixed track access charge was imposed on them.'[4]

The way that railways in Britain had been privatised and financed had never been previously assessed in public hearing by a High Court judge, and perhaps the words 'horse-trading' and 'a wholly artificial construct' should then have been rubber stamped on the cover of the 1993 Railways Act.

So GNER had lost the battle, and it went on to lose the war. As the fortunes of its parent Sea Containers continued to spiral downwards during the autumn of 2006, GNER was forced to tell the DfT that the game was up. Sea Containers CEO Bob McKenzie commented:

'While we are not in breach of the current franchise agreement, GNER will not be able to meet the significant increase in franchise premium obligations due from May 2007. We would have preferred a renegotiation of the current contract, but that was not available.'[5]

GNER's franchise ended in December, but the operator stayed on to run a management contract on behalf of the DfT, in return for a fixed fee, until a successor could take over.

The outcome of this case did not make any obvious difference to the subsequent fortunes of open access operators. Grand Central later gained a second route to Bradford in 2010, but another new operator survived only from April 2008 to January 2011.

This was Wrexham & Shropshire, which offered direct trains from Wrexham and Shrewsbury to London Marylebone. In spite of commendable standards of on-board service, it was particularly hampered by its uncompetitive journey times. It also faced problems imposed by the privatisation rules – particularly those that were a consequence of moderation of competition.

Virgin Trains – which extended two of its own Chester services onwards to Wrexham following the launch of the open access operation – wielded MoC clauses to prevent the Wrexham company calling at some stations between Shrewsbury and

London, particularly Birmingham New Street. It should be added that Virgin said it was bound to protect its operations, because otherwise it would have been in breach of its franchise contract, but as a result Wrexham was forced, for example, to divert its trains away from Wolverhampton to call instead at Tame Bridge Parkway.

This was hardly in the spirit of the 1992 White Paper – in reality a 'right of access' to stations like Wolverhampton or Birmingham New Street could not be demanded – and, perhaps inevitably, its service failed to prosper.

The relationship of the railways and the state evolved yet again after 2006 because the SRA had been abolished, so that direct management of franchises and related matters was now the responsibility of the DfT, although it was then accused of 'micro-management' (in October 2009 the Association of Train Operating Companies described the level of detailed management from the DfT as 'inappropriate'[6]).

Certainly the focus of control moved to the DfT in an unprecedented way (we may recall Sir John Reith's comment in 1940 (Chapter 5) that 'I would rather have private ownership than nationalisation, if nationalisation means the conduct of public services by Government Departments'. Recent orders for rolling stock, such as the replacement Thameslink fleet and the Intercity Express trains, have been masterminded by the DfT, which then writes the specification into the relevant franchise agreements.

As far as the East Coast intercity services were concerned, they were entering a long period of uncertainty. The management contract run by GNER after its formal franchise had ended gave way to a new National Express franchise that began with the usual high hopes in November 2007.

Industry eyebrows were raised when it became clear that National Express had offered premiums worth some £1.4bn – more than GNER. Indeed, as the new franchise was to run for seven years and five months, the equivalent daily premiums payable rose from approximately £350,000 to £500,000.

National Express had beaten rivals who included a consortium of Virgin and Stagecoach, advised by GNER. In response to the news, Sea Containers said the previous GNER franchise had ended because of several factors that 'included the loss of revenue due to the London bombings in July 2005, higher energy and fuel costs, and regulatory permission being granted for a new open access entrant on the route'.[7]

This statement was notable for including the only recorded claim from a failed franchisee that an open access rival had contributed to its downfall, but without moderation of competition there would probably have been more.

Today Grand Central is a subsidiary of Arriva plc, which is in turn now owned by Deutsche Bahn. GC has accrued considerable losses but has made a number of other applications for more routes, most of which have been rejected.

The long-running saga of international rail services reached an important point in November 2007 when the second phase of the high-speed line from the Channel

Tunnel to London was opened and Eurostar services were transferred from Waterloo to St Pancras.

The Channel Tunnel itself had opened in 1994 but its operator, Eurotunnel, would prove to be a financial disaster, being saved only by a major 'restructuring' of its debts in 2006 and 2007.

The question of how London was to be connected to the Tunnel was answered in the early years by equipping the Eurostar fleet with third-rail equipment. Britain now had an international train service that did not rely on ferries but, just like the former boat trains to Folkestone or Dover, it still ran on the former Southern Region of British Railways.

As a result, journeys between London and the Tunnel inevitably seemed slow – particularly so when compared with the 300km/h running that was achieved from the beginning between the French tunnel portal and Paris – and a high-speed Channel Tunnel Rail Link was authorised by Act of Parliament in 1996.

A consortium known as London & Continental Railways was chosen to build the line, but the Channel Tunnel had already proved that conventional sources of private capital were inadequate (Eurotunnel was saved by a complex conversion of debt into equity capital), and so it was with London & Continental, which was only rescued when the Government agreed to fund it with Treasury-guaranteed bonds.

It had been intended that Railtrack would purchase the first section at least, but this idea had to be abandoned when Railtrack failed, and the complete project became the property of London & Continental Railways, which built both sections of the line but became insolvent in 2009. The only possible solution was nationalisation, and once London & Continental Railways had passed into public ownership a 30-year operating concession was let for £2.1bn in November 2010 to a Canadian consortium, which now operates the link (known for most purposes as High Speed 1 since 2006) and its stations.

In short, repeated efforts to fund major railway projects with private capital had failed, and it is only because of public money that passengers can now travel by train between London and Paris in little more than two hours.

We may also note here that open access became a reality on international rail routes in 2010, but that Eurostar has yet to encounter a competitor at St Pancras, in spite of optimistic noises from Deutsche Bahn, which took the trouble to have one of its intercity sets propelled into St Pancras for a single day in October 2010. As these words are written in the summer of 2015, DB has still not returned.

Eurostar itself was owned jointly (if unevenly) by the railway administrations of France, Great Britain and Belgium, but the British share of 40% was sold in March 2015 to a largely Canadian-funded buyer, although a UK investment house has a minor stake.

So private capital has returned to the Channel Tunnel Rail Link and its trains, but not without an intervening period of state intervention.

In some ways, the CTRL saga is a mirror of the domestic railway industry in Britain over the past 20 years – in spite of determined efforts by Government to separate the railway and the state, the divorce has never become absolute.

This reality was underlined in 2009, when GNER's successor National Express was forced to concede that the terms of its East Coast franchise were too onerous. Accordingly, since renegotiation was again ruled out, the operation was transferred to the Department for Transport's subsidiary Directly Operated Railways in November.

This inadvertent renationalisation was not unprecedented because, after Connex had been dismissed from Southeastern in 2003, that franchise had been operated on behalf of the Strategic Rail Authority until Govia won the next private sector contract in 2006.

However, the return of East Coast to the public sector gained more attention – it is one of the country's key intercity franchises, and also the one that has repeatedly defeated its operators.

The original intention was that East Coast would be relet by 2011, according to the Transport Secretary Lord (Andrew) Adonis:

'East Coast will remain in public hands for two years and there will be full continuity of service. But this is not a care and maintenance job – I want to see real improvements in the service and better value for money... This is a profitable railway – it needs to be the pride of its passengers and staff too and that's my aim for East Coast.'[8]

In the event, East Coast was not returned to the private sector until March 2015, when control passed to a consortium of Stagecoach Group and Virgin Trains. In spite of the branding – Virgin Trains East Coast – Stagecoach actually owns 90%, compared with 49% of the Intercity West Coast franchise.

The 'nationalisation' of East Coast inevitably re-ignited the ownership debate, with rail unions pointing out that the profits mentioned by Lord Adonis were now being paid to the Treasury rather than shareholders.

This was true, but there was also room for misunderstanding here as well, thanks to the labyrinth of railway finances. When East Coast announced that it had paid a 'premium' of £190.5m in 2012-13, the figure was greeted with delight by the proponents of public ownership. What they tended to overlook was that East Coast's share of the grant paid to Network Rail was calculated as £206.2m. In other words, Lord Adonis's 'profitable' railway had needed effective public subsidy of £15.7m in 2012-13 alone.

While East Coast was in public hands, the spotlight was turned again on railway costs. The Conservative Government that had been elected in 2010 wanted to control all aspects of public spending more firmly, and it accordingly employed a businessman whose main transport experience had been in the aviation sector, Sir Roy McNulty, to prepare a report on railway finances.

His main conclusion was that railways in Britain were costing more to run than their counterparts on the continent. On 19 May 2011 the Transport Secretary, Stephen Hammond, summarised the McNulty findings in a statement to the House of Commons:

'Spending on the passenger railway has increased by 60% in real terms since 1996/97, that's more than £4bn, and despite significant passenger growth, unit costs in 2009 were almost exactly the same in real terms as in 1996, so that UK rail is now up to 40% more expensive per passenger mile than the railways of our European competitors. After allowing for unavoidable differences, Sir Roy estimates that UK rail costs are 20-30% higher than they should be, and that potential savings amounting to between £740m and £1.05bn a year could be found by 2018/19 without any reductions in services. These savings, when added to the savings Network Rail are already committed to achieving to 2014 and the savings Sir Roy expects the Regulator to seek from Network Rail over the period to 2019, should largely close this efficiency gap.'[9]

The brave words would not be borne out by experience, partly because some of the McNulty recommendations appeared to be logical enough until their practical consequences were considered. One example of this was provided by his controversial contention (bitterly opposed by the unions) that trains should be operated only by a driver; '...the default position for all services on the GB rail network should be DOO, with a second member of traincrew only being provided where there is a commercial, technical or other imperative.'[10]

The reality was that there are a number of potential 'imperatives' that could pose exceptions to the rule. On local lines with unstaffed stations, for example, revenue collection is the responsibility of the conductor. A truly DOO train would offer free rides, although a second member of staff could travel on board to sell and check tickets but take no part in the operation of the train. Such a person would cost less to employ than a fully qualified conductor.

A DOO train could still run if such a second member of staff was not available, even if some of the revenue would then be at risk. But that would not answer the legal requirements for accessibility at unstaffed stations. Who would then place a wheelchair ramp in position?

Four years after McNulty, few reforms have so far been directly linked to his conclusions (some of which which were positive), although there may be more to come. We may note that the new Intercity Express fleets being built for the East Coast and Great Western Main Lines have door controls in every drivers' cab, and that on the Great Western at least it is planned that the driver will be in charge of the doors, although a Train Manager and other staff will still be on board.

We have already said that Sir John Reith did not welcome the direct involvement of government departments in the administration of public services, and one event in 2012 tended to confirm his caution, voiced more than 70 years earlier.

The letting of the West Coast franchise was a high-profile business. It had been run by Virgin Trains (itself a high-profile brand) since 1997, and its status had passed from franchise to management contract and back to franchise again. It had been dogged by Railtrack's failure to modernise the West Coast line properly, but nonetheless had managed to introduce an unprecedented three trains an hour on the routes from London to Birmingham and Manchester in 2008 – which then offered the most frequent intercity services in Europe.

Although also dogged by continuing infrastructure problems that were mostly related to the de-scoped 'upgrade' of its key route, it was undeniably popular with its passengers. There was considerable public surprise, therefore, when the DfT announced on 15 August 2012 that FirstGroup had won the new Intercity West Coast franchise, which would run for up to 15 years.

There were many improvements offered in the FirstGroup bid: new routes and trains, a reduction of 15% in 'Anytime' fares over the first two years, and premiums of £5.5 billion.

Everyone – operator, passengers and taxpayers – seemed set to win as a result. But as with many things that seem almost too good to be true, it was.

The first hint of a storm on the horizon came from the dislodged incumbent Virgin Trains, whose founder Sir Richard Branson was not only disappointed, but doubtful:

'…this is the fourth time that we have been out-bid in a rail tender. On the past three occasions, the winning operator has come nowhere close to delivering their promised plans and revenue, and has let the public and country down dramatically. In the case of the East Coast Main Line, both winners – GNER and National Express – over-promised in order to win the franchise and spectacularly ran into financial difficulties in trying to deliver their plans. The East Coast is still in Government ownership and its service is outdated and underinvested, costing passengers and the country dearly as a result. Insanity is doing the same thing over and over again and expecting different results. When will the Department for Transport learn?'[11]

In fact, the Department was about to learn quite a lot. The reality was that its financial modelling had gone awry, and the award was not sustainable.

After a tense period, during which Virgin Trains started legal action to formally challenge the DfT's figures and a petition of protest attracted more than 100,000 signatures, and while the Department continued to maintain that it would defend any legal challenge 'robustly'[12], the civil servants climbed down.

On 3 October the newly appointed Transport Secretary, Patrick McLoughlin, had to withdraw the decision that had been signed off by his predecessor, Justine Greening:

'I have had to cancel the competition for the running of the West Coast franchise because of deeply regrettable and completely unacceptable mistakes made by my department in the way it managed the process. A detailed examination by my officials into what happened has revealed these flaws and means it is no longer possible to award a new franchise on the basis of the competition that was held. I have ordered two independent reviews to look urgently and thoroughly into the matter so that we know what exactly happened and how we can make sure our rail franchise programme is fit for purpose.'[13]

What had gone wrong? Essentially, the DfT had got its sums wrong, as the House of Commons Transport Committee later explained:

'The Department made a number of mistakes when identifying the amount of risk capital (called the subordinated loan facility) it required from bidders to balance the riskiness of their bid. It failed to include inflation in its calculation and also applied discretion in deciding the amount it asked from bidders which was not allowed in the stated process. These errors led to the Department asking FirstGroup for a lower subordinated loan facility than was needed to protect itself from the recognised additional risk in the bid. A higher subordinated loan facility was requested from Virgin Trains. This opened the Department to the risk of legal challenge and ultimately led to the cancellation of the franchise competition.'[14]

It was not the first time. The introduction of private enterprise on London Underground more than ten years earlier by creating public-private partnerships called Metronet and Tube Lines to maintain and renew the infrastructure had failed to endure for similar reasons – the financial risks had not been properly assessed.

The results of cancelling the West Coast franchise competition were far-reaching. One of the inquiries, led by Centrica Chief Executive Sam Laidlaw, was to concentrate on the details of the errors, while the other, led by former Eurostar Chief Executive and Chairman Richard Brown, would draw up a new franchising programme for the Department.

In the meantime, the DfT had to go through the humiliating process of negotiating a temporary continuation of the Virgin Trains operation on the West Coast Main Line. This was followed by the direct award of a fresh contract, which means that Virgin will now be on the West Coast route until at least 2017.

FirstGroup, which had not been accused of making any mistake (apart, perhaps, from bidding for West Coast at all), had been evidently unaware that trouble was brewing:

'Until this point we had absolutely no indication that there were any issues with the franchise letting process and had received assurances from the DfT that their processes were robust and that they expected to sign the contract with FirstGroup soon. We are extremely disappointed to learn this news and await the outcome of the DfT's inquiries. The DfT have made it clear to us that we are in no way at fault, having followed the due process correctly. We submitted a strong bid, in good faith and in strict accordance with the DfT's terms.'[15]

All four bidders later received a refund of their costs. When Departmental expenditure was added, the total bill for the taxpayer came to more than £50m.

The Department for Transport is still in charge of railway franchising as this book goes to press, but part of the West Coast fallout has been a major reorganisation of the Department and the creation of a subsidiary Rail Executive, which itself contains a Passenger Services division.

When Patrick McLoughlin announced details of the DfT reforms in February 2014, following an internal review, he also signalled that the work of reorganisation was not necessarily complete:

'The review has … recommended we consider a longer term option of a new, more arms-length body with responsibility for rail delivery functions. The creation of the rail executive provides a strong foundation for such future evolution and the government will consider moving to a more arms-length body in 2016.'[16]

The Conservative victory in May 2015 suggests that there will be little to prevent the creation of such an arms-length body in due course. It could be called the Office of Passenger Rail Franchising.

Meanwhile, the wheels continue to go round. The newest major project is HS2, but its evolving story has yet to be told, although if all goes to plan the first trains are due to arrive at 'Birmingham Curzon' – the city's new high-speed station – around 2026.

As for the rest of the network, usage is steadily increasing, although worryingly accompanied by concerns in 2015 about the low rate of progress and high costs of some major projects managed by Network Rail, which were followed by the 'pausing' of some electrification schemes in June and changes of personnel at board level.

The industry may not be untroubled, but it also has a good deal to celebrate – including its own survival.

As Northern Rail Managing Director Alex Hynes told the *Financial Times* on 31 May 2015: 'British Rail was managing decline. It spent years closing stations, depots and lines. Now we spend our time opening things.'

Chapter 29

'A sharp inspection'

Railway finances continue to cause confusion today, partly because the subject is both complex and obscure, but also because there are frequent efforts in some quarters to rewrite the story (to put it kindly) in order to reinforce a particular point of view or objective.

For example, the announcement of the change of status of Network Rail in December 2013, in which the previously 'private' company became a public sector government body from 1 September 2014, was not actually nationalisation – according to the Department for Transport. However, the *Oxford English Dictionary* defines nationalisation as the transfer of a private enterprise to state ownership, which seemed to be what happened.

There is, perhaps, some room for manoeuvre in that Network Rail had not been a private sector enterprise in the conventional sense, but that had not prevented Governments from both sides of the House routinely insisting that it amounted to the same thing.

Thus, when a change of stance in the statistical office triggered a reclassification of the company's liabilities, the semantic chickens came home to roost at the DfT. Nonetheless, the Department continued to maintain that the change did not amount to nationalisation – but did not explain why. Whatever the distinction may have been, it was too fine for the present author to discern, but this type of juggling with railway facts has become commonplace.

One of the most often-heard examples is the frequent assertion that the involvement of the private sector has been the principle cause of railway growth since the mid-'90s.

Here is Transport Secretary Patrick McLoughlin speaking in the House of Commons on 26 March 2013:

'Traffic has doubled since privatisation from 750 million journeys a year to 1.5 billion now. There are more services and record levels of investment. And our railways have the best recent safety record in Europe. That hasn't been achieved despite privatisation. It has been achieved because of privatisation.'[1]

This looks suspiciously like an example of what American statistician Darrell Huff dubbed the 'post hoc fallacy' ('post hoc', literally 'after this', refers to the examination of data after an experiment to seek patterns – such as possible connections between cause and effect). As Mr Duff put it, 'You need to put any statement of relationship through a sharp inspection.'[2]

It is true that passenger figures on National Rail have risen steeply since privatisation, but they had tended to rise during the previous decade as well, having fallen to an historically low point of 630m in 1982.

The cumulative annual increase between then and 1995 had been almost 1.5%, but this average concealed some greater rises and also some retreats. For example, the passenger total in 1988 had been 822m, but it was back down to 735m by 1994, after another period of national economic woe.

In 1995, the last full year before the first private sector operators took over, passenger traffic was up again by just over 3.5% to 761m, yet Mr McLoughlin claimed in 2013 that the Government had privatised an industry that was 'still in decline'[3].

Like the rest of the country, British Rail had experienced mixed fortunes during the 1908s, but it takes some ingenuity to describe an increase in a single year of just over 3.5% as a decline.

However, usage has certainly risen much more significantly since 1995. The ORR quotes the passenger journey total for 2013-14 as almost 1.59bn (although as we shall see this figure also merits a sharp inspection, for slightly different reasons).

What is particularly interesting is the trend in the years immediately after 1995, which saw the totals rise further in 1996 to 801.4m, in 1997 to 845.7m and in 1998 to 891.9m.

On the face of it these figures would appear to vindicate Mr McLoughlin's claim, until we pause to consider what difference privatisation actually made to most rail users in those early years. At this point the argument starts to collapse.

After private sector operators had taken over, the trains they leased bore new logos and in some cases different colours, while publicity was redesigned, but what else happened in the early years?

The industry-led factors that can attract more passengers include new or upgraded trains, electrification, refurbished or additional stations, more frequent services and lower fares.

There had been a famine in new train orders as privatisation unwound, because British Rail was no longer in a position to make any major capital commitments and the new franchise contracts had yet to be awarded. It took several years after 1996-97 to pick up the slack, not least because rolling stock cannot be built overnight.

So a replacement fleet for the London, Tilbury & Southend route, agreed with the new franchisee in 1996 and ordered in 1997, did not start to enter service until 2000.

New tilting trains for intercity services on Virgin West Coast, which began in 1997, took still longer to arrive; a 'Pendolino' was propelled into Euston for a media event in April 2002, and the first ceremonial runs under power were made later that year.

Indeed, some major routes such as the Great Western and East Coast Main Lines have still seen only a few trains that have been built since BR days, although that situation is due to change by 2017-18.

No route was newly electrified in the privatisation era before 2003, while station upgrades and improved timetables were not a strong feature of the initial franchises, at least in their earlier years.

As for fares, it is true that some of the new intercity operators took advantage of modern technology to introduce 'yield management', which in practice means discounted fares on specified trains, but again this took a number of years to achieve.

Even so, by 2000-01 the passenger total had reached 956.6m, an increase of 25.7% on 1995, but to perceive a causal link between that increase and the quality of privatised railway services at the time is a remarkable leap of faith. There could be other reasons for passenger growth, even if they have been officially disregarded.

Jonathan Ely suggested as much in the *Financial Times* on 22 August 2014, when he wrote:

'The government likes to claim that privatisation has resulted in record passenger numbers. This seems rather dubious; how can we know how many of the extra passengers are because of general population growth, rising house prices, more expensive petrol or congestion on the roads?'

The short answer to Mr Ely's very reasonable question is that we can't and we don't. On the other hand, it may be also be wrong to entirely dismiss privatisation – or at least some of the activities of the privatised operators – as a contributory cause of growth.

As the ORR comments:

'There are a number of possible factors behind recent increases in rail usage such as the opening of new lines and stations, additional services/trains, ticketing initiatives including special offers/discounts, and more competitive pricing.'[4]

This usefully sums up some of the industry-inspired causes of growth. Of the four possible factors quoted, the first is rarely due to significant investment by franchised operators, while the second is largely controlled by contracts with local or national government, but the remaining two are more likely to be based on franchisees' commercial decisions.

Even so, there would have been little to prevent British Rail offering similar discounts, particularly had the former railways board been able to make concrete long-term financial plans, equivalent to franchise terms or Network Rail's five-year control periods.

It is probably true that some examples of 'competitive pricing' between rail operators are a result of the franchise structure, although in practice these are far from being industry-wide, being confined in the main to corridors like London-Birmingham.

The other point is that 'bargain' fares that are the product of commercial initiatives are rarely applicable to commuters with season tickets, who make up nearly half of the passenger business.

Advance fares on intercity services may well boost travel in that sector, but total long-distance ridership in 2013-14 was just 129.2m, up from 77.2m in 2002-03.

An increase of 67.3% in just over a decade is laudable, but then the base was very low when compared to the commuter market.

A useful indicative figure for this market is provided by the total for season ticket holders, who made an estimated 691.5m journeys in 2013-14 compared to 411.9m in 2002-03, an increase of 67.8%. The third sector, 'regional' journeys, has grown slightly less, having risen by 60.0% since 2002-03.

But we can see that the growth has been fairly general and is not confined to one sector, so when we try to explain why passenger travel has risen so remarkably, we have look further than discounted fares on long-distance trains.

Of course, discounted fares do play a part, but they are not an exclusive feature of privatisation. British Rail was offering discounted 'Apex' intercity fares in the 1980s, and although there were few opportunities for genuine route competition, where they did (and do) exist, as between London and Birmingham, it is possible to visualise BR's passenger sectors behaving in a similar manner, with a relatively independent InterCity competing with Network SouthEast or a comparable successor.

Of course, it is to be expected that key figures in the transport groups holding rail franchises will favour the present structure.

For example, Tim O'Toole, speaking as Chief Executive of FirstGroup and Chairman of the Rail Delivery Group, used disparaging terms about nationalised organisations when he gave the 2nd Bradshaw Lecture in November 2012, referring to them as 'state-owned monoliths' lacking the 'diversity' to 'fuel innovation'.

Mr O'Toole made a strong plea for the capitalist motive, but between 2002 and 2009 he had been charge of London Underground, which, in spite of a disastrous attempt by Labour Chancellor Gordon Brown to privatise maintenance and renewals, was then and still is in public ownership, as a subsidiary of Transport for London.

London Underground also provides a useful comparison with National Rail. If Mr McLoughlin is right to attribute the dramatic growth in rail demand to privatisation, by the same token we might expect nationalised LU to have grown much more slowly, if at all.

The statistics, however, tell another story. Between 1995 and 2013 the National Rail total increased by 109% from 761m to almost 1,590m, while London Underground recorded 1,265m passenger journeys in 2013, up by 61% from 784m in 1995. However, there is a substantial inflation factor in National Rail totals (see below) which, when discounted, actually brings the two rises even closer together.

So much for the ineffectiveness of state-owned monoliths.

The National Rail passenger total itself is a statistic beloved of politicians and the railway industry, and it is now common to hear official boasts that passenger figures have set yet another record.

It is true that, irrespective of the causes, the trajectory of the total has been almost uniformly upwards since 1995.

There have been two brief departures from this trend. One of these was a noticeable pause in growth after the Hatfield derailment in the autumn of 2000, although it is possible that this was caused at least partly by the consequent disruption rather than the accident itself, while there was an actual (if modest) fall in the annual total as the economic crisis deepened in 2008-09.

Demand on the passenger railway is certainly historically high. The last time so many people used the railway was 1945, a highly atypical year in which demand was swollen artificially by wartime needs, particularly the conveyance of many thousands of 'demobbed' members of the Forces.

The total in 1945 was 1.372bn, including an estimated 316m journeys by season ticket holders. It was the highest total reached during the war years, and would have been even higher had the amount of travel on season tickets not been depressed by wartime conditions. Passenger kilometres were estimated as 56.7bn.

Almost 70 years later, the official (ORR) totals for 2013-14 were 1.587bn journeys, involving 59.2bn passenger kilometres.

At first sight this indeed does appear to be a record, but these figures conceal an important difference.

The traditional method of measuring passenger traffic was by 'originating journeys', so that a journey from, say, Birmingham New Street to Looe would be recorded by the LMS but not the GWR, assuming that a through ticket was issued at Birmingham.

This approach began to change in the 1980s, when each British Rail business sector involved claimed a share, so that the journey from Birmingham to Looe would now be recorded by both InterCity and Provincial.

The immediate effect of this was to inflate passenger totals, which was probably helpful at a time when demand was dangerously low.

Even so, the extent of this statistical exaggeration was fairly limited, as there were only three passenger sectors.

The ORR says that each 'leg' of a journey is now counted using the industry's 'Lennon' database, although the definition of a 'leg' is a little uncertain.

The effect, judging by the comparative measure of rail journeys in and between Government Office Regions (which are counted only once), is to inflate the totals by 20-25%, which implies the figure of 1,586.5m in Table 10 has been exaggerated by at least 265m.

So as far as 'originating journeys' are concerned, the real total is more like 1,320m. This means that 1945 is still just ahead (but may not be for much longer if the current growth trend continues).

Meanwhile, the controversial subject of fares routinely raises its head every January in Britain, when the annual review takes effect.

On 31 December 2013 the author was asked in a radio interview if the new annual season ticket rate from a particular station in South East England was not 'a poor

Table 10: British Rail and National Rail passenger totals, 1993-2014 (million)

1993	740.1	2004	1,039.5
1994	735.1	2005	1,076.5
1995	761.2	2006	1,145.0
1996	801.4	2007	1,218.1
1997	845.7	2008	1,266.5
1998	891.9	2009	1,257.9
1999	931.0	2010	1,353.8
2000	956.6	2011	1,460.0
2001	959.6	2012	1,500.9
2002	975.5	2013	1,586.5
2003	1,011.7	2014	1,653.7

Figures are for April-March: thus, '2013' is April 2013 to March 2014
Source: ORR

deal'. When the alternatives (living in London or driving to the city each day) were costed, it became clear that the railway charge was not particularly outrageous, and indeed appeared to be easily the cheapest of the three.

This fact does not prevent railway commuters from protesting bitterly when their fares rise by almost any amount, although why season ticket rates should be immune to the normal economic pressures that tend to increase the prices of all services and commodities over time is not clear.

A related case of semi-wishful thinking emerged on the same day, when Stephen Joseph of the Campaign for Better Transport observed, with evident disapproval, that given the present trends in passenger fares,

'...by the next Parliament income from fares will not only cover the entire running costs of the railways, [but] the Government will actually begin to start profiting from passengers. The Government must re-examine its fares policy as a matter of urgency and commit to a fairer system in line with the consumer price index so that fares only rise in line with wages.'

Although this may seem to be a fairly standard comment from a pressure group like the CBT, it actually raises the most fundamental point of all: what are the railways for?

The industry began as a collection of separate enterprises that merged over time into successively larger bodies before they were compulsorily bought out by the state in 1948.

As we have seen, railway profits continued to decline after nationalisation and became deficits. That is still the case today, in spite of various upheavals before and since privatisation in 1994-96.

It does not seem conceivable that the industry will ever show a true cash surplus again, given that freight (originally the real moneymaker) has been divorced, apparently for good, from the passenger business.

This does not mean that railways are unimportant, nor that they lack the potential to play an increasingly important role in surface transport. But they are not likely to make much money again, in the direct sense. Indeed, it is interesting that the possibility of even a notional profit from passengers can now be seen as unreasonable by some industry observers.

Of course, such a profit would remain entirely illusory if the industry were to be considered as a whole, given that Network Rail receives direct annual grants of £4bn or so, although the Rail Delivery Group ingeniously argued on 9 July 2014 that 'the railway and its supply chain have an economic footprint of £9.3bn, employ 212,000 people and pay £3.9bn a year in tax, offsetting nearly all of the £4bn the industry receives from government'.

Oh, Dr Beeching, why did you not think of that?

The former companies needed capital and therefore had to use some of their revenues to pay dividends and interest, but modern franchised operators do not need much capital beyond the costs of bidding and, if they are successful, the funds that they must deposit with the DfT (to protect season ticket holders, for example). They are essentially contractors with limited lives who lease or rent most of the tangible assets. These leases and tenancies naturally end when the franchise does.

The question that seems to be neglected by some transport campaigners is how they think railway capital should be raised and serviced now. It would appear that the state, via Network Rail, is the only possible source – certainly the operators can rarely do it, and even then only on a comparatively small scale, so that such projects as major electrification schemes would be quite beyond them. Third party sources of finance are theoretically available, but only at a price. Again, there is no reason for an operator to commit itself in this way, so any serious borrowing has been done in the name of Network Rail – which really means HM Treasury.

As we have seen, shortage of capital has been a major stumbling block for the railways at various times over the past century. It was one of the causes of the Grouping in 1923, but within six years the state was making the first of what would prove to be many grants to help the railways.

Nationalisation, heralded in 1948 as a new dawn, was followed by a chaotic period during which the British Transport Commission struggled to balance its books without success and ended its existence deeply in debt. It was in this period, too, that a major contribution by the state intended to pay for widescale modernisation failed to reverse the industry's fortunes.

From 1963 the British Railways Board was also confronted by financial uncertainties and hostile civil servants, particularly in its first decade, and more than once the industry faced further serious contraction – which in the event was narrowly avoided.

Privatisation in 1993 was a hastily contrived muddle and involved a structure that proved to be unworkable in its original form, but in the second decade of the 21st century we seemed to enter a period of optimism, fostered by greater Government and political support, which is naturally encouraged by the continuing growth in demand.

However, even as Network Rail was beginning its fifth five-year control period in 2014 with a headline budget of £38bn to invest in the new improved railway, some cracks were starting to appear.

Chapter 30

The Railway Dilemma

A consistent theme in this narrative has been the close and often turbulent relationship between the railway and the state.

Having explored some of the detail we can now attempt to assess the progressive effects of this relationship over almost two centuries, before considering its implications for the future.

The heavy hand of government did not make itself felt to any great extent in the earliest days. The railway industry was no more than a modest collection of pioneering, privately funded enterprises in the 1830s, but as its influence grew it inevitably attracted more detailed official attention.

The initial requirement for a railway was usually at least one Private Act of Parliament. This might be avoided – at least at first – if the entire line ran over the property of just one landowner without crossing any highway, but this was almost never the case (although wayleaves provided another solution in some instances).

We have seen that the first major public Act regulating the industry was passed in 1840, while just four years later another Railway Regulation Act forced companies to operate 'Parliamentary' or 'Cheap' trains offering Third Class accommodation at legally capped fares, which called at all stations, protected their passengers from the weather and ran at a minimum speed.[1]

Since such a law could not be retrospective, the relevant section ingeniously provided that this requirement would apply to all newly authorised railways, and also to existing companies when they returned to Parliament at any time in the future seeking further powers – which was usually a necessity sooner or later for all but the smallest.

This kind of legislation could be a force for social good, because until then many companies had barely tolerated Third Class passengers, sometimes providing them with nothing better than crude open wagons. 'Parliamentary' trains improved the situation from the travellers' point of view, but some Directors were still haunted by the suspicion that some of the more prosperous passengers were taking advantage of their liberality:

'The extent to which advantage of the accommodation ... afforded was taken by classes of persons for whom it was not intended, has obliged your Directors ... to reduce the number of Third Class Trains, and so to regulate the times at which they run as to adapt them, as far as circumstances would admit, more exclusively to the wants of the labouring classes.'[2]

This was on the South Devon Railway in 1847, but the SDR Directors were not alone in their view. The law could not be evaded but, as a disincentive to those who were not members of the 'labouring classes', 'Parliamentary' departures could be forbiddingly early, when most of the gentry had hardly descended to their breakfast rooms. The London & South Western timetable for June 1847 showed six trains a day running from London to Southampton, but only one of these – the 07.30 departure from Nine Elms – conveyed Third Class passengers.

Potential control of general passenger fares and goods rates also emerged for the first time in the 1844 Act, although at first this was to apply only to companies incorporated from then on, and those that declared annual dividends of more than 10% after they had existed for 21 years, at which point their profits were presumably regarded as excessive.

Meanwhile, the taxman had already moved in. An Act of 1832 extended a duty on the fares paid by coach passengers on the turnpike roads to those travelling on the new railways 'in or upon carriages drawn or impelled by the power of steam or otherwise.'[2]

This duty was charged at the rate of one halfpenny for each four passengers carried one mile by train, effectively adding just over 3½d to the price of a ticket between Manchester and Liverpool. In response, the railway increased its charges to include the duty, but also took the opportunity to add another 3d to the average fare, an act of commercial initiative that one contemporary commentator said was then nearly balanced by 'the diminution in the number of passengers' – suggesting that the Liverpool & Manchester Railway had made the fatal mistake of charging more than the traffic would bear.[3]

Ten years later this duty was changed to a flat 5% of each fare paid, although when 'Parliamentary' trains were introduced they were exempted from it. Such exemptions (or 'remissions') were gradually extended to Third Class tickets on other trains, and by the 1870s the companies were lobbying for Passenger Duty to be abolished altogether. But their critics did not agree:

'Parliament has armed the Railways with power to take land wherever and in whatever quantity they require, it authorises them even to pull down whole quarters of the most densely peopled parts of our great towns, to block up streets, to cut thoroughfares, and generally to disarrange all other traffics. In addition it invests them with legislative functions, it enables them to maintain a police of their own, and it has actually gone the length of creating special offences for their protection. Is it unreasonable to make them pay a small price for such extensive favours?'[4]

Such arguments did not prevent the duty retreating further in 1883, mainly to encourage the provision of cheap trains for workmen. It was never imposed in Ireland nor on light railways, although elsewhere it continued to apply in First Class and the dwindling Second Class until 1929.

The quotation above (from *The Spectator*) does not tell the whole story. The railways were indeed granted many powers, but at a much greater price than just the payment of Passenger Duty.

As the concept of an industry regulator in the modern sense was foreign to the Victorians, the only tried and tested mechanism they knew was the full weight of statute law, which in the case of railways was mainly enforced by the Board of Trade.

The succession of Acts passed from 1840 onwards obliged the companies to provide detailed operating and commercial statistics at regular intervals, under pain of financial penalties for defaulters. New lines could not be built without the permission of Parliament, nor opened for public traffic without the approval of a railway inspector.

The inspectors, whose department was part of the Board of Trade for many years, were customarily recruited from the Royal Engineers. They were efficient and conscientious gentlemen; when one of them visited a newly constructed railway (the narrow-gauge Talyllyn) in 1866, little seems to have escaped his critical eye:

'There are 7 bridges over and 15 under the Railway, beside a viaduct 51 feet high, and 38 yards long. At a bridge 3½ miles from Towyn the wall plate under the beams should be better secured and the beams in this and other instances be bolted together towards each end. Two brick arches … should be rebuilt… The Company has only two engines of which the heaviest is said to weigh 8 tons in working order … it is desirable that some alteration should be made in them, with a view to check the vertical motion to which … one is liable from its short wheel base…'[5]

The result of this visit was a refusal to allow the line to open until improvements had been made.

The regulation of railways became almost all-embracing. Other requirements approved by Parliament included maintenance of lineside fences, allowing the public to send messages on railway telegraphs, provision of level crossings (and the employment of 'proper persons' to open and close their gates), compulsory conveyance of mail as well as police officers and members of the armed forces ('at fares not exceeding twopence a mile for each commissioned officer proceeding on duty, such officer being entitled to conveyance in a First Class carriage'), and reporting accidents to the Board of Trade ('whether attended with personal injury or not').

Even the longer-term status of newly authorised companies was placed in doubt from 1844; they were not only compelled to run 'Parliamentary' trains from their opening day, but the state could also buy them out after they had existed for 21 years (this power was never exercised, and when nationalisation eventually did come in 1948 it was total).

In 1854 the companies were told that they must provide 'all reasonable facilities' for goods traffic but not give 'undue or unreasonable preference' to particular firms or people.[6]

In other words, although the railways were private enterprises that received no state aid or support, they were not free agents. Unlike other businesses they were forbidden to choose their customers; if they did not accommodate all-comers and deal with them equally, they risked fines and legal injunctions.

The justification for this kind of regulation was that railways had gained an effective monopoly of most inland transport, and although such a monopoly was inevitable until motor vehicles appeared, it could at least be diluted by legal means.

Whatever merit this view may have possessed in the 19th century, it persisted long after the railway's supremacy had disappeared, and would be a major cause of the industry's financial descent after the First World War.

The tightening of the state's grip on the railways continued in the later 19th century, and outright regulation of goods charges (the most important part of railway revenue) was introduced at the end of the 1880s.

However, the first real crisis – apart from occasional confrontations with the expanding unions – did not occur until after the First World War, when it became clear that the railways could not carry on as they were.

The result was the 'Grouping' authorised by the 1921 Railways Act, which allowed four companies to take over nearly all the network from the beginning of 1923.

Goods rates were still tightly regulated, however, and the companies' 'common carrier' obligation also continued (it would not be abolished until 1963).

The strains of another world war, followed by the election of a Labour Government in 1945 that was intent on placing industrial enterprises into the hands of the people, meant that railway nationalisation at last became inevitable, just over a century since the passing of the first Act of Parliament that had provided for (but not achieved) a degree of state railway ownership.

Between the wars the railways had struggled with continuing although outmoded restrictions on their business, but after 1948 their nationalised successor soon discovered that state ownership meant even more control than the Big Four or their predecessors had experienced.

Successive governments from both sides of the House intervened in the business of the British Transport Commission in what they perceived to be the national interest (or when they saw political capital to be gained), and it was not until 1955 that the Government of the day agreed to fund major modernisation of the railways.

This proved to be a mixed blessing, because the British Transport Commission then made a number of poor decisions that often stemmed from the apparent but untested assumption that nearly all the existing system was worth having and should therefore be modernised (see Chapter 10).

An unconvincing 'reappraisal' of the BTC's Modernisation Plan towards the end of the decade, coupled with sharply rising losses, led to growing doubt in official circles about the true role of the railway in the age of the lorry and the motorway.

This was followed by Stedeford, then the appointment of Beeching to lead the new British Railways Board. He had accepted the challenging task of disinterring a profitable railway from the tottering business that the BTC had bequeathed to the BRB, together with a substantial capital debt.

By the time Beeching had arrived the choice had become simple – did the nation want a commercially profitable (but probably quite small) railway, or a larger system whose priority was public service?

In January 1962, former Railway Executive Chairman Sir John Elliot summarised the problem in these words:

'British Railways have had the worst of both deals. You have earnest private sector Conservatives believing that it is possibility to put profitability first and yet put public service first too. Now that is incompatible. There needs to be a clear understanding of what function a public service is to fulfil. And if we take railways they must – and Dr Beeching will have to get this solved if he can – get this clear: "Do you, Mr Government, require us to operate with profitability as No 1 objective? If so, then this is what we are going to do, and you are not going to stop us, or if you do I am going to make a noise."'[7]

Elliot then mentioned the parallel case of London Transport, which he had chaired for six years after the Railway Executive had been abolished. He said he often received complaints from Conservative MPs that there were not enough buses at certain times of day. He had told them:

'You represent the essence of private enterprise; that is what you believe in. We can stand on our heads or we can slide down on our posteriors, but we cannot do both at the same time. If you want us to put profitability first, then there will not be one bus an hour at so and so on Saturday evening, there won't be any…'

This kind of clarity was well overdue.

Indeed, had the situation been defined so accurately in the late 1940s (and accepted by the politicians), much grief could have been avoided, and the BTC could have moved towards its own 'reshaping' a full decade before Beeching. Modernisation capital could then have been invested in the next-generation railway rather than in bolstering the traditional but by now increasingly inappropriate network.

In reality, it was left to Beeching to warn that the railway was still largely functioning, at a vast and unnecessary cost, as it had in the age of the horse and cart.

One further issue, which was less easy to define (and even harder to decide), was what needed to be done to balance the railway books after the extent – and cost – of the railway services that the nation needed for social reasons had been taken into account.

By the early 1960s this public service model had already been accepted in some other countries (France was a good example). Others had either protected railway revenues by permitting a greater degree of control over competing road services (as in the Netherlands at that time) or else allowed the comprehensive passenger railway to wither in the face of competing modes of transport (as in the United States and more recently New Zealand, where railways are only important now as passenger movers in a couple of that country's largest conurbations).

We have already said that the British Transport Commission had allowed itself to wander down some expensive blind alleys, but after Beeching had written what was seen in some quarters as a brutal and destructive prescription (and in others as a vital intervention) some of his senior staff also proved themselves willing to admit that mistakes had been made.

For example, British Railways Board member Frederick (F. C.) Margetts, whose responsibility at that time was to help carry out the Beeching reshaping proposals, told a railway audience in early 1964 that the increasing losses recorded between 1959 and 1962, by which time the annual railway deficit had reached £104m, were 'salutary':

'They are the outcome, on the one hand, of our own inadequacy, our lack of vision, our failure to recognise external change, and consequently the need for parallel changes in our business and, on the other hand, the strength and vision of our competitors, the enterprise of producers, and the development of more suitable forms of transport.'[8]

Margetts was not willing to look further than financial performance, and indeed his speech included a refusal to widen his brief: 'I am not going to talk about social benefits.'

Happily for the railway industry – and the nation as a whole – there would prove to be others who would not merely talk about such benefits, but take account of them.

This particular speech is also interesting because in it Margetts provided a vintage specimen of the *mea culpa* view that seems to have prevailed at the BRB in its earlier days: 'No suggestion has been made, nor should it be, that the railways have been, or are being, unfairly treated.'

After 1964 the British Railways Board continued to struggle with the competing aims that had been set out by Sir John Elliot in 1962. The result was that the Beeching closures continued, while strictly behind the scenes a much smaller network was being envisaged (see Chapter 15).

These plans had reached an advanced stage when a fortuitous change of Transport Minister finally opened the door to the concept that some railway services that could not pay their way were still necessary and should be supported (or bought) by the state.

Barbara Castle's 1968 Transport Act gave that concept a statutory foundation by launching the social railway, supported by a system of grants.

But ministers come and go, and by the start of the 1970s the Board was again trying to define a truly commercial railway in the face of renewed Departmental pressure for cheaper 'bustitution' as a replacement for many smaller lines.

The task proved hopeless, but again the blow did not fall; by the mid-1970s it had been agreed that the railway system was now about the right size, and that it would be supported by the new Public Service Obligation grant created by European law.

Even so, another change of government in 1979 was followed by a long programme of dismantling public sector industries for various reasons – some of which were not made clear at first (see Chapter 19) – and although peripheral parts of the BRB's businesses were 'hived off' to the private sector in the 1980s, the core railway remained in state ownership. However, it was not immune, as the appointment of the Serpell Committee proved in 1982.

The members of this Committee, which was asked to define a range of financial options, were divided in their opinions – demonstrating yet again, perhaps, that if it was easy to deal with the railway problem 'someone would have solved it long ago', to quote Richard Marsh (see Introduction).

Serpell fell flat and was soon buried, but the Committee's main report had at least provided further confirmation, if such a thing was needed after so many years of soul-searching, that the profitable passenger railway did not exist.

This fundamental truth was disregarded yet again within a decade, after a deluge of free market optimism had been unfortunately reinforced by British Rail's dubious claim that its InterCity passenger sector was now managing without any financial support.

The result was privatisation, based on the assumption – in the face of decades of evidence to the contrary – that most of the railway could pay its way so long as socially necessary passenger services continued to be 'bought' by the state.

Railways in Britain were to be freed from the shackles of monopoly. Anyone who had appropriate safety and financial qualifications would be able to run trains, together with franchised operators; the 1992 White Paper spoke glibly of the 'right of access', qualified only by the warning that 'provision will need to be made to reconcile the requirements for franchised services with the opportunities to be provided for liberalised commercial services'.[9]

The open access dream proved to be unachievable in most cases, because the Government soon realised that successful competitors could easily derail their franchised contractors (see Chapter 28).

The architects of railway privatisation knew that their plans rested in part on smoke and mirrors, in any case. BR had trumpeted its achievement of 'profits' from InterCity, but even the White Paper toned down its general air of optimism to admit that 'it is not clear that [InterCity] as a whole could improve its performance sufficiently to allow sale in this Parliament'.[10]

Just so. When the various intercity routes were franchised in 1996 and 1997, the only part of this sector that did not need subsidy from the outset proved to be the small and specialised Gatwick Express, while substantial premiums of more than £1bn, which would have been due from Virgin West Coast, were transformed into subsidies of about the same amount between 2006 and 2012 because Railtrack had failed to modernise the West Coast Main Line.

Thus the hard lesson was learned that dividing the railway into watertight compartments did not work; irrespective of political dogma or management aspirations, each component continued to rely on the others.

So where are we now? As the last parts of this book were being completed, a new crisis emerged that once again threatened to plunge railway affairs into the melting pot.

Network Rail had succeeded Railtrack in 2002 as a 'not for dividend' company, which then proceeded to borrow on the open market. Its borrowings at the time of writing are expected to exceed £40bn by 2019, and they are secured, rather tenuously, on the 'railway estate' itself.

The concept is ingenious, but not on all fours with conventional secured borrowing – an unpaid bond holder can hardly foreclose on Paddington station.

The picture has been complicated by two factors. One is a change to the statistical rules, which has forced Network Rail wholly into the public sector, so that it has been a 'government body' since September 2014.

One effect of this change has been to transfer Network Rail's growing debt to the national balance sheet, which is calculated to cause unrest at the Treasury.

At the same time, Network Rail was committed to a major programme of system 'enhancements' between 2014 and 2019 – particularly the electrification of several long routes, such as Bedford-Sheffield/Nottingham and London-Bristol-Cardiff-Swansea, and also a number of other lines or sections that include Manchester Piccadilly-Preston-Blackpool North, Oxenholme-Windermere and Reading-Newbury, as well as the 'electric spine' intended mainly for freight between Southampton and the Midlands.

The industry was disturbed to learn in 2015 that some of these projects were lagging behind schedule while their costs were rising (Great Western electrification, originally costed at less than £1bn, was said to have reached at least £2.5bn by the autumn of 2015).

Worse followed: in June two of the electrification projects were 'paused', and yet another review of Network Rail's methods was ordered.

This kind of uncertainty recalled the tribulations of Railtrack in the later 1990s over its disintegrating project to modernise the West Coast Main Line, and also had uncomfortable echoes of the British Transport Commission's ill-fated Modernisation Plan.

In both these cases one result was the eventual abolition of the railway body concerned, accompanied by much lamentation – public and political – about the state of the railway and what should be done about it.

It is not too surprising, then, that these new rumours of overruns and spiralling costs were accompanied by talk of restructuring Network Rail, perhaps by dividing it into regional companies or even trying to reprivatise the whole concern.

But what kind of industry would result from reprivatising Network Rail? The company (as it still technically is) relies mainly on government grants of £4bn or more a year – the rest of its revenue comes from track access charges and property rents.

In recent times, track access charges have become a shadow of their former selves. They have been much lower than a free market would demand, so as a result an artificially high number of franchised operators were able to pay premiums to the Government.

In short, the Government has been subsidising the industry largely through Network Rail. Although some franchises still draw direct subsidies as well, these are lower than they would need to be if 'free market' track access charges were payable, although there was some suggestion after the crisis in 2015 that the balance should change yet again, so that the operators paid more realistic track access charges once more. If so, the amount they could pay in premiums would inevitably fall and perhaps disappear entirely, while already-subsidised operators would need greater support.

If Network Rail became Railtrack 2, the present model would surely be unsustainable, not least because the complications of dividends would raise their heads again, potentially recalling the Parliamentary debates of the 1930s about the propriety of subsidising commercial companies with taxpayers' money, and it is tempting to speculate whether the recent suggestions for a change in direction for much of the financial support could therefore be paving the way for a reprivatisation of Network Rail.

Even before the recent tribulations, the author asked a senior figure within the core railway what would happen when Network Rail's borrowing reached its limit (this is set by the ORR at 75% of the theoretical value of the railway estate, rather like that of a prudent mortgage lender).

It is true that the value of the estate does tend to rise, aided by such network enhancements as electrification, but nevertheless the gap is closing.

The answer to the author's query was only that 'the Government would presumably have to look again at how the railway industry is financed'. In other words, there appears to be no master plan.

This recalls the crises of years gone by; one of these ended the careers of more than 100 railway companies and may have helped to open the door to the eventual abolition of their amalgamated heirs; others spelled doom for the British Transport Commission and, much later, Railtrack.

At various times political incompetence (there is no lesser word for it) created the hapless British Transport Commission, then contributed to the belief that the British Railways Board would be able to service and even repay the debts it had inherited from the BTC.

When this patently failed to happen, the Government came close to forcing the closure of much of the remaining network, before the value of the social railway came to be recognised in the nick of time, while another Government, with a nervous eye on the exit door, hurriedly cobbled together a 'privatisation' that proved to be based on hope, fallacies and unrealisable ambitions. In particular, it created feeble Railtrack, whose departure could have had even worse consequences than it did, although its particular brand of incompetence did cause the loss of a number of lives.

The present structure, in which there are numerous Peters paying multitudes of Pauls in a financial merry-go-round that in another sphere could only be described as money-laundering, is the warped result of a foolish privatisation that has repeatedly needed repair and, at times, extensive reconstruction.

Through it all, the trains have somehow continued to run, and there have been many successes along the platforms and in the freight terminals.

The railway does not have a relationship with the nation – it is at the heart of the nation. But once again, the nation is having to decide afresh what price it wants to pay. Another contraction of the network would be far less easy to achieve than it was in Beeching's day and is hopefully unthinkable, but organisational instability always poses risks, and this narrative has often been concerned with the dire results of decisions taken in haste and repented at leisure.

When the panic levels have risen sufficiently in Whitehall and elsewhere, babies have tended to be thrown out with the bath water.

The country may soon be forced to choose between a profitable industry and a public service one, and in doing so finally abandon any lingering pretence that the two might somehow be combined.

The first of these options would be very small at best, as Serpell and others have proved, and will make a minimal contribution to the national economy, with all the losses and problems – not least on the roads – that this would imply.

But a comprehensive public service railway will not come cheap. It currently needs more than £4bn a year (although the Rail Delivery Group has pointed out that the tax and other revenues received from the wider railway industry as a whole are almost as much), and there are alarming indications that the price is likely to go up, accompanied as it is by a looming public debt of at least £40bn and an apparent loss of direction at Network Rail.

This, then, is the Railway Dilemma, and in describing it the present author has attempted to pose a definitive question. It will be for others to find the definitive answer.

Afterword

On 25 June 2015, the Transport Secretary Patrick McLoughlin confirmed what had become an increasingly open secret within the railway industry – that Network Rail's major projects, particularly several electrification schemes, were increasingly endangered by a spiral of rising costs and a dismal sequence of missed deadlines.

Projects were taking longer than expected to complete and costing more – in some cases much more, so that, for example, the cost of electrifying the Great Western Main Line between London and South Wales had trebled within a couple of years to not far short of £3bn.

It emerged that the Network Rail board had been aware of the problems for some time, and that when the directors had considered the matter on 19 March, the minutes of their meeting recorded: 'The Board noted that without further improvements (which the Executive team required further time to work through and identify) there would be a substantial shortfall in funding.'

There then appears to have been a period of confusion, aided and abetted by poor communication. The Transport Secretary Patrick McLoughlin maintained that he had not been aware that some electrification projects could not be funded until 15 June – after a general election in May in which his party's manifesto had spoken of 'better roads, trains and modern communications' to come, helped by 'the biggest investment in rail since Victorian times'.

In particular, 'We will invest £38bn in our railway network in the five years to 2019. Electrification of the railways is a key part of our investment programme, with work already underway across the North, the Midlands, and South Wales; there are plans to go further in the rest of the country, including East Anglia and the South West.'

As in most manifestos there were no awkward details, but even this broad promise was hardly fulfilled by the Transport Secretary's admission in Parliament on 25 June that at least some of the work would have to be 'paused'.

The main casualties were electrification of the Midland Main Line north of Bedford to Nottingham and Sheffield, where Mr McLoughlin said better services could be provided before electrification 'with things such as speed improvement works', and Northern Transpennine between Leeds and Manchester, where Mr McLoughlin maintained there was a need to be 'more ambitious'.

Mr McLoughlin also brought down his ministerial axe in other ways. Network Rail's Chairman Richard Parry-Jones was replaced by Sir Peter Hendy, who would move across from his job as Commissioner at Transport for London. The 'members' who had theoretically taken the place of the non-existent shareholders at Network

Rail were thanked and stood down, while there would be no bonuses for the company's directors.

Two inquiries were ordered. Sir Peter would investigate the state of Network Rail's projects in the present Control Period, while economist Dame Collette Bowe would analyse how the enhancements programme could have been improved and make recommendations intended to improve the future planning of major railway investments.

The Great Western electrification scheme between London and South Wales was saved, however, being a 'top priority' on which the Transport Secretary wanted 'Network Rail to concentrate its efforts on getting that right'.

He did not explain why Great Western was being allowed to keep its place at the head of the queue, but his Permanent Secretary Philip Rutnam filled in some of the details when giving evidence to the House of Commons Public Accounts Committee on 21 October 2015.

The session was a stormy one – there were repeated calls from some of the Committee members for resignations – and just two hours before the hearing started the Committee had received a letter from Network Rail Chief Executive Mark Carne which broke the news that the cost of the Great Western scheme had risen from £1.6bn to a 'range' between £2.5bn and £2.8bn.

Even this was not necessarily the final figure, being based on 2012 prices and not in any case guaranteed, according to the Chief Executive of the Office of Rail and Road Richard Price, who was also giving evidence alongside Philip Rutnam and Mark Carne.

But whatever the final cost, why did Great Western merit priority? The answer, strictly speaking, was to be found in County Durham, where Hitachi was now assembling two fleets of Intercity Express trains intended for Great Western. The first batch would be hybrid – carrying diesel engines but also able to pick up power directly where overhead wires existed – but the second was electric only, and that fleet was due to be delivered from February 2018.

Without electrification such trains would be useless. To quote Philip Rutnam on 21 October: 'To be clear, the Department, as the ultimate customer on behalf of taxpayers and passengers, is liable to pay for the trains whether the electrification is ready or not. So we are clearly concerned—very concerned—not only about the delays to electrification and the cost overruns, but at the prospect that we might have the electric trains designed for the Great Western Main Line ... and not be able to use them.'

The Committee's Chair Meg Hillier suggested the cost of the trains to the taxpayer would be £400,000 a day (or £146m a year). Mr Rutnam did not contradict her.

Anyone who has patiently read earlier chapters in this book recounting the falls from grace of the British Transport Commission and Railtrack will surely be conscious of some *deja vu* by now.

The plights of Messrs Carne, Price and Rutnam at this hearing tend to recall those of hapless Commission Chairman Sir Brian Robertson, challenged without success by another Select Committee (which was also intent on blood, in the financial sense) to define the meaning of 'adequate' railway services, or John Robinson in Stephen Byers' office, when he was told that there would be no more funding for Railtrack.

It is true that Network Rail has yet to endure the fate of either the Commission or Railtrack, but then this story is still only partly told.

Apart from the Hendy and Bowe inquiries, a third was announced on 8 July, in the Summer Budget. Nicola Shaw, the Chief Executive of HS1 Ltd, which owns the concession for the high speed line to the Channel Tunnel, was appointed 'to advise the government on how it should approach the longer term future shape and financing of Network Rail'.

The Midland and Transpennine electrification schemes were 'unpaused' on 30 September (although they will take longer to complete). On 12 November Shaw published her 'scoping' outline of how she proposed to proceed, and caused an immediate flutter in some quarters by refusing to rule out a return to privatisation, either wholly or partly.

The possibilities are wide, and the document did include an assurance that 'the Report Team has not been asked to consider, nor will it be recommending, financing options purely because they would reduce public sector borrowing or debt'.

Sir Peter Hendy published his recommendations concerning Network Rail's outstanding projects on 25 November 2015 (many of which would now take longer to complete). He pointed out that, as a public sector body, Network Rail can no longer borrow on the commercial markets but must rely on the Treasury in future. He told the author: 'It's a very tight financial envelope: NR will have to work hard to achieve it.'

At this point our journey has to stop for now, with the function, structure and even just possibly the survival of Network Rail in the melting pot.

None of the options are easy, and some of them will cause a new and no doubt fervent debate about the future of the industry.

All the lessons of history suggest that the outcome will be another compromise, and that the search for a real solution to the Railway Dilemma will continue for many years to come.

As Sir Peter Hendy said after publishing his report in November 2015: 'The whole issue, ever since the start of BR, is that there has never been enough public money for the railways.'

Notes and Sources

Chapter 1 *pages 18-25*
1 *Illustrated London News*, 15 April 1848
2 Keddell, F. The nationalisation of our railway system. London, 1887
3 Cooper, R A. Free railway travel, a proposal ... London, 1890
4 Kirkcaldy, A.W. and Evans, A.D. The history and economics of transport. London, [1915]
5 Threlfall, T R. Shall the railways be nationalised? London, 1909
6 *Railway Gazette*, 22 September 1911
7 Davies, Emil. The case for railway nationalisation. London, 1912

Chapter 2 *pages 26-32*
1 *Hansard (Commons)*, 2 July 1919; vol. 117 col. 1118
2 *Railway Gazette*, 2 July 1920
3 *ibid*, 9 July 1920
4 *ibid*, 30 June 1922

Chapter 3 *pages 33-42*
1 *Railway Gazette*, 17 January 1928
2 For an example, see *Hansard (Commons)*, 28 February 1928; vol. 214 cols. 301-359
3 *Hansard (Commons)*, 28 February 1928; vol. 214 cols. 309-310
4 *Hansard (Commons)*, 16 March 1927; vol. 203 col. 2014, and 11 December 1935; vol. 307 col. 908-9
5 Nock, O S. History of the Great Western Railway, Vol. 3. Shepperton, 1967
6 The Railway Handbook, 1947-1948
7 Ministry of Transport. Report of the committee on main line railway electrification. [The Weir report]. London, 1931
8 *Hansard (Commons)*, 13 December 1935; vol. 307 cols. 1286-372
9 First report of the royal commission on transport, Cmd. 3365 [1929]
    and Second report of the royal commission on transport, Cmd. 3416 [1929]
10 Third and final report of the royal commission on transport, Cmd. 3751 [1931]
11 Ministry of Transport. Report of the conference [the Salter Conference] on rail and road transport, 29 July 1932. London, 1932
12 *Hansard (Commons)*, 19 July 1933; vol. 280 col. 1896
13 *ibid*, col. 1832
14 *ibid*, col. 1834

Chapter 4 *pages 43-50*
1 London Passenger Transport Board. Fifth annual report and accounts. London, 1938
2 *Hansard (Commons)*, 21 December 1938; vol. 342 col. 2986
3 *ibid*, cols. 2992-3
4 *ibid*, col. 3016
5 Transport Advisory Council. Report on the proposals of the main line railway companies as to the conveyance of merchandise by rail. [London, 1939]

Chapter 5 *pages 51-62*
1 British Railways Press Office. It can now be revealed: more about British Railways in peace and war. London, 1945
2 British Railways Press Office. British Railways in peace and war. London, 1944
3 Longmate, Norman. How we lived then. London, 1971
4 *Hansard (Commons)*, 7 February 1940; vol. 357 cols. 221-5
5 Government control of railways [White Paper], under The Railway Control Order, 1939 (S.R. & O. 1939

No. 1197). London, 1939
6 *Hansard (Commons), op. cit.*
7 British Railways in peace and war, *op. cit.*
8 Nock, O.S. History of the Great Western Railway, vol. 3. Shepperton, 1967
9 *Railway Gazette*, 17 October 1941
10 Bill Greig in the *Daily Mirror*, 16 August 1940
11 History of the Great Western Railway, op. cit.
12 *Railway Gazette*. A national transport programme: the approach to a long-term plan. London, 1943

Chapter 6 *pages 63-70*
1 Gourvish, T.R [Terry]. British Railways 1948-73. Cambridge, 1986
2 London & North Eastern Railway. The state and the railways: an alternative to nationalisation. London, 1946
3 Bonavia, Michael R. A history of the LNER, vol. 3. London, 1983
4 *Commercial Motor*, 7 February 1947
5 *Hansard (Commons)*, 16 December 1946; vol. 431 cols. 1617-722
6 *ibid.*
7 *Hansard (Commons)*, 17 December 1946; vol. 431 cols. 1785-894

Chapter 7 *pages 71-77*
1 Railway Executive. Carry on: staff news magazine of British Railways, London Midland Region [and] Scottish Region. vol. 9 no. 87. [London], 1948
2 British Transport Commission. First annual report ... 1948. London, 1949
3 *ibid.*
4 Modern Transport. Unification of British Railways: administrative principles and practice, by members of the Railway Executive. London, 1951
5 British Transport Commission report and accounts, *op. cit.,* pp40-1

Chapter 8 *pages 78-86*
1 *Cabinet Conclusions*, 6 March 1952
2 British Transport Commission. Fourth annual report ... 1951. London, 1952. p28
3 *Cabinet Conclusions*, 16 April 1952
4 British Transport Commission. Fifth annual report ... 1952. London, 1953. p55
5 *Hansard (Commons)*, 21 October 1953; vol. 518 cols. 1980-1
6 *ibid,* col. 2020
7 British Railways (Western Region) London Lecture and Debating Society. By what means can the net revenue of the British Railways be improved in present circumstances? London, 1951 (privately printed)
8 Joy, Stewart. The train that ran away... Shepperton, 1973
9 *ibid,* p46
10 British Transport Commission. First annual report ... 1948. London, 1949. pp40-1
11 *The Age* [Melbourne, Australia], 6 July 1977
12 Department of Transport. Railway finances [The Serpell report]... London, 1983
13 British Transport Commission. Fourth annual report, *op. cit.* p17
14 British Transport Commission. Eighth annual report ... 1955. vol. II. London, 1956. pp254-5
15 British Transport Commission. First annual report, *op. cit.* p31

Chapter 9 *pages 87-93*
1 Transport policy [White paper] Confidential proof. 18 April 1952
2 *ibid.* Revised confidential proof. 22 April 1952
3 *Cabinet Conclusions*, 28 October 1952
4 *Hansard (Commons)*, 15 December 1952; vol. 509 cols. 1001-2
5 *ibid,* col. 1044
6 *ibid,* col. 1047
7 *ibid,* col. 1048
8 Railway Executive. Report of the committee on types of motive power (Appendix A). [Unpublished]. London, 1951.

9 *ibid,* col. 1060
10 Transport Act 1953, s25

Chapter 10 *pages 96-104*
1 Joy, Stewart. The train that ran away... Shepperton, 1973
2 Railway Executive. A development programme for British Railways. [Unpublished]. London, 1953.
      see also Gourvish, T.R. British Railways 1948-73. Cambridge, 1986
3 British Transport Commission. Modernisation and re-equipment of British Railways. London, 1954
4 British Transport Commission. Annual report and accounts, 1958. vol. I. London, 1959. p24
5 British Transport Commission. Annual report and accounts, 1959. vol. II. London,1960
6 St John Thomas, David. A regional history of the railways of Great Britain. vol. 1: the West Country.
      Newton Abbot, 1960
7 St John Thomas, David. The country railway. Newton Abbot, 1976
8 British Transport Commission. Sixth annual report ... 1953. London, 1954
9 Henshaw, David. The great railway conspiracy. Hawes, 1991
10 Railway Executive. Report of the committee on types of motive power. *op.cit.*

Chapter 11 *pages 105-112*
1 British Transport Commission. Seventh annual report ... 1954. London, 1955
2 Railways reorganisation scheme, Cmd 9191 [White paper]. London, 1954
3 *Hansard (Commons),* 1 November 1954; vol. 532 col. 50
4 British Railways Western Region. Report on dieselisation of passenger and freight services in the West
      of England [unpublished]. London, 1955. [National Archive reference AN 49/21]
5 British Transport Commission. Annual report and accounts, 1959. vol. I. London, 1960
6 St John Thomas, David. The rural transport problem. Newton Abbot, 1963

Chapter 12 *pages 113-120*
1 *Hansard (Commons),* 11 December 1958; vol. 597 col. 546
2 British Transport Commission. Re-appraisal of the plan for the modernisation and re-equipment of
      British Railways. London, 1959
3 Joy, Stewart. The train that ran away...Shepperton, 1973
4 British Transport Commission. Sixth annual report and accounts, 1953. vol. I. London, 1954. p20
5 *Cabinet Conclusions,* 14 December 1953
6 British Transport Commission. Eighth annual report and accounts, 1955. vol. I. London, 1956. p3
7 Joy, Stewart. op. cit.
8 *Hansard (Commons),* 26 October 1960; vol. 627 cols. 2363-4
9 *Cabinet Conclusions,* 8 March 1960
10 *Hansard (Commons),* 10 March 1960; vol. 619 cols. 643-4
11 *Hansard (Commons),* 4 April 1960; vol. 621 cols. 48-9
12 Reorganisation of the nationalised transport undertakings, Cmnd. 1248 [White paper]. London,
      1960

Chapter 13 *pages 121-125*
1 *Hansard (Commons),* 31 January 1961; vol. 633 col. 621
2 *Hansard (Commons), op. cit.,* col. 623
3 BBC interview, 27 March 1963
4 *Hansard (Commons),* 20 November 1961; vol. 649 col. 942
5 British Transport Commission. Eighth annual report and accounts, 1955. vol. I. London, 1956
6 Pearson, A.J. The railways and the nation. London, 1964
7 Joy, Stewart. The train that ran away... Shepperton, 1973

Chapter 14 *pages 126-131*
1 Thomas, David St John. The rural transport problem. London, 1963
2 Thomas, David St John. A regional history of the railways of Great Britain: vol. 1: The West Country,
      5th ed. Newton Abbot, 1981
3 Transport Act 1962, s56(5)
4 Irvine, Kenneth. Track to the future. London, 1988

5 British Railways Board press conference, 27 March 1963
6 Joy, Stewart. The train which ran away... Shepperton, 1973

Chapter 15 *pages 132-140*
1 British Railways Board. The development of the major railway trunk routes. London, 1965
2 Freeman Allen, Geoffrey. British Rail after Beeching. Shepperton, 1966. p71
3 Fiennes, G. F. I tried to run a railway. Shepperton, 1967. p101
4 British Railways Board. Route system maps (confidential). [unpublished]. London, 1965. [National Archive reference AN 159/33]
5 Joy, Stewart. The train that ran away... Shepperton, 1973
6 *Hansard (Commons),* 4 November 1964; vol. 701 cols. 195-203
7 The new Britain: Labour Party election manifesto. London, 1964
8 Rail closures: [Cabinet] memorandum by the Minister of Transport (confidential), 9 March 1965
9 Castle, Barbara. The Castle diaries 1964-70. London, 1984. p84
10 Gourvish, T.R [Terry]. British Railways 1948-73: a business history. Cambridge, 1986. p447
11 British Railways Board. Route system maps (confidential). [unpublished]. London, [1966]. [National Archive reference AN 159/32]

Chapter 16 *pages 141-145*
1 Castle, Barbara. The Castle diaries, 1964-70. London, 1984
2 *ibid.*
3 *Hansard (Commons),* 10 February 1966; vol. 724 cols. 607-10
4 Transport policy (White Paper). Cmnd. 3057. London, 1966
5 Castle, Barbara. *op. cit.,* p154
6 Ministry of Transport [and] British Railways Board. British Railways network for development. March, 1967
7 *ibid.*
8 *The Observer,* 14 July 1969 (quoted by Stewart Joy in The train which ran away.)
9 British Railways Board. Report on organisation. London, 1969

Chapter 17 *pages 146-153*
1 *Hansard (Commons),* 4 July 1973; vol. 859 col. 549

Chapter 18 *pages 154-159*
1 [Department of the Environment]. Transport policy: a consultation document. London, 1976
2 British Railways Board. Annual report and accounts, 1974. London, 1975
3 British Railways Board. An opportunity for change. London, 1976. p27
4 British Transport Films. Belief in the future. London, 1976
5 British Railways Board. Annual report and accounts, 1979. London, 1980
6 Speech by Sir Peter Parker to the NUR Annual General Meeting, 30 June 1981
7 Parker, Sir Peter. For starters: the business of life. London, 1989
8 Advertisement by the Railway Conversion Campaign in The Independent, 26 July 1989
9 British Railways Board. Future rail: the next decade. London, 1991

Chapter 19 *pages 160-167*
1 Economic Reconstruction Group [Conservative Party]. Final report of the nationalised industry policy group, chaired by the Hon. Nicholas Ridley. [unpublished]. [London], 1977
2 Joy, Stewart. The train which ran away ... Shepperton, 1973
3 *Daily Telegraph,* 6 August 2008
4 Railway finances: report of a Committee chaired by Sir David Serpell. London, 1983. Supplementary volume par. 5.87
5 Railway finances: report of a Committee chaired by Sir David Serpell. London, 1983. p87
6 Bonavia, Michael. The twilight of British Rail? Newton Abbot, 1985
7 *Hansard (Commons),* 3 February 1983; vol. 36 col. 439
8 Gourvish, Terry. British Rail, 1974-97: from integration to privatisation. Oxford, 2002. pp367-8

Chapter 20 *pages 170-178*
1 Starkie, David. BR — privatisation without tears, in Economic Affairs. vol.5 issue 1, October 1984
2 Research for the Institute of Economic Affairs. *see also* City AM, 26 November 2013
3 Irvine, Kenneth. The right lines. London, 1987
4 Bagwell, Philip. The Railway Clearing House in the British economy, 1842-1922. London, 1968
5 Rail Accident Investigation Branch. Signal NW36 passed at danger at Norton-on-Tees West, 16 January 2013. (RAIB Bulletin 03/2013)
6 British Transport Commission. Annual report and accounts, 1955. Vol. II. London, 1956
7 House of Commons Library. Railways: privatisation, 1987-1996. London, 2010
8 *Hansard (Lords),* 29 November 2007; col. 1363
9 Redwood, John. Signals from a railway conference. CPS Policy Challenge, November 1988
10 British Railways Board. A cross-London rail link: a discussion paper. London, 1980
11 Department for Transport [and] British Railways Board. Review of main line electrification, final report. London, 1981
12 Speech to the Conservative Party conference, 11 October 1989
13 *The Independent,* 29 August 1993
14 Dudley, Geoffrey and Richardson, Jeremy. Why does policy change? Lessons from British transport policy 1945-99. London, 2000
15 Gourvish, Terry. British Rail, 1974-97: from integration to privatisation. Oxford, 2002 (p369)
16 This speech is referred to in *Hansard (Lords),* 19 October 1993; vol. 549 col. 532

Chapter 21 *pages 179-188*
1 The money programme: BR after 1992 (BBC), 22 July 1991
2 Parker, Sir Peter. For starters: the business of life. London, 1989
3 *Panorama* (BBC), 16 October 1989
4 New opportunities for the railways: the privatisation of British Rail. Cm 2012. London, 1992
5 HM Treasury. Nationalised industries: investment and financing review, 9 July 1979. Confidential.
6 British Coal and British Rail (Transfer Proposals) Act 1993
7 *Hansard (Commons),* 2 February 1993; vol. 218 col. 169
8 *ibid.,* col. 176
9 House of Commons Transport Committee. The future of the railways in the light of the Government's white paper proposals (second report), vol.1. London, 1993
10 *Hansard (Lords),* 1 July 1993; vol. 547 col. 1014
11 *Hansard (Lords),* 5 July 1993; vol. 547 col. 1123
12 British Railways Board. Annual report and accounts, 1992-93. London, 1993

Chapter 22 *pages 189-196*
1 *Commercial Motor,* 10 September 1992
2 BBC Nine o'clock news, 28 August 1992, *quoted in The Independent,* 29 August 1992
3 *Hansard (Commons),* 26 October 1992; vol. 212 col. 762
4 Railtrack Great Western news, February 1994
5 *Hansard (Commons),* 20 December 1995; vol. 268 col. 1177W
6 *The Independent,* 9 February 1996
7 *Hansard (Commons),* 5 February 1996; vol. 271 col. 19
8 *ibid.,* cols. 19-20
9 *ibid.,* col. 20

Chapter 23 *pages 197-203*
1 *The Independent,* 5 February 1996
2 House of Commons Library. Railways: privatisation, 1987-1996. London, 2010
3 *Hansard (Lords),* 1 July 1993; vol. 547 col. 1015
4 *Hansard (Commons),* 24 November 1994; vol. 250 col. 729
5 *ibid.,* cols. 729-30
6 *The Times,* 29 April 1996
7 Derby & Derbyshire Rail Forum annual conference, 4 November 2010
8 Glaister, Stephen. British Rail privatisation: competition destroyed by politics. Madrid, 2004

Chapter 24 *pages 204-212*
1 Rolt, L.T.C. Red for danger, 2nd rev. ed. London, 1966
2 Railway Group Standard. Rule book, module TW1: preparation and movement of trains, issue 9. London, 2013
3 Evidence to the Southall inquiry. (Uff, John. The Southall rail accident inquiry report. London, 2000)
4 Uff, John. The Southall rail accident inquiry report. London, 2000
5 Cullen, Lord. The Ladbroke Grove rail inquiry: part 1, report. London, 2001
6 *Evening Standard,* 6 October 1999
7 Railtrack. Railtrack announces end of year operating improvements. Press release, 17 May 2000.
8 Department of Transport, Local Government and the Regions. Prescott takes safety regulation away fromRailtrack. Press release, 22 February 2000
9 Office of the Rail Regulator. The periodic review of Railtrack's access charges: final conclusions, vol. 1. London, 2000

Chapter 25 *pages 213-220*
1 Shadow Strategic Rail Authority. Annual report, 1999-2000. London, 2000
2 House of Commons Select Committee on Environment, Transport and Regional Affairs. Minutes of Evidence, 1 May 2001
3 Transport Act, 2000. s205
4 Transport Act, 1947. s3(1)
5 Transport Act, 2000. s224(2)
6 Cornwall Centre for Excellence (http://www.cornwall-centre-of-excellence.org.uk/t34.htm)
7 Department of Transport, Local Government and the Regions. Prescott sets out ten-year plan for investment. Press release, 13 December 1999
8 *Hansard (Commons),* 20 December 1994; vol. 341 col. 531
9 *ibid.,* col. 542
10 *ibid.,* col. 552
11 Railtrack. Railtrack statement on Regulator's proposed enforcement order on performance. Press release, 19 August 1999
12 Shadow Strategic Rail Authority. Morton calls on Railtrack to meet challenge of growing rail demand. Press release, 26 August 1999
13 Morton, Sir Alastair. The Strategic Rail Authority's challenge to the British rail industry. Speech delivered on 5 October 1999 at the Savoy Hotel, London
14 Office of the Rail Regulator. Statement re West Coast Main Line. Press release, 5 November 1999
15 Shadow Strategic Rail Authority. SSRA response to Rail Regulator's statement on West Coast Main Line upgrade. Press release, 5 November 1999
16 Railtrack. Statement in response to Rail Regulator's announcement re West Coast Main Line. Press release, 5 November 1999
17 Booz Allen and Hamilton. Railtrack's Performance in the Control Period 1995-2001. London, 1999
18 Office of the Rail Regulator. Railtrack regulation. Press release, 25 November 1999
19 Railtrack. Railtrack response to the Rail Regulator's stewardship of the network document. Press release, 25 November 1999

Chapter 26 *pages 221-229*
1 Shadow Strategic Rail Authority. Building a better railway: Franchising Director invites replacement franchise proposals for Chiltern, Connex South Central and Great North Eastern franchises. Press release, 24 November 1999
2 Connex. Connex sets out its position on South Central franchise. Press release, 24 October 2000
3 Association of Train Operating Companies. Complaint to the Rail Regulator regarding breaches of condition 7 of Railtrack's network licence, 21 December 2000
4 *Today* (BBC Radio 4), 23 October 2000
5 Office of the Rail Regulator. Periodic Review and Hatfield. Press release, 15 January 2001
6 Strategic Rail Authority. Railtrack cost increase forces East Coast Main Line review. Press release, 14February 2001
7 Strategic Rail Authority. SRA approves ECML costs and announces Strategic Agenda approval. Press release, 2 March 2001
8 Office of the Rail Regulator. Regulator takes enforcement action to ensure Railtrack delivers network

recovery. Press release, 20 March 2001

9 Strategic Rail Authority. A strategic agenda. London, 2001

10 Strategic Rail Authority. East Coast Main Line – joint venture. Press release, 2 April 2001

11 Railtrack. Railtrack secures £1.5 bn funding settlement and details final quarter business progress. Press release, 2 April 2001

12 Strategic Rail Authority. ECML replacement franchise. Press release, 9 May 2001

13 Department of Transport, Local Government and the Regions. Speech by Stephen Byers, 18 June 2000.

14 Morton, Sir Alastair. Coming out of the shadow. Speech at the IEA conference 'The future of UK rail', 26 June 2001

15 PricewaterhouseCoopers. Upgrading the rail network: focusing on delivery. London, 2001

16 Department of Transport, Local Government and the Regions. Meeting with John Robinson. Minutes, 27 June 2001.

17 Department of Transport, Local Government and the Regions. Meeting with John Robinson. Minutes, 25 July 2001.

18 *Daily Telegraph,* 27 July 2005

19 *op. cit.*

Chapter 27 *pages 230-241*

1 Office of the Rail Regulator. Railtrack administration order. File/attendence note by Tom Winsor, 6 October 2001

2 *Daily Telegraph,* 8 October 2001

3 Private conversation with the author

4 The Guardian, 31 January 2006

5 Robinson, Colin (ed.). Regulating utilities and promoting competition: lessons for the future. Cheltenham, 2006

6 Lords Select Committee on Constitution . Examination of witness, 11 June 2003

7 Department of Transport, Local Government and the Regions. Paddington to be protected by new train safety systems – Byers. Press release, 5 October 2001

8 Railtrack Group plc.Suspension of shares: Government appointment of administrator to Railtrack plc. Press release, 8 October 2001

9 Railtrack plc. Personal statement from Steve Marshall, CEO of Railtrack. Press release, 8 October 2001

10 *The Guardian,* 10 May 2002

11 *The Observer,* 12 May 2002

12 Strategic Rail Authority.Midland Main Line/East Midlands route utilisation strategy. London, 2003

13 Network Rail. Rail industry agrees new approach to planning Britain's future railway. Press release, 1 June 2012

14 Office of the Rail Regulator. The Regulator's consultation on the proposed track access agreement between Railtrack and Virgin Rail. London, 1997

15 *Railway Gazette International*: Making the Virgin vision happen, 1 November 2000

16 Strategic Rail Authority. Interim agreement between the Strategic Rail Authority and Virgin Rail Group. Press release, 22 July 2002

17 National Audit Office. The Modernisation of the West Coast Main Line. London, 2006

18 House of Commons Transport Select Committee.The future of the railway. London, 2004

19 Winsor, Tom. Letter, 4 July 2004

Chapter 28 *pages 242-253*

1 Office of the Rail Regulator. Competition for railway passenger services: a consultation document. London, 1994

2 Office of the Rail Regulator. Competition for railway passenger services: a policy statement. London, 1994

3 Office of the Rail Regulator. Competition for railway passenger services: a consultation document. London, 1994

4 High Court judgment. R (GNER) v ORR [2006] EWHC 1942 (Admin). 27 July 2005

5 Sea Containers. GNER enters into new management agreement with Department for Transport to operate Intercity East Coast Mainline. Press release, 15 December 2006

6. *Railnews* [website]. ATOC calls for longer franchises and less DfT 'micro-management' of railways.

30 October 2009

7 Sea Containers. Sea Containers disappointed by government decision on East Coast rail line. Press release, 14 August 2007

8 Department for Transport. East Coast Main Line company pledges to improve services and invest for the future. Press release, 13 November 2009

9 *Hansard (Commons)*, 19 May 2011; vol. 528 col. 520

10 Department for Transport [and] Office of Rail Regulation.Realising the potential of GB rail: report of the value for money rail study [by Sir Roy McNulty]. London, 2011

11 Virgin Trains. Press statement: from Sir Richard Branson, founder Virgin Group. Press release, 15 August2012

12 *Hansard (Commons)*, 3 September 2012; vol. 549 col. 14WS

13 Department for Transport. West Coast Main Line franchise competition cancelled. Press release, 3 October 2012

14 House of Commons Transport Committee. Department for Transport: Lessons from cancelling the InterCity West Coast franchise competition. London, 2013

15 FirstGroup. FirstGroup statement re: InterCity West Coast Franchise. Press release, 3 October 2015

16 *Hansard (Commons)*, 26 February 2014; vol. 576 col. 24WS

Chapter 29 *pages 254-261*

1 *Hansard (Commons)*, 26 March 2013; vol. 560 col. 1487

2 Huff, Darrell. How to lie with statistics–4th ed. London, 1954

3 *Hansard (Commons), op.cit.*

4 Office of Rail Regulation. 2013-14 Quarter 4 statistical release: passenger rail usage. London, 2014

Chapter 30 *pages 262-271*

1 Railway Regulation Act 1844. s6

2 Quoted in Thomas, David St John. A regional history of the railways of Great Britain, vol.1: The West Country. London, 1960

3 Grahame, Thomas. A treatise on internal intercourse and communication in civilised states, and particularly in Great Britain. London, 1834

4 The Spectator, 28 August 1875

5 Rolt, L.T.C. Railway adventure. London, 1953

6 Railway and Canal Traffic Act, 1854. s2

7 Elliot, Sir John. Railways in a changing world: British Railways (Western Region) London Lecture and Debating Society [privately printed]. London, 1962

8 Margetts, F.C. The benefits to be derived from a reshaped railway system: British Railways (Western Region) London Lecture and Debating Society [privately printed]. London, 1964

9 New opportunities for the railways: the privatisation of British Rail. Cm 2012. London, 1992. p13

10 *ibid.,* p8

Index